GOD AND GODDESSES IN HINDUISM

GOD AND GODDESSES IN HINDUISM

Dr. Krishan Saigal

KALPAZ PUBLICATIONS
DELHI-110052

God and Goddesses in Hinduism

Rs. 590

ISBN: 81-7835-565-5

Published in 2007 in India by
Kalpaz Publications
C-30, Satyawati Nagar,
Delhi-110052
E-mail: kalpaz@hotmail.com
Phone : 9212729499

Lasser Type Setting by: Quick Media, Delhi
Printed at : Salasar Imaging System, Delhi

CONTENTS

PREFACE

When I was a child all the stories in Ramayana, Mahabharat and the Puranas were related to the children by the elderly ladies of the family. Today with the pace of life speeding up and most wives working children are deprived of this most important part of our culture. As children we were told that these stories told us how to live good and decent lives—how to be a better brother like Rama or Bharata, or devoted like Hanuman and so on.

As I grew up and studied the Vedas and the Upanishads I came to realise how those Puranic stories were really derived from the rich wisdom of the earlier scriptures. I felt that our younger generation needed to imbibe the ancient wisdom as reflected in these 'mythologies'.

There was a difficulty however. The stock of these mythologies was huge what with 18 Puranas, the voluminous Mahabharata and Ramayana. Fortunately there is a unifying thread running through all these mythologies. And the lesson of all was also the same—how to lead a spiritual life in the world and to ultimately get liberated from the cycle of births and deaths.

I have tried to collect some typical mythologies but much has had to be omitted. This was inevitable in a short work like this. I have tried to give the spiritual development from the Vedas though the Upanishads to the Puranas. This is a vast work and has only been cursorily dealt with here. There are however many books available on the subject for those interested.

This work does not profess to give any new translations on the subject. The existing translation have been collected, edited and presented. The symbology of the most popular gods and goddesses is also given as well as the relations between the various deities.

I hope that the reader will not be disappointed. Those who want to delve deeper into the matter can consult the various English translations of the Ramayana, Mahabharata and the Puranas which are available.

1

INTRODUCTION

To those not brought up in the Hindu tradition there is a bewildering profusion of gods and goddesses. To those in the western tradition, including educated Hindu, this is evidence of a degraded and primitive mentality. But these critics have ignored the fact that Hinduism is very strongly a monotheistic religion and that it does not concieve of any other than the one. So, as I shall show, it was the one who himself became the many so that the Divine was not only transcendent but was also immanent in the world.

The Hindu religion founded itself on the conceptions of a timeless, nameless and formless supreme. But it did not deny or abolish all intermediary forms, names, powers and personalities of the Eternal and the Infinite. The one Godhead is worshipped as the all, for all in the unverse is he or made out of his being or his nature. But this concept did not make it into a polytheism, for beyond the various gods Hinduism recognized the supra cosmic Eternal. So that the worshipper of many gods always knew that all the divinities are forms, names, personalities and powers of the one; his gods proceed from the one Purusha, and the goddesses are energies of the one divine Force.

Hindu religion is based on three basic ideas or rather three fundamentals of a high and wide spiritual experience. First is the idea of One Existence of the Veda to which the sages give different names the one without a second of the Upanishads who is all that is and beyond all that is. To discover, approach and enter into whatever kind or degree of unity with this Permanent, this Infinite, this Eternal is the *summum bonum* of spiritual experience.

The second basic idea is the manifold ways of man's approach to the Eternal and Infinite. The Infinity is full of many infinities and each of these infinities is itself the very Eternal. And here in the limitations of the cosmos God manifests and fulfils himself in the world in many ways, linking each as the way of the Eternal. For in each finite we can discover and though all things as his forms and symbols we can approach the Infinite; all cosmic powers all manifestations, all forces are forces of the one. The gods behind the workings of Nature are to be seen and adored as the names, personalties and powers of the one Godhead.

The Infinite creates and is Brahma; it preserves and is Vishnu; it destroys or takes to itself and is Siva. The supreme Energy beneficient in upholding and protection is the Mother of the worlds, Lakshmi or Durga. Or beneficient even in the mark of destruction it is Kali, the dark Mother. The one Godhead manifests in the forms of his qualities in various names and godheads. The God of divine love of the Vaishnavas, the God of the divine power of the Shaktas appear as two different godheads; but in reality they are the are infinite Deity in different forms.

Between the highest unimaginable Existence and our material way of being the spiritual and psychic knowledge of the Hindus did not fix a gulf as between two unrelated entities. For Hinduism was aware of other psychological planes of consciousness and experience and the truths of these supra physical planes were as real to it as the outward truths of the physical experience.

The third idea of great consequence and as the base of Hinduism is the most dynamic for the inner spiritual life. It is that the Supreme can be approached through a universal consciousness and by piercing through all inner and outer Nature, and that he can be met by each individual soul in itself, in its own spiritual part, for there is something in it that is intimately one, or at least intimately related, with the one divine Essence. The essence of Hinduism is to aim at so growing and living that we can grow out of the Ignorance which veils His self-knowledge from our mind and life and become aware of the Divinity within us.

The Hindu sages were aware that the majority of men put emphasis on the outward life and live very strongly in their surface consciousness and very little in the inward existence. To have made the discovery of our deeper being and hidden spiritual nature is the first necessity. But many times this endeavour takes the from of a spiritual exclusiveness which revolts against the outward existence rather than seeks to transform it. But the Vedic and Vedantic rishis reposed on too wide and many sided a concept to admit as its base this narrow view. To them the spirit was not only the highest and inmost thing, but all was manifestation and creation of the spirit. Their aim was not only to raise to inaccessible heights the few elect, but to grow all men and all life upward, to spiritualise life and in the end to divinise human nature.

Now the spirit of Hindu religion and spirituality has been persistently and immovably the same throughout time though its form has undergone remarkable changes. In its earliest form it took its outward foundation on the mind of the physical man whose natural faith is in things physical and the external pursuits and aims of this material world. Man's first and primitive idea of the Divine can only come through his vision of external Nature and the sense of a superior power or Powers concealed behind her phenomena.

The Vedic religion took this natural form and feelings and used the conceptions to which they gave birth, and sought to lead him to the psychic and spiritual truths of his own being and the being of the cosmos. The Vedas accepted also the form in which early man expressed his sense of the relation between himself and the godheads of Nature; it adopted as its central symbols the act and ritual of a physical sacrifice. However crude this concept was it was founded on that constant interchange between the individual and the universal powers of the cosmos which covertly supports all the process of like and develops the action of nature. At the same time the Vedic Rishis gave a psychic function to the godheads worshipped by the people; they spoke to them of a higher truth, Right, law of which the gods were guardians, of the necessity of a truer knowledge and a larger inner living according to this Truth and Right and of a home of Immortality to which the soul of man could ascend by the power of Truth and of right doing. This moral and religious force was the highest reach of the external cult and the most that could be followed or understood by the people.

The deeper truth of these things was reserved for the initiates. For the Veda is full of words which, as the Rishis themselves express it, are secret words that give their inner meaning only to the seer or sage. Only by penetrating into the esoteric sense of this worship can we understand the full flowering of the Vedic religion in the Upanishads.

The Upanishads have always been recognised as the crown and end of Veda as is indicated in the general name Vedanta. The time in which the Vedantic truth was wholly seen and the Upanishads took shape was an epoch of immense and strenuous seeking. The Vedantic seer renewed the Vedic truth by extricating it from its cryptic symbols and casting it into a highest and most direct and powerful language of intuition and inner experience. It was not the language of the intellect, but still it wore a form which the intellect could take hold of and translate into its more abstract terms and concept into a starting-point for an ever widening and deepening philosophic speculation.

The post-Vedic and post-Vedantic age was distinguished by the rise of the great philosophies and by a copious, vivid, many-sided epic literature. Through profound and subtle philosophies there was an attempt to analyse by the reason and logical faculty what had formerly been approached with a much more living force through intuition and the soul's experience. But the philosophic mind started from the data these mightier powers had discovered and was faithful to its parent light. It was always admitted that spiritual experience was a greater thing and its light a truer guide than the clarities of the reasoning intellect.

Buddhism, which arose as the result of an intense stress of the union of the logical reason with a spiritualised mind, laid emphasis on Nirvana and Karma as the way to liberation. But Buddhism with its trenchant affirmations and still more exclusive negations in the long run could not be made sufficiently compatible with the flexibility many-sided susceptibility and rich synthetic turn of the earlier religious consciousness. It was a high creed but not plastic enough to hold the heart of the people.

While absorbing all that it could of Buddhism the new development, while rejecting its exclusive positions, moved forward not by any destruction of principle, but by a gradual feeling of prominent Vedic forms. There was a transformation of symbol and the development of new idea-forms from the seed of the original thinking. And there was a further deepening of psychic and spiritual experience furtherning.

The Vedic gods lost their deep original significance. As first they kept their hold by their external cosmic sense but were overshadowed by the great trinity, Brahma-Vishnu-Siva. A new pantheon appeared which in its outward symbolic aspects expressed a deeper truth and larger range of religious experience. The *yagya* and altar were replaced by the temple and devotional temple ritual. The vague and shifting images of the Vedic gods in the mantras were replaced by more precise conceptual forms of the two great deities, Vishnu and Siva, and of their Shaktis and their mantras. These new concepts resulted in physical images which were made the basis both for internal adoration and external worship. The psychic and mystic aspects which were the inner significance of the Vedic hymns, gave way to the less intensely luminous but the wider, richer and complex psycho-spiritual inner life of the Puranic and Tantric religion.

The Purano-Tantric stage was decried by European crities and Indian reformers as a base and ignorant degradation of the earlier religion. Much of the adverse criticism proceeded from a total ignorance of the sense and intention of the worship and by the concentration on side-paths and observations. In fact the Purano-Tantric development was a catholic attempt to draw towards the spiritual truth minds of all qualities and people of all classes. Though there was a loss of the profound psychic knowledge of the Vedic seers, but much of new knowledge was developed, untrodden ways were discovered and a hundred gates discovered to the Infinite. The essential aim and sense of this new development evolved out of the early Vedic form. For the early religion spoke to the outward physical mind of man and took that an its starting-point to the inner mystical sense. But the new evolution tried to awaken a more inner mind even in the common mass of humanity, to awaken the soul and lead humanity towards the highest spiritual truth.

The Vedic godheads were to the mind of their worshippers divine powers who presided over the workings of the physical cosmos; only the elect few were initiated into the inner mysteries. The Puranic Trinity had even for the multitude a predominant psycho-religious and spiritual significance. The central spiritual truth remained in both systems the same, the truth of the one in many aspects. The Trinity is the triple form of the one supreme Godhead; the Shaktis are energies of the one Energy of the highest divine Being. But this greatest truth was no longer reserved for the select few; it was brought powerfully, widely and intensely home to the general mind and feeling of the people.

There grew out of Vedic dieties the larger and simpler worship of Vishnu or Siva as the one universal and highest Godhead of whom all others are living forms and powers. The idea of Divinity in man was popularised to an extraordinary extent and this developed the various systems of Yoga. All the systems led or hoped to lead through a variety of psycho-spiritual methods to the common aim of Hindu spirituality to a greater consciousness and a more or less complete union with the one and Divine. The Purano-Tantric systems, based on the Vedic spirit, became a wide, assured and many-sided methodology by which man could rise though knowledge, works or love or through any other fundamental power of his nature to a supreme experience and highest absolute state.

We thus see in all the transformations and transmutation that have taken place from the Vedas through Vedanta to the Puranas the same concept of the one in the many and the way through the many to the one being developed. And the ultimate aim is spiritual attainment though its appearance may be physical or mental, temple rituals or philosophical disputation, chanting of mantras or singing of hymns. It is in this context that the gods and goddesses whether Vedic, Vedantic or Puranic have to be viewed.

2. Synopsis

Chapter 2 deals with the Vedic and Vedantic concepts because these are the authority on which all later Hindu systems are based. In the Vedic system there is only the one who is both immanent and transcendent in the universe. The Vedic seers describe the single universal Being as the substrate of the empiricial and multiple godly entities who are called by different names according to their attributes and functions: They also become the All and were the guardians of the Truth, Right and Law. The Vedantic system talks of the one only without a second. The one is inconceivable and indefinable by the finite and defining mind. So it has no name or form and can only be referred to as That. Vedanta also made the various Vedic deities the powers of consciousness in addition to their being the powers of nature. This led to an intense inward turning of the mind and the development of the various yogic disciplines.

Chapter 3 deals with the Vedic deities. Starting from the creation hymn as to how the one made himself into the manifold universe while yet transcending the universe, it deals with the original sacrifice by which the one (Purusha) became all that there is. A description of some of the main Vedic deities-Dyaus and Prithvi (Heaven and Earth), Agni, Surya, Indra, Soma is given and since the description in the Veda is very sketchy some quotation about these deities from some Puranas are also given.

Chapters 4 through 9 deal with the mythology of the Puranic deities. It will be clear from these chapters that every image and symbol, every word and idea of any Hindu myth, in spite of the stress played upon traditional form, each myth celebrates the belief that the universe is boundlessly various, that everything occurs simultaneously, that all possibilities may exist without excluding each other. The pattern that emerges from these myths is the tension between variety and pattern: the resolution of chaos into order, and its dissolution back into chaos.

Chapter 4 deals with Brahm or Brahman the one undying constant in the universe.

Chapter 5 deals with Brahma, the creator, and goddess Saraswati, his consort, and the epitome of wisdom.

Chapter 6 deals with the many myths about Vishnu the preserver, and his consort Lakshmi, the goddess of wealth.

Chapter 7 deals with the incarnations of Vishnu and how He descended into the earth as man to vanquish *adharma* and restore *dharma*. In other words to prevent the spread of chaos and to restore order.

Chapter 8 deal with Siva who is in change of creative destruction so that the universe can renew itself.

Chapter 9 deals with the consort of Siva the goddess Uma who also appears in different forms as Parvati, Durga and Kali. All of them represent the power of *Shakti* of Siva.

Chapter 10 deals with the Tantric or *Shakta* concept whereby the different goddess are conceived as independent powers necessary to battle evil and so prevent the world from degenerating into chaos.

Chapter 11 deals with the sons of Siva and Parvati, Ganesh the leader of the ganas of Siva, and Kartikeya the commander-in-chief of the gods.

Chapter 12 deals with the process of creation and the divine *rishis* who make this possible.

Chapter 13 deals with the symbolisms of the chief gods and why their idols and iconography is what they are with in many cases, a number of hands and weapons.

2

THE VEDIC AND VEDANTIC CONCEPTS

Vedic

The Vedas have for long been the authority on which all later Hindu systems-economic, political, social- are based. The Vedas being fundamentally a record of experiences of intuition and revelation, the observation of the seers tend to be varied, and belong to various stages of human and individual development and exploration. The Vedas record not only the experiences of the poets who have composed the hymns of the Vedas, but also the experiences of the ancestors *(pitarah, poorvajanah).* Vedas thus describe the knowledge contained in the pre-Vedic tradition as also the Vedic tradition proper.

The Vedas probably took their present shape in the second millennium before Christ, but their roots go back to far more ancient times. Perhaps nowhere else can one observe the whole process of human evolution from its primordial utterance to the most elaborate poetic speech and the most profound philosophy.

The Vedas are known as *shruti,* that which has been 'heard'; they are not merely the product of human ingenuity but of revelation, that is an unveiling' that is eternal, signifying that they do not derive from the world of time and change, but are reflections of the eternal. Finally, they are expressions of the eternal word, the *vak,* and the human authors are seers *(drashta),* those who have 'seen' the truth, and 'poets' (*kavi*), those whose utterance is inspired.

Here it may be useful to note what the notion of the Vedas having no author, either human or divine, means for us. The theory of there being no author of the Vedas has often been ridiculed as a contradiction of common sense and a denial of causal thinking. The idea of having no author, in my thinking, seems to imply that at the core of this conception there is a desire to purify man's relationship with the Vedic text. Any one of us is the author of the Vedas when we read, meditate, and understand them. Nobody is the author of living words, like those of Vedas, except the one who utters them. The absence of an author means that there is no one who has laid down a relationship between words and their meaning. It is the reader who establishes this relationship thereby making of the Vedas a real or saving knowledge.

The fact that the Vedas have no author and thus no anterior authority, the fact that they possess only the value contained in the actual existential act of really "hearing" them, imparts to them a universality that makes them peculiarly relevant today. They dispose us to listen and then we hear what we hear, trusting that it is also what was to be heard.

One and the Many

Since the beginning a basic question has persisted "Is the universe monistic or pluralistic?" Whether man is primitive or civilized, illiterate or highly educated, he perceives a pluralistic world, and thus gets *prima facie* evidence of the existence of multiplicity in the world through his five sense-organs.

Man saw the vast earth and the infinite sky. He could not estimate the dimensions of the sky, or conceive of the boundaries of space. He could not make out the millions of galaxies. Even our own galaxy (the Milky Way) was unknown to him. But he could discern the sun, the moon, some planets of our solar system and the innumerable stars in the night sky. He observed diversity on the earth: varieties of human beings, families, genera and species of plants and animals.

Some of the interrelationships between the diverse elements were understood by Vedic man. What he could not understand he attributed to magic, to gods whom he called the possessors of *Maya* or magic. According to the function studied a god was specified. Vedic man correlated gods also to planes of existence or consciousness: The three worlds or planes referred to in the Vedas, being *bhur, bhavar, swar* (earth, atmosphere, heaven). The *Atharva-Veda* (10.9.12) goes on to say that some of the groups of gods (11 each) are celestial, some are atmospheric and the rest are terrestrial, thus correlating gods to the heavens, atmosphere and the earth.

The large number of gods mentioned in the Vedas has led to controversy among scholars as to whether this concept of the Vedas represents monotheism, +, pantheism, henotheism or kathenotheism. None of the above categories really applies. In the Vedas the worship of many gods has always occurred along with a teaching of the identity of the many gods with the one. This unity is conceived as not only being in the external world but also in the internal workings in man whereby all organs of perception and action are united in a supra - sensual entity. This concept of an underlying unity in nature as well as the human being has lead to the development of meditative and yogic practices. The result has been that India has produced a constant stream of sages who sought knowledge of the deeper workings of the mind in mystical states as a means of integrating themselves into holistic personalities.

The Vedic seers are among the more ancient and renowned of these sages of India. The multiplicity of gods in the Vedas and their link with the one has to their vision always reflected not a crude polytheism, pantheism, henotheism or kathenotheism but an abundance of living approaches to the Divine. In this concept the gods were only meant to perform certain functions on behalf of the one.

The Vedic vision of the seers culminates in the great mystical realization "I am one, I am the Brahman." The *Rig-Veda* says.

"All this in the beginning was Brahman. It knew itself as I am Brahman. Seeing this , the Rishi Vamadeva realized "I was the father of the human race and I became the Sun".

This realization is much like what Moses heard at the burning bush in the old Testament, of God as "I am that I am." In the teaching of the Vedas such knowledge is not, however, considered to be the exclusive property of a rare prophet or messiah but is declared to be the heritage and goal of each soul and to the development of various kinds of yoga -- whether based on action, devotion, intellect or concentration -- as a means of attaining to the one. This has given to humanity the great concept of equality of every human being in the spiritual sense irrespective of the work that anyone performs or the path that is followed.

But though the Vedic seer recognizes the transcendental Being which is the one only, but, in his invocations, he praises and worships the functional gods and not the transcendental Being. The phenomenal universe functions under the control of the one Lord *(Ishwar)* who is another aspect of the Transcendental one in the world of name and form. But as regards the Transcendental one, "there sight travels not, nor speech, nor the mind" and from which "words turn away without attaining and the mind also returneth baffled." Since the speech and mind travels not to the one, praise and worship as described in the Veda can obviously be meant for the functional gods only. The functional gods are also described in language by different names in accordance with their attributes and functions. But the functional gods are only different aspects of the one who is "without hue but has obtained manifold hues by His yogic power."

The *Rig-Veda* in a hymn, the *Purusha Sukta,* the Primal Man, also describes the pervasive nature of the immanent *Purusha* as one "who possesses a thousand heads, arms, and feet" as well as to how the "sacrifice" led to creation. The immanent one, is however, at the same time transcendent. Says the *Rig-Veda.*

"Mightier than his might is *Purusha,* one -fourth of whom is all that has come into being, while three- fourths of him resides in the region of immortality.

With three – fourths hath *Purusha* risen up, with one – fourth having become again this, thence spreading over what eats and does not eat."

The might of *Purusha,* the indweller God, is expressed in creation, which by virtue of God's presence abides as a self – renewing and eternal process. But, lest one misunderstand that God thus immanent in the world process is not distinct from it, we are immediately reminded that God, the indwelling *Purusha,* is greater that his might, in the sense that God essentially transcends the world process. It is in his immanent form that all the gods exist and not in his transcendental one.

Deeper probe into the Vedic texts also reveals that in their conception the various gods are not different from one another although they carry different names. They are only differernt forms of the same substance just as water and ice are both H_2O. In spite of their apparent differences in identities, according to the *Rig-Veda* the one is identified with gods such as Mitra, Varuna, Yama and Matarishvan. The *Atharva-Veda* (13.3.13) gives a description of Agni in the following way.

"Agni becomes Varuna in the evening and Mitra in the morning; becoming Savita he moves through the air and becoming Indra he glows in the middle of the sky."

This hymn is clear about the identity of the Vedic gods: They are different in name, but one in reality. According to the hymn Agni becomes Varuna; he becomes Mitra, he also becomes Savita and Indra and all the gods are comprehended in him. He encompasses all the gods as the felly rings the spokes is the simile given in a hymn of the *Rig-Veda* where Agni is invoked,

"Through you, o Agni, Varuna enforces the laws, Mitra dispels darkness and Aryama becomes bounteous. and thus all of them are universally comprehended in you in their functions. You encompass them all who are like spokes in a felly."

The Vedic seers thus poetically describe the single unitary Being as the substrate of the empirical multiple godly entities who are called by different names according to their different attributes and functions. They also become the all.

The Vedic surface thus gives a variegated appearance, a mosaic – like scenario with different forms and colours; but beneath the surface is a homogeneous, undifferentiated, unbroken whole, one, non – dual, without a second. The *Rig-Veda* declares; "Reality (the divine, well – winged Garutmat) is one only, which is verbally expressed by the seers in diverse ways."

Unity and the Multiplicity

Two questions arise concerning the one and the many: How did the one become the many? If there is equality between the one and the many, how is man to proceed from the empirical many to a realisation in identity with the one ?

The first question relates to the devolution or descent of the one into the world of name and form. The second to the return path, the evolution of man into a spiritual being who gets nearer and nearer to the one until he finally realises his identity with the one.

The first question deals with Vedic cosmogony. In the Veda the universe is compared to an inverted tree, with roots above. Below and above spread its branches, nourished by the *gunas;* sense – objects are its buds. The Kathopanisad also uses the same simile; it compares the world with an inverted tree. An infinitesimally tiny seed germinates; a sprout appears; it grows and become the world – tree.

According to the Upanishads, the expansion of the Universe is brought about through *tapas* or meditation. Meditation, according to the Upanishads, is also the instrumentality through which one attains bliss and fearlessness. Says the *Taittirya Upanishad.*

"Desiring that he became many, that he should make of himself many forms, Brahman meditated. Meditating, he created all things. Creating all things, he entered into everything. Entering into all things, he became that which can be defined and that which cannot be defined; he became that which has support and that which has not support; he became that which is conscious and that which is not conscious; he became that which is gross and that which is subtle. He became all things whatsoever; therefore the wise call him the real.

Before creation came into existence, Brahman existed as the Unmanifest. From the Unmanifest he created the Manifest. From himself he brought forth himself. Hence he is known as Self – Existent. The Self – Existent is the essence of all Beatitude. For who could live, who could breathe, if that blissful Self dwelt not within the lotus of the heart? He it is that gives joy. When a man finds his existence and unity in the Self – – who is the basis of life, who is beyond the senses, who is formless, inexpressible, beyond all predicates – then alone does he transcend fear. So long as there is the least idea of separation from him, there is fear. To the man who thinks himself learned, yet knows not himself as Brahman, Brahman, who drives away all fear, appears as fear itself."

But the realistion of Brahman, of the unity is not so easy to realize even if we know how the one became many. For this to come about our individualized nature needs to live in the single consciousness of an inner and outer movement dedicated to something that is beyond us and greater than ourselves. In all action there must be a consciousness that we are presenting it to the one divine Being who is also in all beings. This is the way to the absence of hate and grief, or it put it positively, to love and happiness. Says the *Isha Upanishad.*

"He who sees all beings in the one, and the one in all beings, hates none. To the illumined soul, the one is all. For he who sees everywhere onenss, how can there be delusion or grief."

The Veda has always considered perception of the one as knowledge and perception of the many as ignorance. But the Veda has never considered ignorance or knowledge of the many as irrelevant to life. To turn again to the *Isha Upanishad.*

"To darkness are they doomed who devote themselves only to the ignorance (life in the world), and to a greater darkness they who devote themselves only to the knowledge (meditation on the one).

Life in the world alone leads to one result, meditation alone leads to another. So have we heard from the wise.

They who devote themselves both to life in the world (the many) and to meditation (the one), by life in the world overcome death and by meditation achieve immortality."

The Veda does not demand rejection of the world of plurality but the attaining of harmony between the inward poise and the outword action. This is the path to the psycho – social integration of man and the creation of harmony between his innner self and the outer world: The management of oneself leads to management of the external environment.

Upanishadic (Vedantic) Concept

According to the Upanishadic concept, the subsystem of man is composed of both the gross and the subtle. Its substratum is the same divine consciousness that pervades the universe and its evolution from the gross to the subtle is the way by which the Eternal can be realised. Once the human soul is seized by this compelling desire for the ultimate reality, it is no longer satified with looking upon the world of forms and constant change through those doors of the mind and senses which the Self – existent has made to open outward; but rather it is driven to gaze inward into a new world of realities.

The senses and the sense – objects, belonging to name and form, are within the space – time continuum and subject to causation. The Upanishads hold that the ultimate reality, being beyond name and form, cannot be comprehended or understood by that which is finite and says the Upanishad, "can never be reached by speech nor by the eyes nor even the mind".

The Eternal, which is of the nature of the Infinite, is thus inconceivable and indefinable by finite and defining mind, just as it is inexpressible by mind – created speech. Attainment of the Eternal, says the Upanishad, leads to the cessation of all regrets and all desires.

"The Bliss of the Eternal is that from which words turn back without attaining and the mind also returneth baffled. He who knoweth the Bliss of the Eternal, verily to him cometh not remorse or torment at not having done the right or having done wrong; for he knoweth them both and delivereth his spirit from them on knowing the Eternal".

Here we reach the one who is not the Vedic unified Existence whom the sages call by various names but is the absolute Brahman referred to in the neuter gender as the That The result is that the Upanishadic gods, become unaware of their divine origins so that in the *Kena Upanishad* it is seen even the chief gods, Vayu, Agni and Indra are unable to understand and comprehend the power and might of Brahman. Though the Rig Veda had referred to the God to whom all gods paid worship as well as to the God above all gods nowhere in the Veda had the transcendental absolute become what he was to becme in the Upanishads: The one both immanent in, and transcending the universe, and while being devoid of all qualities and characteristics yet having them all in the absolute and eternal sense.

The Upanishad also made the various Vedic deities the powers of consciousness in addition to their being the power of nature. They correlated the different deities with the various senses following a hint to this effect in the *Atharva-Veda* which speaks of the gods entering into him after they had fused the mortal man complete' and of how 'man is regarded as this Brahman for verily all deities abide in him as cows in a pen'. An Upanishad declares that the self or spirit after deciding to create, first created the different worlds, and then their guardians or the gods. Feeling hunger and thirst they, the gods, asked the spirit for a place where they could establish themselves and eat food. The spirit first found them to be insufficient vehicles; and so the spirit finally created the form of man which the gods found to be excellently made and sufficient, and they entered into it for the performance of their functions. Agni entered the organ of speech, the Sun the eyes, Vayu the nostrils, the deities of the quarters the ears, the deities of herbs and trees the skin, and the moon the mind. In another passge, the *Taittiriya Upanishad* clearly declares Indra as the power and godhead of the purified and intuitive mind.

"He who is the Bull of the Vedas of the universal form, he who was born in the sacred rhythms from the Immortal, may Indra increase my intellect. O God, may I become a vessel of the Immortal. My body be full of vision and my tongue of sweetness, may I hear the much and vast with my ears. For thou art the sheath of Brahman covered over and hidden by the intelligence."

The Upanishads then go on to establish the relationship between the gods and Brahman. In the external world we have already noted how in the *Kena Upanishad* it is said that even the chief gods, including Indra, the godhead of the intelligence, could not get to know and to comprehend Brahman. It required the divine Shakti, Uma to elucidiate the power of Brahman. The *Brihadaranayaka Upanishad* goes on to say that even the gods cannot prevail against the man who has realised Brahman, since he becomes their very self. But he who worships a god thinking him as different from oneself, becomes as an animal to the gods, seving the gods in the same way as animals serve man. The Upanishad goes on to assert that the performance of sacrifices, or *yagya*, to someone regarded as different from oneself makes a person a servant of the gods. While recognising the efficacy of the Vedas and accepting that the Vedas are projected by the Infinite together with sacrifices, spiritual practices and all that the Vedas declare, the Upanishads in the freedom of their thought go beyond the Vedas.

"After studying the Vedas the intelligent one who is solely intent in acquiring knowledge and realisation, should discard the Vedas altogether, as the man who seeks to obtain rice discards the husk."

The approach of the Upanishads to the Vedic thought and system is, thus, not one of rejection, but rather an acceptance of all that the Vedas stand for, whther in their concept of the gods, sacrifices or rituals. Accepting, as the Upanishadic seers did, the presence of graded capabilities in different human beings, all that they do is to place the matter in perspective by delineating the differential results that flow from different kinds of behaviour and actions. Thereafter they leave it to each individual to follow the path considered most suitable by him. And later on the concepts get more and more subtle as the delineation of the Upanishdic system progresses.

The Upanishads also address themselves to the question of harmonising the internal and the external, that is, the subjective and inner world of man with the objective universe. Their approach is that whatever there is in the external is also in the internal. The gods thus become both the powers of nature and of consciousness thereby unifying the external with the internal. The Upanishads also speak of the processes of involution and evolution, with the Divine coming into nature through the process of involution, and man rising out of nature through the process of evolution. Both during the processes of involution and evolution, the milestones to be passed on the way are the same, namely, matter, energy, mind, intuitive thought and bliss for the evolving soul and bliss etc. downwards to matter for the Divine in its process of involution. In the Upanishadic scheme al the external power are controlled by Brahman, and the inner ones by the Atman, the inner controller. The harmonisation is completed by the identify of the Brahman with the Atman.

The Vedic attitude to life and nature was positive and activist making the Vedas to apparently put a somewhat greater stress on the external in contrast to that put on the internal. The Upanishads set out to redress the balance and re-establish harmony between the external and the internal by stressing the neçessity of an inward turning of the mind and consciousness. Says the *Katha Upanishad.*

"The self – born has set the doors of the body to face outwards, therefore the soul of a man gazes outward and not at the Self within; hardly a wise man here and there, desiring immortality, turns his eyes inward and sees the self within him."

The *Mahanarayana Upanishad* carries the matter further. Stating that there are various opinions being held as to what are the means of liberation, it goes on to say that the practice of truthfulness, austerity, withdrawal of senses from forbidden objects, giving of selfless gifts, scriptural duty and procreation (the son being the way to the land of the ancestors, *pitriloka*) are all very difficult to practice and are conducive to the highest good. Those devoted to the Vedic religion stress *agnihotre* and *yagya* and these also lead to the highest good. The wise, however, consider inward worship as the means of liberation with complete renunciation and dispassion, *sannyasa,* as surpassing all the austerities mentioned earlier and therefore being considered the supreme remedy.

As we have noted the Vedas speak of seers who conceive of the one in different ways. The Upanishads, which are post– Vedic, adopt the same liberal attitude. The oneness of the Supreme is insisted on, but variety of description is permitted. The light of absolute truth is said to be refracted as it passes through the imperfect human mind. In the boundless being of the one are all the powers that are worshipped as gods, not as if they were standing side by side in space, but each a facet mirroring the whole, or a hologram if we were to say it in modern language.

Once upon a time, Buddha relates, a certain king of Benares, desiring to divert himself, gathered together a number of beggars blind from birth and offered a prize to the one who should give him the best account of an elephant. The first beggar who examined the elephant got hold of the trunk and said it was like a tree the second, laying hold of the tail, declared that an elephant was like a rope; another, who seized an ear, insisted than an elephant was like a palm – leaf; and so on. The beggars fell to quarrelling with one another, and the king was greatly amused. The moral of the story is : Ordinary teachers who have grasped this or that aspect of the truth quarrel with one another, while only a Buddha knows the whole. In theological discussions we are at best blind beggars fighting with one another. The complete vision is difficult of attainment since Buddhas are rare.

In the above story those who are "blind" to the Reality cannot grasp it; it requires the "opening" of the eyes for them to have the holistic vision. Sri Krishna tells Arjuna in the Bhagvad Gita.

"But thou never canst see Me with these thy mortal eyes: I will give thee divine sight."

It was only when his eyes had been "opened" (the so called Third Eye referred to in many mystical traditions) that Arjuna could exclaim.

"I see in thee all the gods, O my God; and the infinity of the beings of thy creation ...All around I behold thy Infinity: The power of they innumerable arms, the visions from thy innumerable eyes, the world from thy innumerable mouths. Nowhere do I see thy begining or middle or end".

3

THE VEDIC DEITIES

The Vedas

Before speaking of the Vedic Deities, it is necessary that something be said concerning the Vedas themselves, the source of our information concerning them. The root of the word is *vid*, "to know;" hence the term *Veda* signifies *knowledge*; and as these books were not *written* for centuries after they were originally composed, it signifies knowledge that was heard, or orally communicated. The Vedas are not the work of a single person, but, according to popular belief, were communicated to a number of Rishis or saints, who in their turn transmitted them to their disciples. The Seer Vyasa is styled the arranger, or, as we should now say, the editor, of these works.

The instruction contained in these writings is said to have been breathed forth by God Himself. Other writers teach that it issued from Him like smoke from fire. Sometimes the Vedas are said to have sprung from the elements. The accounts of their origin, though differing in form, agree in teaching that they were the direct gift of God to man; and hence they are regarded with the greatest veneration.

The Vedas are four in number; of these the *Rig-Veda* is the oldest, next in order was the *Yajur-Veda*, then the *Sama-Veda*, and last of all the *Atharva-Veda*. Each of these Vedas consists of two main parts: a Sanhita, or collection of mantras or hymns; and a Brahmana, containing ritualistic precept and illustration. In these are found instructions to the priests who conduct the worship of the gods addressed in the hymns. Attached to each Brahmana is an Upanishad, containing secret or mystical doctrine.

Vedic Gods

Yaska (probably the oldest commentator on the Vedas) gives the following classification of the Vedic gods. "There are three deities, according to the expounders of the Vedas: Agni, whose place is on the earth ; Vayu or Indra, whose place is in the air; and Surya, whose place is in the sky. These deities receive severally many appellations in consequence of their greatness, or of the diversity of their function." In the Rig-Veda itself this number is increased to thirty-three, of whom eleven are said to be in heaven, eleven on earth, and eleven in mid-air. "Agni, the wise god, lends an ear to his worshippers. God with the ruddy steeds, who lovest praise, bring hither those three-and-thirty." This is the number usually mentioned, though it is by no means easy to decide which are the thirty-three intended, as the lists found in various places vary considerably; whilst in another verse it is said that "three hundred, three thousand, thirty-and-nine gods have worshipped Agni."

These deities, though spoken of as immortal, are not said to be self-existent beings; in fact their parentage in most cases is given; but the various accounts of their origin do not agree with each other. Agni and Savitri are said to have conferred immortality upon the other gods; whilst it is also taught that Indra obtained this boon by sacrifice. An interesting account is given in the *Satapatha Brahmana* of the means by which the gods obtained immortality, and superiority over the asuras or demons. All of them, gods and demons alike, were mortal, all were equal in power, all were sons of Prajapati, the Creator. Wishing to be immortal, the gods offered sacrifices liberally, and practised the severest penance; but not until Prajapati had taught them to offer a particular sacrifice could they become immortal. They followed his advice, and succeeded. Wishing to become greater than the asuras, they became truthful. Previously they and the asuras spoke truthfully or falsely, as they thought fit; but gradually, whilst they ceased from lying, the asuras became increasingly false; the result was that the gods after protracted struggles gained the victory.

It will be noticed that each of the gods is in turn regarded by the worshipper as superior to all the others. In the Vedas this superlative language is constantly employed, and identical epithets are indiscriminately given to various deities. Max-Muller says, "When these individual gods are invoked, they are not conceived as limited by the power of others, as superior or inferior in rank. Each god, to the mind of the supplicants, is as good as all the gods. He is felt at the time as a real divinity, as supreme and absolute, in spite of the limitations which, to our mind, a plurality of gods must entail on every single god. All the rest disappear for a moment from the vision of the poet, and he only who is to fulfil their desires, stands in full light before the eyes of the worshippers. … It would be easy to find, in the numerous hymns of the Rig-Veda, passages in which almost every single god is represented as supreme and absolute."

The will of these gods is sovereign; no mortal can thwart their designs. They exercise authority over all creatures. In their hands is the life of mortals. They know the thoughts and intentions of men, and whilst they reward the worshipper, they punish those who neglect them.

When the Puranic deities are described it will be noticed that the representations of the deities of that age are far more clearly defined than those of earlier times. Though the Vedic gods are spoken of as possessing human forms and acting as human beings, there is considerable vagueness in the outline. But as time goes on this is lost. The objects of worship are no longer indistinct and shadowy, but are so minutely described that their portraits could be easily painted. And as their physical features are no longer left to the imagination, so their mental and moral characters are fully delineated.

Creation in the Scriptures

The vision of the hymn (given in its entirety later) comes out of a profound insight into the mystery of reality. It is the product of a mystical experience that far transcends the limits of logical thinking. This hymn, while trying to plumb the depths of the mystery, formulates no doctrinal system but expresses itself by means of a rich variety of different symbols related to the one single insight. We are dealing here, in the first place, not with a description of a succession of stages through which the world has passed. The starting point of the hymn is an intuitive vision of the whole. This hymn does not attempt to communicate information but to share a mystical awareness that transcends the sharpest lines of demarcation of which the human mind is capable: the divine and the created, Being and Non being. It seeks to give expression to the insight of the oneness of reality which is experienced as being so totally one that it does not need the horizon of nonreality or the background of a thinking process to appear in its entire actuality.

The first verse brings us straightaway to the heart of the mystery and is composed of a series of questions. Neither an affirmation nor a negation is capable of carrying the weight of the ultimate mystery. Only the openness of an interrogation can embrace what our mere thinking cannot encompass. The Ultimate is neither real nor non-real, neither being nor nonbeing, and thus neither is nor is-not.

The seer then continues by a series of negatives: there was neither death nor nondeath, nor any distinction between day and night. All the opposites, including the contradictories, are on this side of the curtain. At this point we have not yet reached Being and thus we have not yet the possibility of limiting Being by Non-being.

This One is not even a concept. It is not a concept limit like truth, goodness, beauty, and similar concepts when applied to the Absolute; it is rather the limit of a concept, unthinkable in itself and yet present on the other side of the curtain as the necessary condition for the very existence and intelligibility of everything. Whereas the concepts of being, goodness, truth, and the like admit degrees of approximation to the fullness of that to which they refer, the One does not. There are degrees of being, of goodness, of truth. There are no degrees of oneness. The One represents the peak of mystical awareness, which India developed later in her Advaitic philosophy, and the West in Trinitarian theology.

Darkness and emptiness are also symbols of the first moment. This darkness is not, however, the moral darkness of the world, but the primordial darkness of the Origin. The negative as well as the positive aspect of existence belongs to the Ultimate. Evil and good, the positive and the negative, both are embraced in the One that encompasses everything. Furthermore, it is said that desire, love, fervor, were the dynamic forces that brought reality to a temporal process of originating something out of something. Out of nothing, nothing can come. Nothingness is not previous to, but coextensive with Being. The source of Being is not another Being or anything that can be considered as *being* an origin out of which things come to be. The process, according to the intuition of the Vedic *rishi* is one of concentration, and of an emergence by the power of love. This love cannot be a desire toward "something" that does not exist, or even a desire coming out of a nonexisting Being. Primordial love is neither an act directed toward the other (which in this case does not exist) nor an act directed toward oneself (which in this case is also nonexistent), but it is the constitutive act by which existence comes into being. Without love there is no being, but love does not happen without ardor or *tapas*. It is fervor, *tapas*, that makes the being be; they are not separable. The relation between *kama*, desire and love, on the one hand, and *tapas*, ardor and heat, on the other, is one of the universal cosmic laws linking Being and the whole realm of beings (V. 3–4).

The poets, those sages who seek to penetrate the mystery of reality, discover in Nonbeing the gravitational center of Being; only when this is realized can the cord that differentiates them be extended. The rope connecting Being and Nonbeing is the ultimate rope of salvation (V. 5).

The two last stanzas voice several agonized queries and give expression to a deep-rooted—uncertainty for which no reply is vouchsafed, because reality is still on the move and any definite answer would preclude its constant newness. This insight brings us again to that ultimate level where the One is situated. From that depth the sage expresses the most fundamental question about the essential enigma of the universe: What, he asks, is the origin of this universe, of all this, *idam*? Who, or what, is its purpose, its end, its direction? It cannot be the Gods, for they themselves belong on this side of the curtain. To say that we do not know can be as assertive as to say that we do know. The last question is not the expression of a renunciation of knowledge or a declaration of agnosticism, which would here amount to a dogmatic affirmation, but the declaration that the problem—and not only the answer—is beyond the subject and object of knowledge itself. The hymn concludes with this query, this constitutive uncertainty which is of infinite magnitude, because we are all involved in it. To answer the query would amount to killing the very unfolding of reality. It is the openness of this interrogation which allows the universe to emerge and to exist.

Nasadiya Sukta (Rig Veda)

At first was neither Being nor Nonbeing.
There was not air nor yet sky beyond.
What was its wrapping? Where? In whose protection?
Was Water there, unfathomable and deep?

There was no death then, nor yet deathlessness;
of night or day there was not any sign.
The One breathed without breath, by its own impulse.
Other than that was nothing else at all.

Darkness was there, all wrapped around by darkness,
and all was Water indiscriminate. Then
that which was hidden by the Void, that One, emerging,
stirring, through power of Ardor, came to be.

In the beginning Love arose,
which was the primal germ cell of the mind.
The Seers, searching in their hearts with wisdom,
discovered the connection of Being in Nonbeing.

A crosswise line cut Being from Nonbeing.
What was described above it, what below ?
Bearers of seed there were and mighty forces,
thrust from below and forward move above.

Who really knows ? Who can presume to tell it ?
Whence was it born ? Whence issued this creation ?
Even the Gods came after its emergence.
Then who can tell from whence it came to be ?

That out of which creation has arisen,
whether it held it firm or it did not,
He who surveys it in the highest heaven,
He surely knows—or maybe He does not!

Dismemberment : The Primeval Man is Sacrificed (Rig Veda)

One cosmogonic myth is the subject of an entire Rig Vedic hymn, which explains original creation as the result of a primeval sacrifice—not a true blood sacrifice, but a dismemberment and distribution; not an actual creation of something out of nothing, but rather a re-arrangement, another instance of order out of chaos. The primeval Man is not *changed* into the various forms of life; rather, he *is* those forms, always. It is worthy of note that creation produces not only the physical elements of the universe but also the social order, the basis of life in the Hindu view, as well as the seasons and the parts of the very sacrifice from which creation proceeds.

"The Man [Purusha] has a thousand heads, a thousand eyes, a thousand feet. He pervades the earth everywhere and extends beyond for ten fingers' breadth. The Man himself is all this, whatever has been and whatever is to be. He is the lord of immortality and also lord of that which grows on food. Such is his greatness, and the Man is yet greater than this. All creatures make up a quarter of him; three quarters are the immortal in heaven. With three quarters the Man has risen above, and one quarter of him still remains here, whence he spread out everywhere, pervading that which eats and that which does not eat. From him Viraj was born, and from Viraj came the Man, who, having been born, ranged beyond the earth before and behind. When the gods spread the sacrifice, using the Man as the offering, spring was the clarified butter, summer the fuel, autumn the oblation. They anointed the Man, the sacrifice, born at the beginning, upon the sacred grass. With him the gods, Sadhyas, and sages sacrificed. From that sacrifice in which everything was offered, the clarified butter was obtained, and they made it into those beasts who live in the air, in the forest, and in villages. From that sacrifice in which everything was offered, the verses and the chants were born, the metres were born, and the formulas were born. From it horses were born, and those other animals which have a double set of incisors; cows were born from it, and goats and sheep were born from it.

When they divided the Man, into how many parts did they disperse him? What became of his mouth, what of his arms, what were his two thighs and his two feet called? His mouth was the brahmin, his arms were made into the nobles, his two thighs were the populace, and from his feet the servants were born. The moon was born from his mind; the sun was born from his eye. From his mouth came Indra and Agni, and from his vital breath the wind [Vayu] was born. From his navel the atmosphere was born; from his head the heaven appeared. From his two feet came the earth, and the regions of the sky from his ear. Thus they fashioned the worlds."

From the *Vishnu Purana*

Although all creatures are destroyed at each cosmic dissolution, they are not released from rebirth, but are reborn according to their former good or bad *karma*. Therefore when Brahma performs creation mentally, from him are born the four-fold creatures, varying from gods to inanimate objects. When Brahma desired to create the four types – gods, demons, ancestors, and men – he harnessed the forces within his own self. When he was thus concentrated, desiring to create, the quality of darkness became manifest in Prajapati, and first the demons were born from his thigh. Brahma then abandoned his own body which had the quality of darkness, and that body which he had abandoned became night. Still desiring to create, he took another body and found pleasure; then the gods, in whom the quality of goodness was predominant, were born from the mouth of Brahma. He abandoned that body too, and it became the day, in which the quality of goodness is paramount; therefore at night the demons are powerful, and by day the gods. Then he took another body in which the quality of goodness formed the essence, and as he thought of himself as being like a father, the ancestors [*pitris*, 'fathers'] were born from him. The lord then abandoned that body when he had created the ancestors, and that cast-off body became the evening twilight which stands between day and night. Then he took another body in which the quality of passion was the essence, and from him was born the race of men, in whom the quality of passion abounds. Prajapati quickly abandoned that body too, and it became the light of the early twilight, the dawn. Therefore when this light arrives, men are powerful, and the ancestors become powerful at the time of evening twilight. The light of dawn, night, day, and evening twilight – these four are the bodies of the lord Brahma which served as vessels for the three qualities.

The lord Brahma, having created these creatures when he was impelled by their own capabilities and powers, then created others of his own will. He made the birds from his own youthful energy; he made sheep from his breast, goats from his mouth; Prajapati created cows from his stomach and his two sides. From his feet he made horses, elephants, donkeys oxen, deer, camels, mules, antelopes, and other species. Grasses, fruits, and roots were born from the hairs of his body.

Thus the lord Brahma, the First Creator and lord, created; and whatever *karma* they had achieved in a former creation, they received this *karma* as they were created again and again, harmful or benign, gentle or cruel, full of *dharma* or *adharma*, truthful or false. And when they are created again, they will have these qualities; and this pleased him. The lord Creator himself diversified the variety and differentiation of all the objects of the senses, properties, and forms. By the authority of the Vedas, he fashioned in the very beginning the name and form of creatures, gods and others, the diversity of their functions, and the appellations of the sages in the Vedas. In this way he made other creatures with the properties appropriate to their purpose.

Dyaus and Prithivi

The general opinion respecting Dyaus (Heaven) and Prithivi (Earth) is that they are amongst the most ancient of the deities, hence they are spoken of in the hymns of the Rig-Veda as the parents of the other gods. They are described as "great, wise and energetic;" those who "promote righteousness, and lavish gifts upon their worshippers". And in another place they are said to have "made all creatures", and through their favour "immortality is conferred upon their offspring." Not only are they the creators, but also the preservers of all creatures; and are beneficent and kind to all. In other passages Heaven and Earth are said to have been formed by Indra, who is declared to transcend them in greatness, whom they follow "as a chariot follows the horse." They are described as bowing down before him; as trembling with fear on account of him; and as being subject to his control. Again, they are said to have been formed by Soma; and in other verses other deities are said to have made them.

Some are of the opinion that Indra gradually superseded Dyaus in worship. As the praises of the newer god were sung, the older one was forgotten; and in the present day, whilst Dyaus is almost unknown, Indra is still worshipped, though in the Vedas both are called the god of heaven. Of Prithivi the *Vishnu Purana* gives the following account of her birth. There was a king named Vena, notorious for his wickedness and general neglect of religious duties. When the Rishis of that age could bear with his impiety no longer, they slew him. But now a worse evil happened; anarchy prevailed, and they felt that a bad king was better than none at all. Upon this they rubbed the thigh of Vena, when there came forth a black dwarf, resembling a negro in appearance. Immediately after his birth the dwarf asked, "What am I to do?" He is told, "Nisida" (sit down), and from this his descendants are called "Nisidis" unto this day. The corpse was now pure, as all sin had left it in the body of this black dwarf. The right arm was then rubbed, and from it there came a beautiful shining prince, who was named Prithu, and reigned in the place of his father. Now during his reign there was a terrible famine. As the Earth would not yield her fruits, great distress prevailed. Prithu said, "I will slay the Earth, and make her yield her fruits." Terrified at this threat, the Earth assumed the form of a cow, and was pursued by Prithu, even to the heaven of Brahma. At length, weary with the chase, she turned to him and said, "Know you not the sin of killing a female, that you thus try to slay me?" The king replied that "when the happiness of many is secured by the destruction of one malignant being, the slaughter of that being is an act of virtue." "But," said the Earth, "if, in order to promote the welfare of your subjects, you put an end to me, whence, best of monarchs, will thy people derive their support?" Overcome at length, the Earth declared that all vegetable products were old, and destroyed by her, but that at the king's command she would restore them "as developed from her milk." "Do you, therefore, for the benefit of mankind, give me that calf by which I may be able to secrete milk. Make also all places level, so that I may cause my milk, the seed of all vegetation, to flow everywhere around."

Prithu acted upon this advice. Before his time there was no cultivation, no pasture, no agriculture; no highways for merchants; all these things (or all civilization) originated in the reign of Prithu. Where the ground was made level, the king, induced his subjects to take up their abode. Thence proceeded all kinds of corn and vegetables upon which people now subsist. By granting life to the Earth, Prithu was as her father, and she thence derived the appelation Prithivi.

Aditi and the Adityas

Aditi is almost the only goddess mentioned by name in the Rig-Veda, as the mother of many of the gods; but it is by no means an easy task to delineate her character, as the most contradictory statements are made concerning her. She was invoked as the bestower of blessings on children and cattle; and she is declared to be the mother of Varuna, and other deities, sometimes eight, sometimes twelve in number. She is supposed to be the impersonation of "infinity, especially the boundlessness of heaven, in opposition to the finiteness of earth." Another supposition is that Aditi is the personification of "universal, all-embracing Nature or Being."

In the account of the Creation given in the *Rig-Veda*, Aditi is said to have sprung from Daksha, and in the same verse Daksha is called her son. There is also a reference to her other sons. In the *Vishnu Purana* we have no less than three somewhat differing accounts of the origin of Daksha the father of Aditi. In the first account, his name appears amongst the mind-born sons of Brahma; and in this connection he is said to have had twenty-four daughters; but Aditi is not mentioned as one of them. In the second account of Daksha, Aditi is said to have been one of his sixty daughters, and was given in marriage to Kasypa, by whom she had twelve sons—the Adityas. Elsewhere we read that Vishnu, when incarnate as the Dwarf, was a result of this marriage. In the third account of Daksha, Aditi is again mentioned as his daughter, and the mother of Vivasat (the Sun).

The Adityas

This name signifies simply the descendants of Aditi. In one passage in the *Rig-Veda* the names of six are given: Mitra, Aryaman, Bhaga, Varuna, Daksha and Amsa. In another passage they are said to be seven in number, though their names are not given. In a third, eight is the number mentioned; but "of the eight sons of Aditi, who were born from her body, she approached the gods with seven, and cast out Marttanda (the eighth)." As the names of these sons given in different parts of the Vedas do not agree with each other, it is difficult to know who were originally regarded as Adityas. Judging from the number of hymns addressed to them, some of these deities occupied a conspicuous position in the Vedic Pantheon; whilst others are named once or twice only, and then in connection with their more illustrious brethren. In the *Satapatha Brahmana*, and the *Puranas*, the number of the Adityas is increased to twelve. In addition to the six whose names are given above, the following are also described in some hymns of the Rig-Veda as the offspring of Aditi: Surya, as an Aditya identified with Agni, is said to have been placed by the gods in the sky; Savitri, and Indra too, are in one passage addressed as Aditya along with Varuna and the Moon. In the Taittiriya Texts, the following are described as Adityas:—Mitra, Varuna, Aryaman, Amsu, Bhaga, Indra, and Vivasvat (Surya).

As noticed above, the *Rig-Veda* says, "Of the eight sons who were born from the body of Aditi, she approached the gods with seven, but cast away the eighth." In the commentary, the following explanation of this circumstance is given. "The eighth son was deformed. His brothers, seeing his deformity, improved his appearance. He was afterwards known as Vivasvat (the Sun). From the superfluous flesh cut off his body an elephant was formed, hence the proverb, 'Let no man catch an elephant, for the elephant partakes of the nature of man.' "

According to a passage from the *Satapatha Brahmana*, Agni, Indra, and Surya, obtained superiority over the other gods by means of sacrifice. By whatever means this position was obtained, it is certain that they were the most popular deities of the Vedic Age. Agni stands in a class by himself; but with Indra and Surya there are other deities closely associated, and possessing very similar attributes.

Agni

Agni, the god of Fire, is one of the most prominent of the deities of the Vedas. With the single exception of Indra, more hymns are addressed to him than to any other deity.

Various accounts are given of the origin of Agni. He is said to be a son of Dyaus and Prithivi; he is called the son of Brahma, and is then named Abhimani; and he is reckoned amongst the children of Kasyapa and Aditi, and hence one of the Adityas. In the later writings he is described as a son of Angiras, king of the Pitris (fathers of mankind), and the authorship of several hymns is ascribed to him. In pictures he is represented as a red man, having three legs and seven arms, dark eyes, eyebrows and hair. He rides on a ram, wears a *poita* (brahmanical thread), and a garland of fruit. Flames of fire issue from his mouth, and seven streams of glory radiate from his body. The following gives a good idea of the character and functions of this deity in the Vedic Age.

Agni is an immortal who has taken up his abode with mortals as their guest. He is the domestic priest who rises before the dawn, and who concentrates in his own person and exercises in a higher sense all the various sacrificial offices which the Indian ritual assigns to a number of different human functionaries. He is a sage, the divinest among the sages, immediately acquainted with all the forms of worship; the wise director, the successful accomplisher, and the protector of all ceremonies, who enables men to serve the gods in a correct and acceptable manner in cases where they could not do this with their own unaided skill. He is a swift messenger, moving between heaven and earth, commissioned both by gods and men to maintain their mutual communication, to announce to the immortals the hymns, and to convey to them the oblations of their worhsippers; or to bring them (the immortals) down from the sky to the place of sacrifice. He accompanies the gods when they visit the earth, and shares in the reverence and adoration which they receive. He makes the oblations fragrant; without him the gods experience no satisfaction.

Agni is the lord, protector, king of men. He is the lord of the house, dwelling in every abode. He is a guest in every home; he despises no man, he lives in every family. He is therefore considered as a mediator between gods and men, and as a witness of their actions; hence to the present day he is worshipped, and his blessing sought on all solemn occasions, as at marriage, death, etc.

The highest divine functions are ascribed to Agni. Although in some places he is spoken of as the son of heaven and earth, in others he is said to have stretched them out; to have formed them, and all that flies or walks, or stands or moves. He formed the sun, and adorned the heavens with stars. Men tremble at his mighty deeds, and his ordinances cannot be resisted. Earth, heaven, and all things obey his commands. All the gods fear, and do homage to him. He knows the secrets of mortals, and hears the invocations that are addressed to him.

The worshippers of Agni prosper, are wealthy, and live long. He watches with a thousand eyes over the man who brings him food, and nourishes him with oblations. No mortal enemy can by any wondrous power gain the mastery over him who sacrifices to this god. He also confers and is the guardian of immortality. In a funeral hymn, Agni is asked to warm with his heat the unborn (immortal) part of the deceased, and in his auspicious form to carry it to the world of the righteous. He carries men across calamities, as a ship over the sea. He commands all the riches in earth and heaven; hence he is invoked for riches, food, deliverance, and in fact all temporal good. He is also prayed to as the forgiver of sins that may have been committed through folly. All gods are said to be comprehended in him; he surrounds them as the circumference of a wheel does the spokes.

The main characteristics of Agni are brought out in the following verses.

"Great Agni, though thine essence be but one,
Thy forms are three; as fire thou blazest here,
As lightning flashest in the atmosphere,
In heaven thou flamest as the golden sun.

"It was in heaven thou hadst thy primal birth;
By art of sages skilled in sacred lore
Thou wast drawn down to human hearths of yore,
And thou abid'st a denizen of earth.

"Sprung from the mystic pair, by priestly hands
In wedlock joined, forth flashes Agni bright;
But, oh! ye heavens and earth, I tell you right,
The unnatural child devours the parent brands.

"But Agni is a god; we must not deem
That he can err, or dare to comprehend
His acts, which far our reason's grasp transcend;
He best can judge what deeds a god beseem.

"And yet this orphaned god himself survives:
Although his hapless mother soon expires,
And cannot nurse the babe as babe requires,
Great Agni, wondrous infant, grows and thrives.

"Smoke-bannered Agni, god with crackling voice
And flaming hair, when thou dost pierce the gloom
At early dawn, and all the world illume,
Both heaven and earth and gods and men rejoice.

"In every home thou art a welcome guest,
The household tutelary lord, a son,

A father, mother, brother, all in one,
A friend by whom thy faithful friends are blest.

"A swift-winged messenger, thou callest down
From heaven to crowd our hearths the race divine.
To taste our food, our hymns to hear, benign,
And all our fondest aspirations crown.

"Thou, Agni, art our priest: divinely wise,
In holy science versed, thy skill detects
The faults that mar our rites, mistakes corrects,
And all our acts completes and sanctifies.

"Thou art the cord that stretches to the skies,
The bridge that scans the chasm, profound and vast,
Dividing earth from heaven, o'er which at last
The good shall safely pass to Paradise.

"But when, great god, thine awful anger glows,
And thou revealest thy destroying force,
All creatures flee before thy furious course,
As hosts are chased by overpowering foes.

"Thou levellest all thou touchest; forests vast
Thou shear'st, like beards which barber's razor shaves.
Thy wind-driven flames roar loud as ocean's waves,
And all thy track is black when thou hast past.

"But thou, great Agni, dost not always wear
That direful form; thou rather lov'st to shine
Upon our hearths, with milder flame benign,
And cheer the homes where thou art nursed with care.

"Yes! thou delightest all those men to bless
Who toil unwearied to supply the food
Which thou so lovest—logs of well-dried wood,
And heaps of butter bring, thy favourite mess.

"Though I no cow possess, and have no store
Of butter, nor an axe fresh wood to cleave,
Thou, gracious god, wilt my poor gift receive:
These few dry sticks I bring—I have no more.

"Preserve us, lord; thy faithful servants save

From all the ills by which our bliss is marred;
Tower like an iron wall our homes to guard,
And all the boons bestow our hearts can crave.

"And when away our brief existence wanes,
When we at length our earthly homes must quit,
And our freed souls to worlds unknown shall flit,
Do thou deal gently with our cold remains.

"And then, thy gracious form assuming, guide
Our unborn part across the dark abyss
Aloft to realms serene of light and bliss,
Where righteous men among the gods abide."

In the *Mahabharata,* Agni is represented as having exhausted his vigour by devouring too many oblations, and desiring to consume the whole Khandava forest, as a means of recruiting his strength. He was [at first] prevented from doing this by Indra; but having obtained the assistance of Krishna and Arjuna, he baffled Indra, and accomplished his object.

According to the *Ramayana,* in order to assist Vishnu when incarnate as Rama, Agni became the father of Nila by a monkey mother; and according to the *Vishnu Purana*, he married Swaha, by whom he had three sons—Pavaka, Pavamana, and Suchi.

Agni has many names; those more generally known are the following:—

Vahni, "He who receives the *hom*, or burnt sacrifice."

Vitihotra, "He who sanctifies the worshipper."

Dhananjaya, "He who conquers (destroys) riches."

Jivalana, "He who burns."

Dhumketu, "He whose sign is smoke."

Chhagaratha, "He who rides on a ram."

Saptajihva, "He who has seven tongues."

Surya

Surya and Savitri are two names by which the Sun is commonly addressed in the Vedic hymns. Sometimes one name is used exclusively, sometimes they are used interchangeably, and sometimes they are used as though they represented quite distinct objects. It is said that Savitri refers to the sun when invisible; whilst Surya refers to him when he is visible to the worshippers.

Although the hymns in which Surya is addressed are not very numerous, his worship was most common in the olden time, and has continued to the present hour. It is to him that the Gayatri, the most sacred text of the Vedas, is addressed. Simple in its phraseology, this short verse is supposed to be powerful. It is as follows:—

> Let us meditate on that excellent glory of the divine Vivifier;
> May he enlighten (or stimulate) our understandings.

As a specimen of the language employed in some of the later writings in reference to this verse, there are the following from the *Skanda Purana*:— "Nothing in the Vedas is superior to the Gayatri. No invocation is equal to the Gayatri, as no city is equal to Kasi (Benares). The Gayatri is the mother of the Vedas, and of Brahmans. By repeating it a man is saved. By the power of the Gayatri the Kshatriya Vishvamitra became a Brahmarishi, and even obtained such power as to be able to create a new world. What is there indeed that cannot be effected by the Gayatri? For the Gayatri is Vishnu, Brahma, and Siva, and the three Vedas." With promise of such blessings, it is not to be wondered at that the worship of Surya should continue.

The following hymns from the *Rig-Veda* gives a fair specimen of the language used for Surya:

> "Behold the rays of Dawn, like heralds, lead on high
> The sun, that men may see the great all-knowing god.
> The stars slink off like thieves, in company with Night,
> Before the all-seeing eye, whose beams reveal his presence,
> Gleaming like brilliant flames, to nation after nation.
> With speed, beyond the ken of mortals, thou, O Sun!
> Dost ever travel on, conspicuous to all.
> Thou dost create the light, and with it dost illume
> The universe entire; thou risest in the sight
> Of all the race of men, and all the host of heaven.

Light-giving Varuna! the piercing glance dost scan,
In quick succession, all this stirring, active world,
And penetrateth too the broad ethereal space,
Measuring our days and nights, and spying out all creatures.
Surya with flaming locks, clear-sighted god of day,
Thy seven ruddy mares bear on thy rushing car.
With these, thy self-yoked steeds, seven daughters of thy chariot
Onward thou dost advance. To thy refulgent orb
Beyond this lower gloom, and upward to the light
Would we ascend, O Sun! thou god among the gods."

Surya, as we have already noticed, is regarded as a son of Aditi; at other times he is said to be a son of Dyaus. Ushas (the Dawn) is called his wife, though in another passage he is said to be produced by the Dawn. Some texts state that he is the Vivifier of all things; whilst others state that he was formed and made to shine by Indra, Soma, Agni, and others.

From the character ascribed to Savitri in some hymns, it seems more natural to regard him as the sun shining in his strength and Surya as the sun when rising and setting. Savitri is golden-eyed, golden-handed, golden-tongued. He rides in a chariot drawn by radiant, white-footed steeds. He illuminates the earth; his golden arms stretched out to bless, infusing energy into all creatures, reach to the utmost ends of heaven. He is leader and king in heaven; the other gods follow him, and he it is who gives them immortality. He is prayed to for deliverance from sin, and to conduct the souls of the departed to the abode of the righteous.

In the Puranic Age, Surya sustains quite a different character. He is there called the son of Kasyapa and Aditi. He is described as a dark-red man, with three eyes and four arms: in two hands are water-lilies; with one he is bestowing a blessing, with the other he is encouraging his worshippers. He sits upon a red lotus, and rays of glory issue from his body. In addition to the daily worship that is offered him by Brahmans in the repetition of the Gayatri, he is worshipped once a year by the Hindus of all castes, generally on the first Sunday in the month of Magh; and in seasons of sickness it is no uncommon thing for the low-caste Hindus to employ a Brahman to repeat verses in his honour, in the hope that thus propitiated he will effect their recovery.

In the *Vishnu Purana* there is the following account of Surya. He married Sangna, the daughter of Visvakarma; who, after bearing him three children, was so oppressed with his brightness and glory that she was compelled to leave him. Before her departure, she arranged with Chhaya (Shadow) to take her place. For years Surya did not notice the change of wife. But one day, in a fit of anger, Chhaya pronounced a curse upon Yama (Death), a child of Sangna's, which immediately took effect. As Surya knew that no mother's curse could destroy her offspring, he looked into the matter and discovered that his wife had forsaken him, leaving this other woman in her place. Through the power of meditation, Surya found Sangna in a forest in the form of a mare; and, in order that he might again enjoy her society, he changed himself into a horse. After a few years, growing tired of this arrangement, they returned in proper form to their own dwelling. But in order that his presence might be bearable to his wife, his father-in-law Visvakarma, who was the architect of the gods, ground the Sun upon a stone, and by this means reduced his brightness by one-eighth. The part thus ground from Surya was not wasted. From it were produced the wonder-working discus of Vishnu, the trident of Siva, the lance of Kartikeya (the god of war), and the weapons of Kuvera (the god of riches).

The *Bhavishya Purana* says, "Because there is none greater than he (*i.e.*, Surya), nor has been, nor will be, therefore he is celebrated as the supreme soul in all the Vedas." Again, "That which is the sun, and thus called light or effulgent power, is adorable, and must be worshipped by those who dread successive births and deaths, and who eagerly desire beatitude." In the *Brahma Purana* is a passage in which the sun is alluded to under twelve names, with epithets peculiar to each, as though they were twelve distinct sun-deities :

"The first form of the sun is Indra, the lord of the gods, and the destroyer of their enemies; the second, Dhata, the creator of all things; the third, Parjanya, residing in the clouds, and showering rain on the earth from its beams; the fourth, Twasta, who dwells in all corporeal forms; the fifth, Pushan, who gives nourishment to all beings; the sixth, Aryama, who brings sacrifices to a successful conclusion; the seventh derives his name from almsgiving, and delights mendicants with gifts; the eighth is called Vivasvan, who ensures digestion; the ninth, Vishnu, who constantly manifests himself for the destruction of the enemies of the gods; the tenth, Ansuman, who preserves the vital organs in a sound state; the eleventh, Varuna, who, residing in the waters, vivifies the universe; and the twelfth, Mitra, who dwells in the orb of the moon, for the benefit of the three worlds. These are the twelve splendours of the sun, the supreme spirit, who through them pervades the universe, and irradiates the inmost souls of men."

Surya is said to have Aruna, the Dawn, the son of Kasyapa and Kadru, as his charioteer.

According to the *Ramayan,* Sugriva, the king of the monkey host which assisted Rama in his great expedition to regain possession of Sita his wife, was a son of Surya by a monkey. According to the Mahabharata, the hero Karna also was the son of this deity ; and when he was in the form of a horse, he became father of the Asvins, and communicated the *White Yajur -Veda.*

When referring to the planets, Surya is known under the name of Ravi.

Among the many names and epithets by which this deity is known, the following are the most common :

Dinakara, "The Maker of the day."

Bhaskara, "The Creator of light."

Vivaswat, "The Radiant one."

Mihira, "He who waters the earth;" *i.e.*, he draws up the moisture from the seas so that the clouds are formed.

Grahapati, "The Lord of the stars."

Karmasakshi, "The Witness of (men's) works."

Martanda, "A descendant of Mritanda."

Pushan

Pushan is the name of a sun-god to whom some hymns are exclusively addressed, and whose praise at other time is sung in connection with that of Indra and other gods. In these hymns his character is not very clearly defined. He is said to behold the entire universe; is addressed as the guide of travellers, and the protector of cattle. He is called upon to protect his servants in battle, and to defend them as of old. He is invoked in battle, and to defend them as of old. he is invoked in the marriage ceremonial, and asked to take the bride's hand, to lead her away, and to bless her in her conjugal relations. He is said also to conduct the spirits of the departed from this world to the next. In one text he is called "the nourisher," as Vishnu in later times was called "the preserver." By far the greater number of prayers addressed to him seem to regard him as the guide and protector of travellers, both along the ordinary journeys of life and in the longer journey to the other world; and as he is supposed to be constantly travelling about, he is said to know the road by which they have to go.

The following is a hymn addressed to Pushan in the *Rig-Veda* :

"Conduct us, Pushan, over our road; remove distress, son of the deliverer; go on before us. Smite away from before us the destructive and injurious wolf which seeks after us. Drive away from our path the waylayer, the thief and the robber. Tread with thy foot upon the burning weapons of that deceitful wretch, whoever he be. O wonder-working and wise Pushan, we desire that help of thine wherewith thou didst favour our fathers! O god, who bringest all blessings, and art distinguished by the golden spear make wealth easy of acquisition! Convey us past our opponents; make our paths easy to travel; gain strength for us here. Lead us over a country of rich pastures; let no new trouble (beset our) path. Bestow, satiate, grant, stimulate us; fill our belly. We do not reproach Pushan, we praise him with hymns; and we seek riches from the wonder-working god."

In the Puranas Pushan occupies a far less exalted position. He, who in the Vedas is reverently approached as the giver of good to his worshippers, described as being obliged to feed upon gruel, because his teeth have been knocked out of his mouth.The earliest form of the legend describing this event is found in the *Taittiriya Sanhita.* Rudra, the name by which Siva was then known, not being invited to a great sacrifice that Daksha, his father-in-law, was celebrating, in his anger shot an arrow which pierced the sacrificial victim. Pushan ate his share, and in doing so broke his teeth.

Mitra and Varuna

These deities are most frequently named together in the hymns; Varuna is often addressed alone, but Mitra very seldom. The idea of the older commentators was that Mitra represented and ruled over the day, whilst Varuna was ruler of the night. Varuna is sometimes visible to the gaze of his worhsipers; he dwells in a house having a thousand doors, so that he is ever accessible to men. He is said to have good eyesight, for he knows, what goes on in the hearts of men. He is king of gods and men; is mighty and terrible; none can resist his authority. He is sovereign ruler of the universe. It is he who makes the sun to shine in heaven; the winds that blow are but his breath; he has hollowed out the channels of the rivers which flow at his command, and he had made the depths of the sea. His ordinances are fixed and unassailable; through their operation the moon walks in brightness, and the stars, which appear in the nightly sky, vanish in daylight.

The following is one of the hymns of the *Rig-Veda* :

"The mighty lord on high our deeds as if at hand espies;
The gods know all men do, though men would fain their deeds disguise:
Whoe'er stands, whoe'er moves, or steals from place to place,
Or hides him in his secret cell, the gods his movements trace.
Wherever two together plot, and deem they are alone,
King Varuna is there, a third, and all their schemes are known.
This earth is his, to him belong those vast and boundless skies,
Both seas within him rest, and yet in that small pool he lies.
Whoever far beyond the sky should think his way to win,
He could not there elude the grasp of Varuna the king.
His spies descending from the skies glide all this world around;
Their thousand eyes, all scanning, sweep to earth's remotest bound.
Whate'er exists in heaven and earth, whate'er beyond the skies,
Before the eye of Varuna the king unfolded lies.
The secret winkings all he counts of every mortal's eyes;
He wields this universal frame as gamester throws his dice.
Those knotted nooses which thou flingst, O god! the bad to snare,
All liars let them overtake, but all the truthful spare."

In other hymns we learn that the affairs of men are under his control; he is asked to prolong life, to punish transgressors; and a hope is held out that the righteous shall see him reigning in the spirit world in conjunction with Yama, the ruler of that region. Varuna in fact has attributes and functions ascribed to him in the Vedas, of a higher moral character than any other of the gods, and therefore men call upon him for pardon and purity. "Release us," they say, "from the sins of our fathers, and from those which we have committed in our own persons."

And again, "Be gracious, O mighty god, be gracious. I have sinned through want of power; be gracious."

In the hymns addressed to Mitra and Varuna together, almost the same terms are employed as when Varuna is addressed alone. Both are spoken of as righteous, and as the promoters of religion. They are said to avenge sin and falsehood.

In the Vedic literature, though Varuna is not regarded chiefly as the god of the ocean, as he is in the later writings, but rather, as the above hymns show, as one of the gods of light, yet there are passages which describe him as being connected with the waters of the atmosphere and on the earth, which afford some foundation for the later conceptions of his kingdom. Thus, for instance, we read, "May these waters in the midst of which Varuna goes preserve me.

In the *Brahmana* of the *Rig-Veda* is an interesting legend showing that probably human sacrifices were at one time offered to Varuna. A certain king named Harischandra had no son. Being greatly distressed on this account, as a son was necessary to the due performance of his funeral ceremonies, the king, acting upon the advice of Narada the sage, went to Varuna, saying—

"Let but a son be born, O king! to me,

And I will sacrifice that son to thee."

Varuna heard the prayer, and granted a son. When the boy grew up, his father told him of the vow he had made; but unfortunately the son was not willing to be sacrificed, and left his home. Varuna, not being at all pleased at the non-fulfilment of the king's vow, afflicted him with dropsy. For six years the boy wandered in the forest; at length, happening to meet with a poor Brahman with his three sons, the prince proposed to purchase one of them to offer to the god as a substitute for himself. The father could not give up his firstborn, the mother would not yield her youngest; the middle one was therefore taken. The prince then returned home, taking with him the Brahman's son. At first the king was delighted at the prospect of being able to keep his promise to the deity; but a difficulty now arose as to who would slay the boy. After some time, on the consideration of a large present being made to him, the boy's father consented to do this. The boy was bound, the father ready to strike, when the boy asked permission to recite some texts in praise of the gods. Of course this was granted; and as a result the deities thus lauded were so pleased with the boy's piety, that they interceded with Varuna to spare him. Varuna granted their request, suffered the boy to live, and Harischandra recovered from his sickness.

In the Puranas, as mentioned before, Varuna is described as the god of the ocean. After a great conflict between the powers of heaven and earth, when order was again restored, the *Vishnu Purana* records the position assigned to the various deities. In that account Varuna is said to rule over the waters. In the same Purana we read that an old Brahman named Richika was most anxious to obtain in marriage a daughter of King Gadhi, wo was really an incarnation of Indra. Gadhi refused to give his daughter to Richika except on one condition: that he would present him with a thousand fleet horses, each having one white ear. Horses of this colour were special favourites of Indra; hence those sacrificed to him usually had this peculiarity. The Brahman is said to have propitiated Varuna, the god of the ocean, who gave him the thousand steeds, by means of which he was able to obtain the princess in marriage.

Varuna is represented in pictures as a white man sitting upon a fabulous marine monster called a *makara*. This animal has the head and front legs of an antelope, and the body and tail of a fish. In his right hand he carries a noose. He is occasionally worshipped in seasons of drought, and by fishermen as they cast their nets, but nowadays no images of him are made.

Although Varuna is described in the Vedas as a holy being, according to the teaching of the Puranas his heaven is a place of sensual delights. He sits with his queen Varuni on a throne of diamonds; Samudra (the sea), Ganga (the Ganges), and the gods and goddesses of different rivers, lakes, springs, etc., form his court. And stories are told of conduct the very opposite to what would be expected in one who once was addressed in such language as is found in the Vedic hymns. He is said, conjointly with Surya, to have been enamoured of Uravasi, a nymph of Indra's heaven, by whom they had a son named Agastya, one of the most eminent of Hindu ascetics.

Varuna is also known as Prachetas, the wise; Jalapati, the lord of water; Yadapati, the lord of aquatic animals; Amburaja, the king of waters; Pasi, the noose-carrier.

The Asvins

From the hymns addressed to these deities it is not at all easy to know who or what they are. Yaska, the commentator of the Vedas, deriving the name from a root meaning "to fill," says they are called Asvins because they pervade everything, the one with light, the other with moisture. Another commentator says they are called Asvins because they ride upon horses. Some say that by them heaven and earth are indicated; others that they are day and night; others, again, that they are the sun and moon. In some hymns they are said to be sons of the sun (Surya); in others are called children of the sky; in others, again, as the offspring of the ocean. They seem to represent the transition from night to morning—night when it is passing into day.

The Asvins are said to have had Surya, the daughter of Savitri, as their common wife. She chose them, as her life was lonely. Her father had intended her to marry Soma; but, as the gods were anxious to obtain so beautiful a bride, it was agreed that they should run a race, Surya being the prize of the winner. The Asvins were successful, and she ascended their chariot. In another passagge Soma is said to have been her husband ; the Asvins being friends of the bridegroom.

The Asvins are regarded as the physicians of the gods, and are declared to be able to restore to health the blind, the sick, the lame, and the emaciated amongst mortals. They are the special guardians of the slow and backward; the devoted friends of elderly women who are unmarried. They are said to preside over love and marriage, and are implored to bring together hearts that love.

A number of legends are found illustrating the power of the Asvins in healing the sick and assisting those in trouble, from which we learn that they could restore youth and vigour to the aged and decrepit; they resclued a man from drowning, and carried him in safety to his home. The leg of Vispala, that was cut off in battle, they replaced by an iron one. At the request of a wolf, they restored sight to a man who had been blinded by his father as a punishment for slaughtering a hundred and one sheep, which he gave to the wolf to eat. They restored sight and power to walk to one who was blind and lame. As a result of these and other similar legends, the Asvins are invoked for "offspring, wealth, victory, destruction of enemies, the preservation of the worshippers themselves, of their houses and cattle."

Ushas

This goddess, representative of the Dawn, is a favourite object of celebration with the Vedic poets, and the hymns addressed to her are among the most beautiful—if not the most beautiful—in the entire collection. She is described as the daughter of the Sky, has Night for her sister, and is related to Varuna. She is at times spoken of as the wife of the Sun; at other times Agni is given as her lover; the Asvgins are her friends. Indra is at one time regarded as her creator; at another time he assumes a hostile position, and even crushed her chariot with his thunderbolt.

Ushas is said to travel in a shining chariot drawn by ruddy horses or cows. Like a beautiful maiden dressed by her mother, a dancing girl covered with jewels, a gaily attired wife appearing before her husband, or a beautiful girl coming from her bath, she smiling and confiding in the irresistible power of her attractions, unfolds her bosom to the gaze of the beholders. She dispels the darkness, disclosing the treasures it concealed. She illuminates the world, revealing its most distant extremities. She is the life and health of all things, causing the birds to fly from their nests, and, like a young housewife awaking all her creatures, sends them forth to the pursuit of their varied occupations. She does good service to the gods, by causing the worshippers to awake, and the sacrificial fires to be lighted. She is asked to arouse only the devout and liberal, while she allows the niggardly to sleep on. She is young, being born every day; and yet she is old, being immortal, wearing out the lives of successive generations, which disappear one after another, whilst she continues undying. The souls of the departed are said to go to her and to the sun.

In the following hymn will be found the main teaching of the Vedas respecting this goddess:—

"Hail, ruddy Ushas, golden goddess, borne
Upon thy shining car, thou comest like
A lovely maiden by her mother decked,
Disclosing coyly all thy hidden grace
To our admiring eyes; or like a wife,
Unveiling to her lord, with conscious pride.
Beauties which, as he gazes lovingly,
Seem fresher, fairer, each succeeding morn.
Through years and years thou hast lived on, and yet
Thou'rt ever young. Thou art the breath and life
Of all that breathes and lives, awaking day by day

Myriads of prostrate sleepers, as from death,
Causing the birds to flutter in their nests,
And rousing men to ply with busy feet
Their daily duties and appointed tasks,
Toiling for wealth, or pleasure, or renown."

Indra

Indra, together with Agni and Surya, by means of sacrifice obtained supremacy over the other gods; and judged from the number of hymns addressed to him in the Vedas, he was a most popular diety.

He is the god of the firmament, in whose hands are the thunder and the lightning; at whose command the refreshing showers fall to render the earth fruitful. When it is borne in mind that in India for months together the earth, exposed to the scorching rays of the sun, becomes so hard that it is impossible for the fields to be ploughed or the seed to be sown, it will not be regarded as wonderful that the god who is supposed to bestow rain should frequently be appealed to, and that the most laudatory songs should be addressed to him. To the poetic minds of the Vedic age, the clouds that the winds brought from the ocean were enemies who held their treasures in their fast embrace until, conquered by Indra, they were forced to pour them upon the parched soil. And very naturally when, in answer to the cry of his worshippers, the genial rains descended, and the earth was thereby changed from a desert to a garden, songs of thanksgiving and praise, couched in the strongest terms, were addressed to him. The attributes ascribed to him refer principally to his physical superiority; and the blessings sought from him are chiefly of a physical rather than a spiritual character.

Indra is not regarded as an uncreated deity. In some hymns he is spoken of as the twin-brother of Agni, and therefore the son of Heaven and Earth; whilst, in other hymns, heaven and earth are said to have been formed by him. Although his parents are often referred to, it is but seldom that they are named; and when they are named, they are not always the same. He is the king of the gods; and in post-Vedic ages his reign is said to extend for a hundred divine years only; at the end of which time he may be superseded as king by some other of the gods, or even by man, if any be able to perform the severe penance necessary to obtain this exalted position.

In pictures, Indra is often represented as a man with four arms and hands; with two he holds a lance, in the third is a thunderbolt, whilst the fourth is empty. He is also sometimes painted with two arms only, and, having eyes all over his body, is then called Sahasraksha (the thousand-eye). He is generally depicted as riding upon the wonderful elephant Airavatu, who was produced at the churning of the ocean, carrying a thunder bolt in his right hand and a bow in his left. In the Vedic Age his worship was far more popular than it is at present.

The position and attributes of Indra as in the Vedas can be seen from the following description :—

"Come, Indra, come, thou much invoked,
Our potent hymn thy steeds has yoked.
Friend Indra, from the sky descend,
Thy course propitious hither bend.
But, Indra, though of us thou thinkest,
And our libations gladly drinkest,
We, mortal men, can only share
A humble portion of thy care.
We know how many potent ties
Enchain thee in thy paradise.
Thou hast at home a lovely wife,
The charm and solace of thy life.
Thou hast a ceaseless round of joys
Which all thy circling hours employs;
Joys such as gods immortal know,
Unguessed by mortals here below."

Ready prepared for him is a feast, the principal attraction of which is the Soma juice. Indra was particularly fond of this intoxicating drink. It is a most strange circumstance that, whilst the Hindus of the present day are prohibited from the use of intoxicants, Indra is described as being addicted to the Soma; whilst the drink itself is deified and worshipped as a god. Indra on his arrival is invited to quaff the invigorating cup:—

"Thou, Indra, oft of old hast quaffed
With keen delight our Soma draught.
All gods the luscious Soma love,
But thou all other gods above.

Thy mother knew how well this juice
Was fitted for her infant's use.
Into a cup she crushed the sap,
Which thou didst sip upon her lap.
Yes, Indra, on thy natal morn,
The very hour that thou wast born.
Thou didst those jovial tastes display,
Which still survive in strength to-day."

Indra, after singing the praises of the Soma juice, drinks the proffered cup, and as a result is most graciously disposed towards the worshippers, ready to give whatever they ask. When thus strengthened by the draught, he goes forth to meet the great enemy he came to conquer. This enemy is Vritra. And in the conflict and victory are seen the preculiar blessings to the earth and man that Indra is able to grant. Vritra is thus described:—

"He whose magic powers
From earth withhold the genial showers,
Of mortal men the foe malign,
And rival of the race divine;
Whose demon hosts from age to age
With Indra war increasing wage,
Who, times unnumbered crushed and slain.
Is ever newly born again,
And evermore renews the strife
In which again he forfeits life."

The battle is described at length; in which we have a graphic description of the commencement of the rainy season, with the severe thunderstorms which usually accompany this change of the seasons. At last the conflict is over:

"And soon the knell of Vritra's doom
Was sounded by the clang and boom
Of Indra's iron shower.
Pierced, cloven, crushed, with horrid yell,
The dying demon headlong fell
Down from his cloud-built tower."

As a result of the victory of the god, the rains descend and the earth is made fruitful:

"Now bound by Sushna's spell no more,
The clouds discharge their liquid store;
And long by torrid sunbeams baked
The plains by copious showers are slaked;
The rivers swell, and seawards sweep
Their turbid torrents broad and deep.
The peasant views with deep delight,
And thankful heart, the auspicious sight.
His leafless fields, so sere and sad,
Will soon with waving crops be glad;
And mother Earth, now brown and bare,
A robe of brilliant green will wear."

After this blessing has been received, the sun shines, and earth again is bright; the gods come with their congratulations to their king, and men present their thanksgivings.

Such was Indra in ancient times; and though worshipped still, he occupies a very inferior position today. As mentioned previously, according to the teaching of the later books, his rule over the gods continues for a hundred divine years; at the expiration of which time he may be superseded by another god, or even by a man. The Puranas teach that, in each age of the world, a different being has enjoyed this position. In the *Vishnu Purana* is the story of a man raising himself to the throne of Indra.

There was a war between the gods and demons; both parties inquired of Brahma which would be victorious. Brahma replied, "The side for which Raji (an earthly king) shall take up arms." The demons called first upon Raji to invoke his aid. He promised to assist them provided they would make him their Indra or king. They could not promise this, as Prahlada, their Indra's, term of office was not yet expired. The same condition being proposed to the gods, they consented, and Raji became their Indra. He fought for them, and conquered. Upon this, Indra bowed down before him, and, placing Raji's foot upon his head, said, "Thou hast preserved me from a great danger. I acknowledge thee as my father:

thou art king over all; I am thy son." Raji, however, was contented to remain as king on earth, and appointed Indra to continue as his representative on the throne of heaven. On the death of Raji, his sons wished to assume the position their father had declined. This Indra opposed, but was at length compelled to yield. After a time, being sad because deprived of his share in the sacrifices of mortals, Indra met with his spiritual preceptor Brihaspati, and asked him for a morsel of the sacrifical butter. The teacher replied that, had Indra applied to him earlier, he would not have been reduced to such straits; but "as it is," he said, "I will regain your sovereignty in a few days." Upon this he commenced a sacrifice, with the special purpose of obtaining power for Indra. The result was, that Raji's sons were led into sin, they became enemies of the Brahmans, despised the Vedas, and neglected their religious duties. When thus weakened, Indra fell upon and slew them.

In the *Vishnu Purana*, there is a legend of a conflict between Indra and Krishna, in which Indra is overcome. Krishna, accompanied by his wife Satyabhama, visits Indra in his heaven. On her arrival, this lady was most anxious to obtain possession of the wonderful Parijata tree, which was produced at the churning of the ocean, and planted in Indra's heavenly garden. This tree was beautiful in form, was adorned with lovely and sweet-scented flowers, and bore most luscious fruit. At the request of his wife, Krishna took the tree, and placed it upon Garuda, his wonderful bird-vehicle. Immediately there was an uproar in heaven; but though Indra and his attendant deities tried to prevent the removal of his property, they could not do so. Krishna caught a thunderbolt of Indra in his hand, and, returning home unhurt, planted the tree in his garden.

The *Ramayana* has a story showing that Indra was believed to have been guilty of the grossest immorality—the seduction of the wife of his spiritual teacher. He is said to have visited the house of Gautama, in the form of a sage, hoping to be mistaken by the preceptor's wife for her husband, who was absent from home. But although Ahalya knew him to be Indra, she yielded to his wishes. As Indra was about to leave, Gautama returned, and knowing what had happened, cursed the god and his wife. Indra in consequence lost his manhood; and Ahlaya was doomed to live for many years invisible in a forest, until Rama should come to restore her to her former state. Another account of this curse of Gautama was that Indra was compelled to carry a thousand disgraceful marks upon his body, that all might know the sin of which he had been guilty. At the god's earnest request these were changed from their original form into eyes, which by the ignorant came to be regarded as an indication of his omniscience.

The heaven of Indra must not be passed over without notice, as it is there the good on earth hope to go for a time, as a reward of their holy lives. To go to *Swarga,* as his heaven is named, is not the highest happiness a man can obtain, because he cannot remain there for ever. When his allotted years of happiness are over, he must return to earth and live other lives, until he becomes perfect and fit to enjoy the highest felicity—absorption into the Divine Being.

The more common of Indra's other names are the following:—Sakra, the able one; Divapati, the lord of the gods; Bajri, he who wields the thunderbolt; Vritraha, the destroyer of Vritra; Meghavahana, he who rides on the clouds; Mahendra, the great Indra; Swargapati, the lord of heaven.

Indrani

Of Indrani, the wife of Indra (called also Sachi), very little is said. In the Rig-Veda we read, "Among all females Indrani is the most fortunate; for her husband shall not at any future time die of old age." This may be explained by the fact that Indrani is wife to all who successively attain to the throne of Indra. There is always some one ruling in heaven; the office is perpetual, and as she is the wife of the reigning king, whoever he may be, her husband can never die of old age. Though kings may come and go, she continues queen. She is said to have a son, Chitragupta by name, who was born of a cow; for, owing to a curse pronounced by Uma, none of the goddesses could become a mother. She practised austerities, in order that she might not be childless; and by means of this expedient her desire was gratified. At the birth of this child, the reputed mother suffered all the pains attendant on childbirth, and was able to nurse him.

Parjanya

There are a few hymns addressed to this deity in the Rig-Veda; but from the character and functions ascribed to him it is difficult to see wherein he differs from Indra. Seeing that the hymns addressed to this deity are very similar to those sung to Indra. In these hymns are the following passages, all of which are in perfect harmony with those in honour of Indra:— "Laud Parjanya, worship him with reverence—the procreative and stimulating fructifier. ...He splits the trees; he destroys the Rakshasas. The whole creation is afraid of his mighty stroke; even the innocent man flees before the vigorous god, when Parjanya thundering smites the evildoers. Like a charioteer urging forward his horses with a whip, the god brings into view his showery scouts. From afar, the lions roarings arise when Parjanya charges the clouds with rain. The winds blow, the lightnings fall, the plants shoot up, the heaven fructifies; food is produced for all created things when Parjanya thundering replenishes the earth with moisture. Raise aloft thy vast water-vessel, and pour down showers; let the discharged rivulets roll on forward, moisten the heaven and earth with fatness; let there be well-filled drinking-places for the cows."

In all this there is not a single idea that is not expressed in the hymns to Indra. In the Puranas Indra is generally styled the king of the gods; whilst Parjanya is spoken of as the ruler over, and as dwelling in, the clouds.

Vayu

Vayu is the god of the winds. He is often associated with Indra, and is regarded, equally with him, as representing or ruling over the atmosphere. He won the race for the first draught of the Soma juice; and, at Indra's request, allowed him to have a quarter of it. He does not occupy a very prominent position in the Vedic hymns. He is said to be the son-in-law of Tvastri (Visvakarma); but here a difficulty occurs: only one daughter of Tvastri is mentioned, and, as was noticed in the account of Surya, he was said to be husband of this girl.

Vayu is described as being most handsome in form; one who moves noisily in a shining car, drawn by a pair of red or purple horses. At times the number of horses is increased to ninety-nine, a hundred, or even a thousand.This latter number would probably be employed during a cyclone. He is seldom mentioned in connection with the Maruts (storm-deities), though in one place he is said to have begotten them by the rivers of heaven.

Another name for Vayu in the Vedas is Vata. The praise of Vata is sung in the following hymn:

"(I celebrate) the glory of Vata's chariot; his noise comes rending and resounding. Touching the sky, he moves onward, making all things ruddy; and he comes propelling the dust of the earth. The gusts of air rush after him, and congregate upon him as women in an assembly. Sitting along with them on the same car, the god [Indra] who is king of this universe is borne along. Hasting forward … he never rests. Friend of the waters, first-born, holy, in what place was he born? His sounds have been heard, but his form is not (seen)."

In a later age, when it was thought necessary to connect the heroes, whose exploits are then sung, with the gods, Vayu, or Pavan as he is then called, is said to have had a son, Hanuman, by a monkey mother. Hanuman played a most conspicuous part in Rama's expedition in search of Sita. In the *Mahabharata,* Bhima (the Strong) one of the bravest of the warriors whose history is given there, is also said to be a son of Vayu-Kunti, the mother of Bhima, had a boon granted as a reward of her devotion, that she could obtain a child by any of the gods she might wish. As her husband, owing to a curse, could not become a father, she employed this charm, and so Vayu became the father of Bhima.

Vayu or Pavan (the Purifier) is represented in pictures, as a white man riding on a deer and carries a white flag in his hand. In the Purnas he is said to be son of Aditi.

Other names by which this deity is known are the following:—Anila, breath; Marut, air that is necessary to life; Sparsana, he who touches; Gandhavahu, he who carries odours.

The Maruts

In one passage in the Rig-Veda these gods are said to be one hundred and eighty in number; in another text, twenty-seven is the number given; whilst in the Purnas they are said to be forty-nine. In the Vedas they are called the sons of Rudra. They are the companions of Indra; at times they worship him, and thus acknowledge his superiority; at others they seem to assert their inherent power, and remind Indra of the aid they have given him. They are armed with golden weapons and lightnings; they dart thunderbolts, gleam like flames of fire, and are borne along with the fury of boisterous winds. They split Vritra to pieces, are clothed with rain, create darkness during the day, water the earth, and avert heat. They cause the earth and the mountains to quake. They were accustomed to the use of the soma; and were appealed to, to bring healing remedies, which are described as abiding in the (river) Sindhu, the seas, and the hills.

In the *Vishnu Purana* we find quite a different account of the Maruts. They are there said to be the sons of Kasyapa and Diti. Diti having lost her children, propitiated her husband, who promised her a boon. She asked that she might have a son of irresistible prowess and valour, who should destroy Indra. The Muni promised to grant this request on one condition. "You shall bear a son," he said, "who shall slay Indra, if with thoughts wholly pious, and person entirely pure, you carefully carry the babe in your womb for a hundred years." Diti accepted the boon with this condiiton. Indra hearing of this, tried his best to distract her mind, and so prevent the birth of this wonderful child. When ninety-nine years had passed, an opportunity offered itself. Diti retired to rest one night without having washed her feet, and thus violated a rule of ceremonial purity. Indra, ever-watchful, availing himself of this neglect, was able to accomplish his purpose. With his thunderbolt he cut the embryo into seven parts. The children cried bitterly, and Indra was unable to console them. Incensed at their obstinacy in crying, he cut each of these seven parts into seven, and thus formed the forty-nine Maruts. The name Maruts was given to them from the words "Ma rodih" (Weep not), used by Indra when trying to quiet them; and they became subordinate deities—the associates of the wielder of the thunderbolt.

Soma

Soma, according to the Vedic hymns, is the god who "represents and animates the juice of the Soma plant." Not only are all the hymns of the ninth book of the Rig-Veda, one hundred and fourteen in number, besides a few in other places, dedicated to his honour, but constant references occur to him in a large proportion of other hymns. In some of these hymns he is extolled as the Creator, or Father of the gods. Evidently at that time he was a most popular deity. Indra, as was stated before, was an enthusiastic worshipper of Soma.

The following lines show the warmth of feeling towards him :—

"This Soma is a god; he cures
The sharpest ills that man endures.
He heals the sick, the sad he cheers,
He nerves the weak, dispels their fears;
The faint with martial ardour fires,
With lofty thoughts the bard iuspires;
The soul from earth to heaven he lifts:
So great and wondrous are his gifts,
Men feel the god within their veins

And cry in loud exulting strains:
'We've quaffed the Soma bright
And are immortal grown:
We've entered into light,
And all the gods have known.
What mortal now can harm,
Or foeman vex us more?
Through thee, beyond alarm,
Immoral god, we soar."'

From the Vedas the following account of Soma is derived. In some passages the plant is said to have been brought from a mountain and given to Indra; in others, King Soma is said to have dwelt amongst the Gandharvas, a race of demi-gods that form the choir in Indra's heaven. The gods, knowing the virtues of this king or plant—for the two terms seem to be indiscriminately applied—wished to obtain it. Not knowing how to get it, Vak (the goddess of speech) said, "The Gandharvas are fond of women; let me go, and I will obtain it for you." The gods said, "How can we spare you?" She replied, "Obtain the god; and I will then return to you, whenever you may want me."

Another account of this affair is, that whilst the gods were living on earth, Soma was in the sky. Wishing to possess it, they sent Gayatri (a name of Brahma's wife or daughter) to fetch it. She went in the form of a bird, and was returning with it, when the Gandharvas seized it, and only gave it up when the goddess Vak went amongst them as narrated above.

When Soma was brought to the gods, a dispute arose as to who should have the first draught. At length, this was decided by a race. Vayu first reached the goal, Indra being second. Indra tried hard to win, and when near the winning post proposed that they should reach it together, Vayu taking two-thirds of the drink. Vayu said, "Not so! I will be the winner alone." Then Indra said, "Let us come in together, and give me one-fourth." Vayu consented to this, and so the juice was shared between them.

Soma is said to have had thirty-three wives, the daughters of Prajapati; of these Rohini was the favourite. Being dissatisfied with the partiality shown to their sister, the other wives returned to their father. Soma asked that they might come back to him ; the father consented to restore them, provided Soma would treat them all alike. Soma promised to do this; but, failing to keep his promise, he was smitten with consumption for breaking his word.

In the verses and songs in praise of Soma, the actual juice, and the god supposed to dwell in it, are not at all distinct. All the gods drink of it; and Soma, the god in the juice, is said to clothe the naked and heal the sick. Many divine attributes are ascribed to him. He is addressed as a god in the highest strains of adulation and veneration. All powers belong to him; all blessings are besought of him, as his to bestow. He is said to be divine, immortal, and also to confer immortality on gods and men. In a passage where the joys of paradise are more distinctly anticipated and more fervently implored than in most other parts of the *Rig-Veda,* Soma is addressed as the god from whom the gift of future felicity is expected. Thus it is said, "Place me, O purified god, in that everlasting and imperishable world, where there is eternal light and glory. O Indu (Soma), flow for Indra! Make me immortal in the world where Vaivasvata lives, where is the universal sphere of the sky, where those great waters flow."

In later years the name Soma was, and still is, given to the moon. How and why this change took place is not known; but in the later of the Vedic hymns there is some evidence of the transition. In the following passage Soma seems to be used in both senses—as god of the intoxicating juice, and as the moon ruling through the night. "By Soma the Adityas are strong; by Soma the earth is great; and Soma is placed in the midst of the stars. When they crush the plant, he who drinks regards it as Soma. Of him whom the priests regard as Soma (the moon) no one drinks." In another passage this prayer is found: "May the god Soma, he whom they call the Moon, free me." Again, "Soma is the moon, the food of the gods." "The sun has the nature of Agni, the moon of Soma."

In the *Vishnu Purana* we read, "Soma was appointed monarch of the stars and plants, of Brahmanas and plants, of sacrifices and penance." In this Purana we have quite a different account of the origin of Soma; but it must be borne in mind that in this account the term refers only to the moon. At the time the *Vishnu Purana* was written, intoxicants were strictly forbidden; hence Soma, as the god of the intoxicating juice, was no longer known and praised. According to that *Purana* Soma was the son of Atri, the son of Brahma. He performed the Rajasuya sacrifice, and from the glory thence acquired, and the immense dominion with which he had been invested, became so arrogant and licentious, that he carried off Tara, the wife of Brihaspati, the preceptor of the gods. In vain Brihaspati sought to recover his bride; in vain Brahma commanded, and the holy sages remonstrated. In consequence of this there was a great war; the gods fighting with Indra on the one side trying to recover Tara; Soma with the demons on the other. At length she appealed to Brahma for protection, who thereupon commanded Soma to restore her. On her return, Brihaspati finding she was pregnant, refused to receive her until after the birth of her child. In obedience to his orders, the child was immediately born; who being wonderful in beauty and power, both Brihaspati and Soma claimed him as their son. Tara being referred to, was too much ashamed to speak. The child was so indignant at this, that he was about to curse her, saying, "Unless you declare who is my father, I will sentence you to such a fate as shall deter every female from hestitating to speak the truth." On this Brahma again interfered, pacifying the child, and saying to Tara, "Tell me, my child, is this the child of Brihaspati or Soma?" "Of Soma," she said, blushing. As soon as she had spoken, the lord of the constellations, his countenance being bright, embraced his son and said, "Well done, my boy; verily thou art wise;" and hence his name was Budha (Mercury).

Tvastri or Visvakarma

Tvastri, or, as he is called in the later works, Visvakarma, is the architect and workman of the gods. The heavenly places were formed by him, and the warlike gods are indebted to him for their wonder-working weapons. He sharpens the iron axe of Brahmanaspati (Agni), and forges the thunderbolts of Indra. He is intimately associated with men; he forms husband and wife for each other from the womb, and blesses the married couple with offspring. This accounts for the fact that the wives of the gods are his most constant companions. He made the world and all that is in it; and he is the protector of the creatures he has made. He shares with the other gods in the sacrifices offered by mortals.

Tvastri is in several passages connected with the Ribhus. These were sons of a man named Sudhanvan; who, owing to their great skill in working, obtained immortality and divine honours. The Ribbus made Indra's chariot and horses; also by their great austerities restored their parents to youth. They are spoken of as the pupils of Tvastri. It was through their skill in manufacturing four sacrificial cups out of one their master had fashioned that they became divine. This exhibition was made at the command of the gods, and exaltation to deity the promised reward. Tvastri was very angry at their success; and, ashamed of being seen, hid himself amongst the women. It is said that he even tried to slay his pupils. According to other accounts, he admired their skill and was pleased at the result. Tvastri was the father-in-law of Vivasvat (the Sun).

Indra is occasionally described as being in a state of hostility towards Tvastri and his son Visvarupa, and ultimately caused the death of both. This Visvarupa had three heads, called respectively, the Soma-drinker, the Wine-drinker, and the Food-eater. On one occasion he declared in public that the sacrifices should be shared by the gods only; but in private he said the asuras (demons) should share them too. And as it is customary to keep promises that are privately made, Indra was afraid that the asuras, obtaining a share of the sacrifices, would be so strengthened as to be able to overthrow his kingdom; he therefore cut off the heads of Visvarupa with his thunderbolt. The three heads were turned into birds: the Soma-drinker became a Kapinjala (a francoline partridge), for Soma was of a brown colour; the Wine-drinker became a Kalavinka (sparrow), because when men are intoxicated they make a noise like a sparrow; the Food-eater became a Tittiri (partridge), which consequently has a great variety of colour, for its body appears to be sprinkled with *ghee* and honey. Tvastri, enraged because Indra had slain his son, made a libation to the gods but did not invite Indra to it. Indra, noticing this slight, by force took the vessel containing the Soma juice, and drank it. But he drank more than was good for him. Tvastri, being angry, at once broke off the sacrifice, and used the few drops of Soma left to give effect to a curse. He employed the right formula for accomplishing the death of Indra, but unfortunately laid stress upon the wrong word. So, instead of slaying Indra, he was himself slain by him.

In the Puranas, Tvastri appears under the name of Visvakarma. In the *Vishnu Purana* he is styled the author of a thousand arts, the mechanist of the gods, the fabricator of ornaments, the chief of artists, the constructor of the self-moving chariots of the deities, by whose skill men obtain subsistencc. Though not named as an Aditya in the Vedas, he is generally reckoned as one in the Puranas. In other places he is called a son of Brahma. In pictures he is represented as a white man with three eyes. In his right hand he carries a club. He wears a crown, and is adorned with a necklace and bracelets of gold. He is worshipped once, twice, thrice, or four times each year, according to the devotion of his worshippers. Nowadays, no images of him are set up; each man worships the implements of his trade, as representatives. The carpenter bows down to his hammer, saw, etc.; the bricklayer to his trowel; the peasant to his plough; the student to his books; the clerk to his pen. When the worship is over, the day is spent in feasting and enjoyment.

Though, as we have seen in the Vedas, he is regarded in some hymns as the Creator and the Preserver, in the later books he occupies a much lower position. Brahma is styled the Creator, and Vishnu the Preserver —whilst Visvakarma becomes a valued servant who fulfils the behests of his superiors. It is for skill and power to work in their ordinary avocations that his aid is now sought.

Yama

Yama, the judge of men and king of the unseen world, was the son of Vivasvat (the sun) and Saranya, the daughter of Tvastri. He was born before his mother had become afraid of her glorious husband. He was twin-brother of Yami, and they were regarded as the primeval pair from whom the human family has sprung. In another verse of the Rig-Veda they are described as the offspring of the heavenly singers, the Gandharvas. As there were no others to perpetuate the race, Yami entreated Yama to become her husband. She urged the fact that Tvastri had formed them as man and wife in the womb; and therefore it was useless for him to refuse her request, as none can act contrary to the ordinances of Tvastri. But Yama was firm, and resisted her overtures on the ground that it was monstrous for those who are preachers of righteousness to act unrighteously.

Yama was the first of mortals who died, and, having discovered the way to other world, is the guide of those who depart this life, and is said to conduct them to a home which is made secure for them for ever. He is a king, and dwells in celestial light in the innermost sanctuary of heaven. He grants bright homes to the pious who dwell with him.

In the *Rig-Veda,* Yama is nowhere represented (as he is in the later mythology) as having anything to do with the punishment of the wicked. Nevertheless he is still to some an object of terror. He is said to have two insatiable dogs, with four eyes and wide nostrils, which guard the road to his abode, and which the departed are advised to hurry past with all possible speed. These dogs are said to wander about among men as messengers, no doubt for the purpose of summoning them to the presence of their master, who in another place is identified with death, and is described as sending a bird as the herald of doom.

When the remains of the deceased have been placed upon the funeral pile, and the process of cremation has commenced, Agni, the god of Fire, is prayed not to scorch or consume the departed, not to tear asunder his skin or his limbs, but, after the flames have done their work, to convey to the fathers the mortal who has been presented to him as an offering. Leaving behind on earth all that is evil and imperfect, and proceeding by the paths which the fathers trod, invested with a lustre like that of the gods, it soars to the realms of eternal light in a car, or on wings, and recovers there its ancient body in a complete and glorified form: meets with the forefathers who are living in festivity with Yama; obtains from him, when recognized by him as one of his own, a delectable abode and enters upon more perfect life, which is crowned with the fulfilment of all desires, is passed in the presence of the gods, and employed in the fulfilment of their pleasure.

In this kingdom, over which Yama reigns, friends meet with their departed friends—husband with wife, children with parents—and together live in a state of blessedness, free from the evils and infirmities that belong to the present life. As the gods are described as enjoying the pleasures common to men on earth, the kingdom of Yama, the abode of the departed, is not at all less sensual than the present world; and when mortals have been privileged to enter this happy land, they become objects of veneration to their descendants still living, and joyfully partake of the oblations they offer to them.

In the following lines the teaching of the Vedas respecting Yama:

"To great King Yama homage pay;
    Who was the first of men that died,
    That crossed the mighty gulf and spied
For mortals out the heavenward way.

*   *   *   *

"By it our fathers all have passed;
    And that same path we too shall trace,
    And every new succeeding race,
Of mortal men, while time shall last.

"The god assembles round his throne
    A growing throng, the good and wise—
    All those whom, scanned with searching eyes.
He recognizes as his own.

"Departed mortal, speed from earth
By those old ways thy sires have trod;
Ascend, behold the expectant god
Who calls thee to a higher birth.

*　　*　　*　　*

"And calmly pass without alarm
The four-eyed hounds that guard the road
Which leads to Yama's bright abode;
Their master's friends they dare not harm.

"All imperfections leave behind:
Assume thine ancient frame once more—
Each limb and sense thou hadst before,
From every earthly taint refined.

"And now with heavenly glory bright,
With life intenser, nobler, blest
With large capacity to taste
A fuller measure of delight.

"Thou there once more each well-known face
Shalt see of those thou lovedst here;
Thy parents, wife, and children dear,
With rapture shalt thou soon embrace.

"The father, too, shalt thou behold,
The heroes who in battle died,
The saints and sages glorified,
The pious, bounteous kings of old.

"The gods whom here in humble wise
Thou worshippedst with doubt and awe,
Shall there the impervious veil withdraw
Which hid their glory from thine eyes.

"The good which thou on earth hast wrought,
Each sacrifice, each pious deed,
Shall there receive its ample meed;
No worthy not shall be forgot.

"In those fair realms of cloudless day,
Where Yama every joy supplies,
And every longing satisfies,
Thy bliss shall never know decay."

In the Puranas Yama is called the judge of men, and is said to rule over the many hells in which the wicked are made to suffer. Thus the *Padma Purana* says: Yama fulfils the office of judge of the dead, as well as sovereign of the damned; all that die appearing before him, and being confronted with Chitragupta the recorder, by whom their actions have been registered. The virtuous are then conveyed to Swarga (Indra's heaven), whilst wicked are driven to the different regions of Naraka (hell). In the *Vishnu Purana* the names of the different hells are given, and it is there stated that there are many other fearful hells which are the awful provinces of Yama, terrible with instruments of torture and fire. In the same Purana it is said that all men at the end of their existence (life) become slave to the power of Yama, by whom they are sentenced to painful punishments. Inquiry is then made as to how men can be free from his authority. The answer is that Yama is the lord of all men, excepting the worshippers of Madhusudan (Vishnu). Worship him in one of his many forms, and Yama can exert no authority over you.

According to the popular ideas now prevailing, Yama is represented as a green man, clothed in red garments. He has a crown on his head, and a flower in his hair; is armed with a club, and rides upon buffalo. He is regularly worshipped once a year; and daily a little water is poured out to him. For a whole month each year unmarried girls present offerings to him in the hope that he will provide them with a husband; and that, having granted this boon, he will not recall his gift, and leave them widows. In his presence the good and evil deeds of the departed are weighed: according to the turn of the scale, the soul goes to heaven or hell. The soul is believed to reach Yama's abode in four hours and forty minutes; consequently a dead body cannot be burned until that time has passed after death.

In the *Mahabharata* is a most interesting story, showing that sometimes Yama is propitious to prayer, and will allow those who have entered his abode to return to earth.

A princess named Savitri loved Satyavan, the son of an old hermit, but was warned by a seer to overcome her attachment, as Satyavan was a doomed man, having only one year to live. Savitri replies:

"Whether his years be or many, be he gifted with all grace.

Or graceless, him my heart hath chosen, and it chooseth not again."

They were married, and the bride strove to forget the prophecy; but, as the last day of the year approached, her anxiety became irrepressible. She exhausted herself in prayers, and penances, hoping to stay the hend of the destroyer, yet all the while dared not reveal the fatal secret to her husband. At last the dreaded day arrived, and Satyavan set out to cut wood in the forest. His wife asked leave to accompany him, and walked behind him, smiling, but with a heavy heart. Satyavan soon made the wood resound with his hatchet, when suddenly a thrill of agony shot through his temples, and, feeling himself falling, called his wife to support him.

"Then she received her fainting husband in her arms, and sat herself
On the cold ground, and gently laid his drooping head upon her lap:
Sorrowing, she called to mind the sage's prophecy, and reckoned up
The days and hours. All in an instant she beheld an awful shape
Standing before her, dressed in blood-red garments, with a glittering crown
Upon his head; his form, though glowing like the Sun, was yet obscure,
And eyes he had like flames, a noose depended from his hand; and he
Was terrible to look upon, as by her husband's side he stood
And gazed upon him with a fiery glance. Shuddering she started up,
And laid her dying Satyavan upon the ground, and with her hands
Joined reverently, she thus with beating heart addressed the shape:
'Surely thou art a god; such form as thine must more than mortal be!
Tell me, thou god-like being, who thou art and wherefore art thou here?'"

The figure replied that he was Yama, king of the dead; that her husband's time was come, and that he must bind and take his spirit.

"Then from her husband's body forced he out, and firmly with his cord
Bound and detained the spirit, clothed in form no larger than a thumb.
Forthwith the body, reft of vital being and deprived of breath,
Lost all its grace and beauty, and became ghastly and motionless."

After binding the spirit, Yama proceeds with it towards the quarter of which he is guardian—the south. The faithful wife follows him closely. Yama bids her go home and perform the funeral rites; but she persists in following, till Yama, pleased with her devotion, grants her any boon she pleases, except the life of her husband. She chooses that her husband's father, who is now blind, may recover his sight. Yama consents, and bids her now return home. Still she persists in following. Two other boons are granted in the same way, and still Savitri follows closely on the heels of the king of death. At last, overcome by her constancy, Yama grants a boon without exception. The delighted Savitri exclaims :

> " 'Nought, mighty king, this time hast thou excepted: let my husband live;
> Without him I desire not happiness, nor even heaven itself ;
> Without him I must die.' 'So be it, faithful wife,' replied the king of death:
> 'Thus I release him ;' and with that he loosed the cord that bound his soul."

Amongst the many names by which Yama is known, the following are the most common :

Dharmaraja, "King of righteousness."

Pitripati, "Lord of the fathers."

Samavurti, "He who judges impartially"

Kritanta, "The finisher."

Samana, "The leveller."

Kala, "Time."

Dandadhara, "He who carries the rod."

Sraddhadeva, "The god of funeral ceremonies."

Vaivasvata, "The son of Vivasvata."

Antaka, "He who puts an end to life."

Kama (Love)

Later speculations within the Indian tradition have somewhat blurred the powerful, sober, and transparent conception of *Kama,* love, desire, which appears in the Vedas. It would be of little avail and merely retrograde to revert to a cosmic conception of love or to the unearthing of old myths; but, equally, we would be falsifying and impoverishing human experience if we were to ignore that area of human existence which is powerfully indicated in the that area of human existence which is powerfully indicated in the texts of the Vedas. Here we have perhaps some of the deepest sayings regarding that fundamental human archetype.

Kama, is considered to be the first principle of activity, the creative and procreative force leading the supreme Being out of the closed circle of its own existence. It is a cosmic force, but not be understood as a kind of blind energy or impersonal urge. On the contrary, the personal is so much included in the transpersonal element that *kama* is said to be the first seed of mind, the firstborn of the Absolute and thereafter the loftiest characteristic of all created beings, and more particularly of human beings. *Kama* is the driving force in any enterprise, the highest of all human qualities. There is one and the same urge stimulating the entire range of reality, one and the same energy pushing the universe to expand—and it is *kama.* Without it there would be only death; time would shrink and reality would collapse. *Kama* is not a hankering after what is lacking in the individual; it is not an imperfection and thus a cause of suffering. *Kama* is not the proof that we have not yet arrived, that we are imperfect and enmeshed in unfulfilled longings and unsatisfied urges. *Kama* is, on the contrary, the perfection of expansion, the quality of creativity, the positive dynamism to be more, to reach higher, to overcome what still stands in front of us, because the adventure of existence is not yet finished, although this unfinished character is just the opposite of the imperfect. A "finished " universe would be in fact finished, limited, finite, deadly, and not divine. *Kama* proves not that we are poor pilgrims, still on the way, displaced persons in search of a paradise lost, but that we are divine sparks full of creative energy with our own part to play in the structuring of the world. Sharing in this power is indeed the first sign of awakening and coming of age. The adolescent is afraid to love to the extent that he is afraid to be.

The Vedic hymn starts by addressing *kama* as a powerful ally whose aid a man seeks to secure in his struggle against enemies of all sorts. The last part of the hymn (given below) is devoted to an address to *kama,* extolling him above all else. He has the primacy over all things, people, and Gods. He who has *kama* has all; all goods come with him. Where *kama* is, there no thoughts of evil intrude.

(From Atharva Veda)

Love is the firstborn, loftier than the Gods,
the Fathers and men.

You, O Love, are the eldest of all,
altogether mighty.
To you we pay homage!
Greater than the breadth of Earth and Heaven
or of Waters and Fire,
you O Love, are the eldest of all,
altogether mighty.
To you we pay homage!
Greater than the quarters and directions, the expanses
and vistas of the sky,
you, O Love, are the eldest of all,
altogether mighty.
To you we pay homage!
Greater than all things moving and inert,
than the Ocean, O Passion,
you, O Love, are the eldest of all,
altogether mighty.
To you we pay homage!
Beyond the reach of Wind or Fire,
the Sun or the Moon,
you, O Love, are the eldest of all,
altogether mighty.
To you we pay homage!
In many a form of goodness, O Love,
you show your face.
Grant that these forms may penetrate
within our hearts.
Send elsewhere all malice!

Kama is not here seen, as in later speculation, as a psychological desire, much less as a mere desire for individual pleasure; desire has here no pejorative connotation. Desire is the dynamism inherent in the whole creation, in whatever way we may like to explain it. If it were not for this striving that we call love, the whole universe would be not only cold, but dead, and would not exist at all.

The other hymn given below recalls that *kama* existed from the beginning and was the first seed of mind. It then proceeds to express a rather subtle identification of and differentiation between the cosmic and primeval *kama* and that of the individual. Sacrifice is here again the clue.

There is an internal and almost inaudible dialogue going on in this hymn, from Love to love, from Desire to desire, from Heart to heart. Without *kama* it is not possible to achieve anything whatsoever; but *kama*, unlike other values, is the most universal gift bestowed upon the whole of creation.

(From Atharva Veda)

In the beginning was Desire (*Kama*)
the first seed of mind.
O desire, twin of Desire,
grant wealth to me!

Powerful, unshakable,
shining, companionable,
formidable victor,
grant power to me!

He who longed from afar
to furnish a pledge
in response to the eternal
was heeded by the regions.
By means of Desire
they generated light.

From Desire springs desire,
leaps from Heart of heart.
The mind of my people,
let that mind be mine!

Now prosper, Desire,
the desires of our hearts,
that we may succeed,
Accept this oblation!

4

THE PURANIC DEITIES

The Puranas

The chief sources of information respecting the present day mythology of the Hindus are the two great Epics—the *Ramayana* and the *Mahabharata*—the Puranas, or "old traditional stories," eighteen in number, and the five principal Tantras.

There is nothing definitely known as to the date of the Epics, beyond the fact that they are later than the Vedas, and earlier than the Puranas. Some place the *Ramayana* as early as B.C. 500, whilst others affirm that it could not have been composed before B.C. 100, and that a considerable portion was added much later. The *Mahabharata* is supposed to be fully a century later. Each of these books is of immense bulk, and the same stories frequently reappear in them. Yet to this day they retain a firm hold of the faith of the mass of the people of India.

It is almost equally difficult to determine the date of the Puranas. It is, however, believed that none of them are older than the 8th century A.D., though some of the lengends incorporated in them may have come from much earlier times. That they are considerably later than the two great Epics is evident from the fact that many Epic heroes in the Puranas are said to be divine beings. These books differ from the Vedas that whilst the older scriptures treat of the religion common to the Hindus each Purana is chiefly concerned to extol one god. There is a general respect shown to the rest of the gods; yet the particular deity to whose praise the Purana is devoted, is declared to be supreme. Now Brahma, now Siva, now Vishnu in some of his many forms, is the great god, whose will is that all men should worship him.

The Puranas may be classified as follows :—

(*i*) Those which are devoted to the praise of Brahma; *viz.* the Brahma, the Brahmanda, the Brahmavaivarta, the Markandeya, the Bhavishya, and the Vaman.

(*ii*) Those which relate to Vishnu; *viz.* the Vishnu, the Bhagavata, the Naradiya, the Garuda, the Padma, and the Varaha.

(*iii*) Those which are chiefly connected with Siva; *viz.* the Siva, the Linga, the Skanda, the Agni, the Matsya, the Kurma. For the Agni Purana another called the Vayu is sometimes substituted.

These Puranas are the authority for nearly the whole of the popular Hinduism of the present day. They are largely read by the people. Parts of some and the whole of others have been translated into the vernaculars from the Sanskrit; and where the people cannot read, it is a common practice for their Guru or teacher to read a portion to them at his periodic visits. By this means the contents of these books are widely known.

The last class of religious books to be mentioned here are the Tantras. The word signifies "a means of faith," and they teach that faith in the revelations they record will save from the greatest sin. They are in the form of a dialogue between Siva and his wife. In answer to her questions, the god gives manifold instructions concerning worship. The date of these works is involved in great obscurity; but as far as can be known they probably are not earlier than the 6th century of our era. They form the authority for the faith and ceremonies of the Saktas, as the worshippers of the wife of Siva are called, and are by them regarded as a fifth Veda. The doctrines, or at least a part of the doctrines, of these sects is kept secret and communicated to those only who receive solemn initiation into the mysteries.

In describing the Puranic deities, I shall follow the common order. The Hindus speak of three great gods—Brahma, Vishnu, Siva, who form what is often spoken of as the Hindu Triad. After giving an account of each of these and their consorts, I shall describe those who are regarded as their incarnations, or descendants; and then proceed to speak of others who have no formal connection with any of them. It will be seen that most of the principal deities are connected with one or other of these three.

Thereafter will be given a description of the goddesses of the Tantric/ Shakti tradition.

Brahm or Brahman

Brahman is regarded as the Supreme Being, of whom Brahma, Vishnu, and Siva are manifestations. It is true that, in some verses of the Vedas, attributes ascribed to him are also ascribed to other deities, and in some of the Puranas various gods are said to be identical with the supreme, nevertheless Brahman is regarded by the Hindus as the Supreme God—the origin of all the others, and of whom they are manifestations. Thus we read in the *Atharva-Veda*; "All the gods are in (Brahm) as cows in a cow-house. In the beginning Brahm was this [universe]. He created gods. Having created gods, he placed them in these worlds, *viz.* Agni in this world, Vayu in the atmosphere, and Surya in the sky. And in the worlds which are yet higher, he placed the gods which are still higher. Then Brahm proceeded to the higher sphere [which is explained by the commentator to mean the Satyaloka, the most excellent and limit of all the worlds]. The gods were originally mortal; but when they were pervaded by Brahm, they became immortal." In the *Taittiriya Brahmana* it is said : "Brahm generated the gods, Brahm (generated) this entire world. Within him are all these worlds. Within him is this entire universe. It is Brahm who is the greatest of beings. Who can vie with him? In Brahm, the thirty-three gods; in Brahm, Indra and Prajapati; in Brahm all things are contained as in a ship."

A few hymns of the Vedas appear to contain the simple conception of one divine self-existent, omnipresent being; and even in these, the idea of one god present in all nature is somewhat nebulous and undefined. In the Purusha Sukta of the *Rig-Veda,* the one spirit is called Purusha. The more common name in the later system is Brahman, neuter (nom. Brahm), derived from the root *brih,* 'to expand,' and denoting the universally expanding essence, or universally diffused substance of the universe ... Brahman, in the neuter, being 'simple infinite being'—the only real eternal essence—which, when it passes into actual manifested existence is called Brahma; when it develops itself in the world, is called Vishnu; and when it again dissolves itself into simple being, is called Siva; all the other innumerale gods and demi-gods being also mere manifestations of the neuter Brahman, who is eternal.

In the *Vishnu Purana* Brahm is translated as "abstract supreme spirit." Later on the question is asked, "How can creative agency be attributed to Brahm, who [as abstract spirit] is without qualitities, illimitable, and free from imperfection?" The answer is, that "the essential properties of existent things are objects of observation, of which no foreknowledge is attainable; and creation and hundreds of properties belong to Brahm as inseparable parts of his essence, as heat is inherent in fire." The Purana goes on to say that creation is effected through the agency of Brahma, the first manifestation of Brahm; and then declares that Vishnu is one with Brahma.

Again, the same Purana says : "There are two states of this Brahm—one with, and one without shape; one perishable, one imperishable; which are inherent in all beings. The imperishable is the supreme being; the perishable is all the world. The blaze of fire burning in one spot diffuses light and heat around; so the world is nothing more than the manifested energy of the supreme Brahm; and inasmuch as the light and heat are stronger or feebler as we are near to the fire or far off from it, so the energy of the supreme is more or less intense in the beings that are less or more remote from him. Brahma, Vishnu, and Siva are the most powerful energies of God; next to them are the inferior deities; then the attendant spirits; then men; then animals, birds, insects, vegetables; each becoming more and more feeble as they are farther from their source."

The *Vishnu Purana* gives the following derivation of the word Brahm: It "is derived from the root *vriha* (to increase), because it is infinite (spirit), and because it is the cause by which the Vedas (and all things) are developed." Then follows this hymn to Brahm : "Glory to Brahm, who is addressed by that mystic word (*Om*), associated eternally with the triple universe (earth, sky, and heaven), and who is one with the four Vedas. Glory to Brahm, who alike in the destruction and renovation of the world is called the great and mysterious cause of the intellectual principle, who is without limit in time or space, and exempt from diminution and decay.... He is the invisible, imperishable Brahm; varying in form, invariable in substance; the chief principle, self-engendered; who is said to illuminate the caverns of the heart; who is indivisible, radiant, undecaying, multiform. To that supreme Brahm be for ever adoration."

In perfect harmony with this teaching of the *Vishnu Purana* is the common belief of the Hindus. No phrase is more commonly used by them when speaking of the divine being than this : "God (Brahm) is one without a second." The word used by them for God as distinguished from his manifestations, is Brahm; and when charged with polytheism, and of violating the primary law respecting the unity of God, they reply that Brahma, Vishnu, Siva, etc., are only manifestations of the supreme Brahm.

In the earliest writings Brahm signified a hymn or mantra, whilst Brahma was the term used to denote a priest or worshipper. It is in the later parts of the Vedas that Brahm is identified with the supreme, and Brahma becomes his great manifestation. Prajapati, the lord of creatures, was the Creator according to the earlier teaching of the Vedas, and occupied the position in the earlier Pantheon that Brahma did in the later. In several texts of the Vedas the two are identified, and thus authority is found for the idea that Brahma is to be worshipped as the Maker of all things.

This Brahma, though satisfactory to the priests, was not so to the common people. In process of time local gods absorbed their worship, and the deities of the people exercised their influence. Rather than lose their hold of the people, the priests adopted these new deities, and found a parentage for them from amongst the old Vedic gods. By the time the Epics were composed, Vishnu and Siva had been thus assimilated. The different names by which these deities are now known may possibly have been the local names of local or tribal gods; by retaining these the priests also retained their hold upon the people. In the "Satapatha Brahmana" attempts are made to identify Siva with Agni, as though the writer wished to show that the later triad—Brahma, Vishnu, and Siva—was identical with the older one composed of Agni, Indra-Vayu, and Surya.

5

BRAHMA AND SARASVATI

Brahma

Brahma, the first of the three great Hindu gods, is called the Creator; he is the father of gods and men, the Vedic Prajapati, the lord of creatures. All the writers of the Puranas seem to regard it a duty to describe the work of creation as performed by this god, and each account differs in detail from the others. Manu's account of it, which is largely founded upon the teaching of the Vedas, is as below.

"This universe was enveloped in darkness—unperceived, undistinguishable, undiscoverable, unknowable, as it were, entirely sunk in sleep. The irresistible self-existent lord, undiscerned, creating this universe with the five elements, and all other things, was manifested dispelling the gloom. He who is beyond the cognizance of the senses, subtile, undiscernible, eternal, who is the essence of all things, and inconceivable, himself shone forth. He, desiring, seeking to produce various creatures from his own body, first created the waters, and deposited in them a seed. This (seed) became a golden egg, resplendent as the sun, in which he himself was born as Brahma, the progenitor of all worlds. The waters are called *narah*, because they are the offspring of Nara; and since they were formerly the place of his movement (*ayana*), he is therefore called Narayana. Being formed by that First Cause, undiscernible, eternal, which is both existent and non-existent, that male is known in the world as Brahma. That lord having continued a year in the egg, divided it into two parts by his mere thought." In the Mahabharata, and some of the Puranas, Brahma is said to have issued from a lotus that sprang from the navel of Vishnu.

The egg referred to above is thus described in the *Vishnu Purana* : "Its womb, vast as the mountain Meru, was composed of the mountains, and the mighty oceans were the waters which filled its cavity. In that egg were the continents, seas, and mountains; the planets and divisions of the universe; the gods, the demons and mankind. Brahma is said to be born; a familiar phrase to signify his manifestation." This wonderful egg, after the Creator had inhabited it for a thousand years, burst open, and Brahma issuing forth by meditation commenced the work of creation. Seeing that the earth was sunk beneath the waters, he assumed the form of a boar, and, diving, raised it upon his tusks. After this, he continued the work of creation.

In pictures Brahma is represented as a red man with four heads, though in the Puranas he is said to have had originally five. He is dressed in white raiment, and rides upon a swan. In one hand he carries a staff, in the other a dish for receiving alms. A legend in the *Matsya Purana* gives the following account of the formation of his numerous heads : "Brahma formed from his own immaculate substance a female who is celebrated under the names of Satarupa, Savitri, Sarasvati, Gayatri, and Brahmani. Beholding his daughter, born from his body, Brahma became wounded with the arrows of love, and exclaimed, 'How surpassingly lovely she is!' Satarupa turned to the right side from his gaze; but as Brahma wished to look after her, a second head issued from his body. As she passed to the left, and behind him, to avoid his amorous glances, two other heads successively appeared. At length she sprang into the sky; and as Brahma was anxious to gaze after her there, a fifth head was immediately formed. Brahma then said to his daughter, 'Let us produce all kinds of animated beings, men, *suras* (gods), and *asuras* (demons). Hearing this, she descended, and Brahma having espoused her, they withdrew to a secluded spot where they dwelt together for one hundred divine years; at the expiration of which time was born Manu, who is also called Swayambhuva and Viraj."

The following legend occurs, with some variations, in several Puranas, showing why Brahma was deprived of his fifth head :

Once when they were assembled on the top of Meru, the holy sages, having saluted Brahma, requested him to declare the true nature of the godhead; but the Creator, influenced by the delusion of Mahesha (a demon), and his mind obscured by spiritual darkness, asserted his own pre-eminence, and said : 'I am the womb of the universe, without beginning or end, and the sole and self-existent lord; and he who does not worship me shall never obtain beatitude.' On hearing this, Kratu, a form of Narayana (Vishnu), smiled and said : 'Hadst thou not been misled by ignorance, thou wouldst not have made an assertion so contrary to truth; for I am the framer of the universe, the source of life, the unborn, eternal and supreme Narayana; and, had I not willed it, creation would not have taken place.'

Thus Vishnu and Brahma disputed, and at length they agreed to allow the matter to be decided by the Vedas. The Vedas declared that Siva was creator, preserver, destroyer. Having heard these words, Vishnu and Brahma, still bewildered by the darkness of delusion, said, 'How can the lord of goblins, the delighter in graveyards, the naked devotee covered with ashes, haggard in appearance, wearing twisted locks ornamented with snakes, be the supreme being?' The incorporeal Prana (Life), then assuming a form, said, 'This is not the real form of Siva; but when united to his energy, he sometimes, under the figure of Rudra, delights himself in various illusive sports.' But even these words dispelled not the spiritual darkness of Vishnu and Brahma; when suddenly appeared between them a wondrous effulgence filling the heavens, earth, and mid air. In the midst of this they beheld a human form, vast, uncreated, of a dark hue, holding in his hand a trident and a rosary, and wearing a serpent for a Brahmanical thread. On seeing whom, the fifth head of Brahma glowed with anger and said, 'I know thee well, O Chandra Shekera, for from my forehead didst thou spring, and because thou didst weep I called thee Rudra. Hasten then to seek the refuge of my feet, and I will protect thee, O my son!' At these proud words of Brahma, Siva was incensed; and from his anger sprang into existence a terrific form (Bhairava), whom he thus addressed : 'Chastise this lotus-born!' No sooner did Bhairava receive this order, then instantly he cut off the head of Brahma with the thumb of his left hand. That member which had committed the fault received punishment; and therefore Brahma was deprived of his fifth head. Upon this Vishnu and Brahma praised Siva.

In another part of the same Purana is another legend, giving a somewhat different account of this circumstance :

Formerly all things movable and immovable having been destroyed, nought remained but one boundless ocean; nor fire, nor air, nor sun, nor atmosphere, nor stars, nor planets, nor light, nor earth, nor heaven, nor gods nor demons existed then; and all was involved in impenetrable darkness. One being alone, Maha Kala (Siva), pervaded all space; who being desirous of creation, churned his left arm with his right forefinger; whence issued a bubble, which increasing in size became an egg resembling gold. This egg Maha Kala divided with his hand; of the upper part he formed the heavens, and of the lower half the earth, and in the centre of it appeared Brahma with five heads and four arms, to whom Maha Kala thus said, 'Through my favour effect creation.' Having thus spoken, he disappeared.

Brahma having then considered in what manner he could accomplish this object, propitiated his lord Bhava with a severe *tapas* (meditation), and in consequence received from him the four Vedas, and was thus enabled to become the Creator. But as Siva had not revealed himself, Brahma continued his meditation in order that he might behold that god. Siva was propitiated; but, still invisible, thus said, 'O Brahma, choose whatever boon thou choosest!' Brahma craved that Siva would become him son. Siva replied : 'Propitiated by thy piety, I will become thy son under the form of Rudra; but as thou hast craved a boon which ought not to have been asked, I shall on this account hereafter cut off one of thy heads. Nevertheless, though thou shalt afterwards possess but four heads, yet as thou hast been formed by me, from my own substance which is that Brahm, thou shalt in remembrance of this circumstance be denominated Brahma. Also from my becoming thy son, shalt thou be called Pitamaha (the great father).'

Brahma having obtained both a boon and a curse, proceeded, in order to effect creation, to sacrifice to that fire which had sprung from his own effulgence; and from the heat, perspiration collected on his forehead. In wiping this off with a small piece of wood, a drop of blood fell into the fire, from which by the will of Siva sprang Rudra, of a dark hue, with five heads, ten hands, and fifteen eyes; having a serpent for his Brahmanical thead, wearing twisted locks, and the moon on his head, and clothed in the skin of a lion. Having seen such a son, Brahma was delighted, and bestowed on him various appellations. Brahma having created various classes of beings, they all adored him, except Rudra; to whom Brahma said, 'Why dost thou not also adore me?' Rudra replied, 'I worship none other than that effulgence from which I sprang!' Having thus spoken, he departed to Siva's abode. But Brahma from the impurity of his nature became immersed in spiritual darkness, and thought that it was by his own power alone that he had effected creation, and there was no other god equal to him. His fifth head also having read the Vedas, which the other four heads had delivered, acquired a splendour which neither suras (gods) nor asuras (demons) could endure.

The *Padma Purana* thus concludes this story : "Unable therefore to approach or behold it, they determined to apply to Siva for relief. Being propitiated by them, Siva granted their request, and proceeded with them to where Brahma remained inflated with pride. On seeing Siva, Brahma did not pay him the customary honours. Siva, seeing Brahma's fifth head inflicting distress on the universe by its effulgent beams, brighter than a thousand suns, approached him and said, 'Oh! this head shines with too much splendour,' and immediately cut it off with the nail of his left thumb, with as much ease as a man cuts off the stem of a plantain tree."

The *Mahabharata* says that Siva did not actually cut off Brahma's head on this occasion, but was only prevented from doing so through the intercession of the gods. It was because of his attempting to seduce his own daughter that Siva decapitated him. This crime was attempted when in a fit of intoxication; hence Brahma pronounced a curse upon the gods who should hereafter drink spirits.

In the passages just quoted, Brahma is represented as worshipping Siva for his own personal benefit; in the *Vishnu Purana,* he is described as joining with gods and men in the worship of this same deity, and as officiating as priest on that occasion. And in another part of the Purana is the following hymn addressed to Vishnu by Brahma : "Thou art the common centre of all, the protector of the world, and all things exist in thee. All that has been, or will be, thou art. There is nothing else but thee, O lord; nothing else has been, or will be. Thou art independent, and without beginning." The object of this laudation was to induce Vishnu to save the earth from its load of sorrow; in answer to it, Vishnu appeared as Krishna.

At the present time Brahma is not largely worshipped by the Hindus. The Brahmans in their morning and evening worship repeat an incantation containing a description of the image of Brahma; at noon they present to him a single flower; at the time of burnt-offering, *ghi* is presented to him. In the month of Magh, at the full moon, an earthen image of him is worshipped, with that of Siva on his right hand, and Vishnu on his left. Brahma as Creator is supposed to have finished his work; hence, excepting in one place, viz. at Pushkara in Ajmer there is no temple to him now existing. It is evident that for centuries the worship of Brahma has not been common, for in the *Skanda Purana* is an indelicate legend, in which the charge of falsehood is proved against him, and this fact is given to account for the fact that his worship had ceased. It concludes as follows : "Since thou hast childishly and with weak understanding asserted a falsehood, let no one henceforth perform worship to thee."

The *Mahabharata* says that Brahma's heaven is eight hundred miles long, four hundred wide, and forty high. Narada declared himself incompetent to describe it. In two hundred years he could not mention all its excellences. He said that it contained in a superior degree all the excellences of the other heavens; and that whatever existed in the creation of Brahma on earth, from the smallest insect to the largest animal, was to be found there.

In the later, mythology, a deity named Dhata (the Creator), who in the *Rig-Veda* has no very clearly-defined powers, but is there said to operate in the production of life and the preservation of health, is identified with Prajapati, or Brahma; and in the sense of "maker" the term is also applied to Vishnu and Krishna. Sometimes he is said to be a son of Brahma.

In addition to the names of Brahma already referred to, the following are those most commonly known :

Atmabhu, "The self-existent."

Paramesthi, "The chief sacrificer." He was the first Brahman who performed all the great sacrifices of the Hindu religion.

Lokesha, "The god of the world."

Hiranyagarbha, "He who came from the golden egg."

Savitripati, "The husband of Savitri."

Adikavi, "The first poet."

Sarasvati

Brahmas wife is Sarasvati, the goddess of wisdom and science, the mother of the Vedas, and the inventor of the Devanagari letters. She is represented as a fair young woman, with four arms. With one of her right hands she is presenting a flower to her husband, by whose side she continually stands; and in the other she holds a book of palm-leaves, indicating that she is fond of learning. In one of her left hands she has a string of pearls, called Sivamala (Siva's garland), which serves as a rosary; and in the other is a *damaru*, or small drum. At other times she is represented with two arms only, seated on a lotus, playing a veena. She dwells on earth amongst men, but her special abode is with her husband in Brahmaloka.

Sarasvati having been produced from Brahma, was regarded as his daughter; hence her union with him was said to be criminal by the other gods. Sometimes she is called the wife of Vishnu, but this difficulty is explained by a legend. Sarsvati, by the standard mythological authorities, is the wife of Brahma. The Vaishnavas of Bengal have a popular legend that she was the wife of Vishnu, as were also Lakshmi and Ganga. The ladies disagreed, Sarasvati, like the other type of learned ladies, being something dominating and Vishnu, finding that one wife was as much as even a god could manage, transferred Sarasvati to Brahma and Ganga to Siva, and contented himself with Lakshmi alone.

Sarasvati is a goddess of some, though not of very great, importance in the Vedas .... She is celebrated both as a river and a goddess. Allusion is made in the hymns, as well as in the Brahmanas, to sacrifices being performed on the banks of this river, and of the adjoining Drishadvati; and the Sarasvati in particular seems to have been associated with the reputation for sanctity which was ascribed to the whole region called Brahmavartta, lying between these two small streams, and situated immediately to the westward of the Jumna. The Sarasvati thus appears to have been to the early Indians what the Ganges (which is only twice named in the Rig-Veda) is to their descendants. When once the river had acquired a divine character, it was quite natural that she should be regarded as the patroness of ceremonies which were celebrated on the margin of her holy waters, and that her direction and blessing should be invoked as essential to their proper performance and success. The connection into which she as thus brought with sacred rites may have led to the further step of identifying her with Vak, the goddess of speech.

In many passages where she is celebrated, her original character is, distinctly preserved. Thus in two places she is mentioned along with rivers, or fertilizing waters : 'Ye opulent waters, command riches; ye possess excellent power and immortality; ye are mistresses of wealth and progeny; may Sarasvati bestow this vitality on her worshipper.' And she is mentioned with the other well-known streams which are there named, the Sindhu, the Ganges, &c. In another place she is said to 'surpass all other rivers, and to flow pure from the mountains to the sea.' In other verses she is called upon to 'descend from the sky, from the great mountain, to the sacrifice;' and is supplicated to combine with the spouses of the other gods to afford secure protection to the worshippers.

In the later mythology, as is well known, Sarasvati was identified with Vak, and became under various names the spouse of Brahma, and the goddess of wisdom and eloquence. In the *Mahabharata* she is called the mother of the Vedas, and the same is said of Vak In the *Taittariya Brahmana* where she is said to be the wife of Indra, to contain within herself all worlds, and to have been sought after by the Rishis who composed the Vedic hymns, as well as by the gods through austerity.

In the Puranas, Sarasvati is spoken of under other titles. A verse in the *Matsya Purana* gives authority for the belief that one goddess only is intended, though she is called by several names : "Brahma next formed from his own immaculate substance a female, who is celebrated under the names of Satarupa, Savitri, Sarasvati, Gayatri, and Brahmani." In the following legend from the *Skanda Purana,* Iswara (Siva) is addressing Devi (Parvati).

'Listen, O Devi, and I will tell you how Savitri forsook Brahma, and he in consequence espoused Gayatri. The Vedas have declared the great advantages which are derived from sacrifice, by which the gods are delighted, and therefore bestow rain upon the earth.... To secure therefore the verdure and vitality of the three worlds, I perform sacrifices; and, in imitation of me, sacrifices are performed by gods and men. For the same purpose Brahma and his wife Savitri, the immortals, and holy sages repaired to Pushkara; but when all the preparations had been made, with all due rites and ceremonies, for performing the sacrifices, Savitri, detained by some household affairs, was not in attendance. A priest accordingly went to call her; but she replied, I have not yet completed my dress, nor arranged several affairs. Lakshmi, and Bhavani, and Ganga, and Svaha, and Indrani, and the wives of the other gods and of the holy sages, have not yet arrived, and how therefore can I enter the assembly alone ?'

The priest returned, and thus addressed Brahma : 'Savitri is engaged and will not come; but without a wife what advantage can be derived from these rites?' The god, incensed at the conduct of Savitri, thus spoke to Indra : 'Hasten, and, in obedience to my order, bring a wife from wherever you can find one.' Indra proceeded accordingly; and as he passed hastily along, saw a milkmaid, young, beautiful, and of a smiling countenance, carrying a jar of butter. He seized her and brought her to the assembly, when Brahma thus spoke : 'O gods and holy sages, if it seem good unto you I will espouse this Gayatri, and she shall become the mother of the Vedas, and the cause of purity to these worlds!' Upon this Brahma was united to Gayatri, who was led into the bower of the bride, and there arrayed in silken garments, and adorned with the costliest ornaments.

At this time Savitri, accompanied by the wives of Vishnu, Rudra, and the other gods, came to the place of sacrifice. Seeing the milkmaid in the bride's bower, and the priests engaged in the performance of the sacred rites, incensed with anger, she thus addressed Pitamaha : 'O Brahma! hast thou conceived so sinful an intention as to reject me, who am they wedded wife? Thou art called the great father of gods and holy sages, and yet thou have acted in a manner which must excite the derision of the three worlds. But how can I now show my face; or, deserted by my husband, call myself a wife?' Brahma replied : 'The priests informed me that the time for the sacrifice was passing away, and that it could not profitably be performed unless my wife were present, ... and Indra having brought Gayatri, Vishnu and Rudra gave her in marriage to me. Forgive, therefore, this one act, and I will never again offend thee!'

On hearing these words, Savitri exclaimed, 'By the powers which I have obtained by the performance of *tapas*, may Brahma never be worshipped in temple or sacred place, except one day in each year.... And, Indra, since thou didst bring that milkmaid to Brahma, thou shalt be bound in chains by thine enemies, and confined in a strange country; and thy city and station shall be occupied by thine enemies.' Addressing Vishnu, she said, 'Since thou gavest her in marriage to Brahma, shalt thou, in consequence of Bhrigu's curse, be born amongst men, and shalt endure the agony of being human. To Rudra she said : 'By the curse of the holy sages, shalt thou be deprived of thy manhood!' To Agni : 'Mayest thou be a devourer of all things, clean and unclean!'

Having pronounced these curses, Savitri left the assembly, and was accompanied for a short distance by Lakshmi and the other goddesses, when they all declared their intention of returning. On hearing this, Savitri was incensed, and thus addressed them : 'Since you now forsake me, O Lakshmi! mayest thou never remain stationary in one place; and mayest thou always abide with the vile, the inconstant, the contemptible, the sinful, the cruel, the foolish, and the barbarian! And, Indrani, when Indra incurs the guilt of Brahmanicide by slaying Tvastri's son, then shall Nahusha acquire his kingdom, and, desirous of obtaining thee, shall exclaim, "Am I not Indra? Why then does not the young and lovely Indrani wait upon me? If I do not obtain her, I will slay all the gods." Thou on learning his wishes shalt remain in thy house immersed in grief, and borne down by the weight of my curse!' Savitri then pronounced this curse on the wives of the gods collectively : 'May you all remain barren; and may you never enjoy the pleasure of having children!' Vishnu then tried in vain to appease her."

After Savitri's angry departure from the assembly, Gayatri modified the curses that had been pronounced. She promised all kinds of blessing, including final absorption into him, to all the worshippers of Brahma. Though Indra be bound, his son should release him. Though Vishnu lose his wife, he should regain her. Though Rudra be deprived of his manhood, the Linga as his representative should be universally worshipped. And though the goddesses could not have children of their own, this would not cause them regret.

The *Padma Purana* gives a happier termination to the story. Vishnu and Lakshmi, at Brahma's request, followed Savitri when she left the assembly, and induced her to return. On re-entering, Brahma asked what she wished him to do with Gayatri. Savitri was too bashful to speak; whereupon Gayatri threw herself at her feet. Savitri raised her, and embracing her said : "A wife ought to obey the wishes and orders of her husband; for that wife who reproaches her husband, who is complaining and quarrelsome, and instead of being his life, deprives him by her conduct of length of years, shall, when she dies, most assuredly go to hell. Considering this, the virtuous wife will do nothing displeasing to her husband; therefore let us both be attached to Brahma." "So be it," said Gayatri; "thy orders will I always obey and esteem thy friendship precious as my life. Thy daughter am I, O goddess! Deign to protect me!" It would appear that between the time when the *Matsya Purana* was composed and the date of the Padma, considerable change had come in the character of the ideal woman. Or it may be that the writer of the Padma wished to give a better ideal to the wives of his day.

In the *Varaha Purana* Sarasvati is addressed as Gayatri, Sarasvati, Maheshvari (one of the names of Parvati), and also Savitri. Her most common name is Sarasvati, by which name, as the goddess of learning, she is regularly worshipped once a year.

6

VISHNU AND LAKSHMI

Vishnu

Vishnu is called the second person of the Hindu Trimurti, or Triad : but though called *second,* it must not be supposed that he is regarded as in any way inferior to Brahma. In some books Brahma is said to be the first cause of all things, in others it is as strongly asserted that Vishnu has this honour; while in others it is claimed for Siva. As Brahma's special work is creation, that of Vishnu is preservation. In the following passage from the *Padma Purana*, it is said that Vishnu is the supreme cause, thus identifying him with Brahma, and also that his special work is *to preserve* : "In the beginning of creation, the great Vishnu, desirous of creating the whole world, became threefold; Creator, Preserver, Destroyer. In order to create this world, the Supreme Spirit produced from the right side of his body himself as Brahma; then, in order ,to preserve the world, he produced from his left side Vishnu; and in order to destroy the world, he produced from the middle of his body the eternal Siva. Some worship Brahma, others Vishnu, others Siva; but Vishnu, one yet threefold, creates, preserves, and destroys : therefore let the pious make no difference between the three."

The essence of the teaching of the *Vishnu Parana* is given in a few lines. "Listen to the complete compendium of the Purana according to its tenor. The world was produced from Vishnu; it exists in him; he is the cause of its continuance and cessation; he is the world." Immediately afterwards is a hymn addressed to him which commences as follows : "Glory to the unchangeable, holy, eternal, supreme Vishnu, of one universal nature, the mighty over all; to him who is Hiranyagarbha (Brahma), Hari (Vishnu), and Sankara (Siva); the Creator, Preserver, and Destroyer of the world." As will be noticed later on, Siva is commonly called Mahadeva (the great god). By those who make him the supreme object of worship, Vishnu is commonly called Narayana, though this was originally a name of Brahma. These generally, to a large extent, disregard his incarnations, and address their praise to him as the greatest of all. And frequently he is indicated by the word Ishwar (God), as though he were *the* God. But this term is far more frequently employed for Siva.

In the *Bhagavata Purana* is the following legend to show the superiority of Vishnu : "Once when the holy sages were performing a sacrifice on the banks of the Sarasvati, a dispute arose amongst them as to which of the three gods was greatest. They sent Bhrigu, the son of Brahma, to ascertain this point. He first went to the heaven of Brahma, and, desirous of discovering the truth, entered his court without paying him the usual honours. Incensed at this disrespect, Brahma glowed with anger; but recollecting that it was caused by his own son, he assuaged the fire of wrath which had risen in his mind. Bhrigu then proceeded to Kailasa; but when Maheshwara (Siva) hastened to embrace him as a brother, he turned away from the proffered embrace. Enraged at such misconduct, the god, seizing his trident, prepared to kill the divine sage; but Parvati fell at his feet, and by her words appeased the anger of her lord. Bhrigu next went to Vishnu's heaven, and kicked the god's breast, as he lay slumbering in the lap of Lakshmi. The lord, rising from his couch, and bowing respectfully to Bhrigu, thus addressed him : 'Welcome to thee, O Brahman! Be seated for a little, and deign to excuse the fault which through ignorance I have committed [in not performing duties due to a guest], and the hurt which your tender foot must have received!' Having thus spoken, he rubbed the foot of Bhrigu with his own hands, and added, 'To-day am I a highly honoured vessel, since thou, O lord ! hast imprinted on my breast the dust of thy sin-dispelling foot.' When Vishnu had finished speaking, Bhrigu was so affected by these benevolent words, that he was unable to reply, and departed in silence, whilst tears of devout emotion rushed from his eyes. On his narrating his adventures to the saints on the banks of the Sarasvati, their doubts were immediately dispelled; they believed Vishnu to be the greatest of the three gods, because he was exempt from impatience and passion."

In the *Varaha Purana* the special work of Vishnu as preserver is described : "The supreme god Narayana having conceived the thought of creating this universe, considered also that it was necessary that it should be protected after it was created; 'but as it is impossible for an incorporeal being to exert action, let me produce from my own essence a corporeal being, by means of whom I may protect the world.' Having thus reflected, the pre-existing Narayana created from his own substance an ungenerated and divine form, on whom he bestowed these blessings: 'Be thou the framer of all things, O Vishnu ! Be thou always the protector of the three worlds, and the adored of all men. Be thou omniscient and almighty; and do thou at all times accomplish the wishes of Brahma and the gods.' The Supreme Spirit then resumed his essential nature. Vishnu, as he meditated on the purpose for which he had been produced, sank into a mysterious slumber; and as in his sleep he imagined the production of various things, a lotus sprang from his navel. In the centre of this lotus Brahma appeared; and Vishnu, beholding the production of his body, was delighted."

In pictures Vishnu is represented as a black man with four arms : in one hand he holds a club; in another a shell; in a third a chakra, or discus, with which he slew his enemies; and in the fourth a lotus. He rides upon the bird Garuda, and is dressed in yellow robes.

This deity is worshipped not only under the name and in the form of Vishnu, but also in one of his many incarnations. Whenever any great calamity occurred in the world, or the wickedness of any of its inhabitants proved an unbearable nuisance to the gods, Vishnu, as Preserver, had to lay aside his invisibility, come to earth in some form, generally human, and, when his work was done, he returned again to the skies. There is no certainty as to the number of times he has become incarnate. Some Puranas describe ten Avataras, as they are called; some mention twenty-four; and sometimes declare that they are innumerable. Ten is the commonly received number, and these are the most important ones. They will be considered in due order. Of these ten, nine have already been accomplished; one, the Kalki, is still future. In the *Matsya Purana* is the following legend, which gives a reason for the manifold and varied appearances of this deity :—

"The *asuras* (demons) having been repeatedly defeated by the *suras* (gods), and deprived of all share of the sacrifices, were meditating to withdraw from the unavailing contest, when Sukra, their preceptor, determined to propitiate Siva by a severe *tapas* (penance), and procure from him a charm by means of which they could conquer. Having left them for this purpose, the asuras said amongst themselves, 'As our preceptor has laid aside his arms and assumed the ascetic dress, how shall we be able to gain a victory over the *suras* ? Let us seek refuge with the mother of Kavya (Sukra), and endure this distress till he shall return; and then let us fight!' Having thus resolved, they hastened to Kavya's mother, who, protecting them, said, 'Fear not! remain near me, and no danger shall approach you!'

"The suras, *seeing* the *asuras* thus protected, were about to attack them, when the goddess in anger thus addressed Indra : 'If thou desist not, I will deprive you of the sovereignty of heaven.' Alarmed at her angry words, and dreading her magic power, Indra was yielding to her desire, when Vishnu appeared and said to him,' Yield not, for I will assist you!' The goddess observing that Indra was protected by Vishnu, angrily said, 'Now let the contending foes behold how the power of my devotions shall subdue both Indra and Vishnu.' Finding themselves likely to be overcome, they asked each other, 'How shall we liberate ourselves from this difficulty ?' Indra then said to Vishnu, 'Hasten to conquer before she has finished her invocations, or we shall be defeated !' Then Vishnu, considering the detriment that must be incurred by the gods should the mother of Kavya bring her incantations to a successful issue, deemed that the slaying of a woman under such circumstances was allowable, seized his discus, and smote off her head. Bhrigu, seeing this horrid deed of the slaughter of a woman and the death of his wife, was violently incensed, and thus cursed Vishnu : 'Since thou hast knowingly murdered a woman, thou shalt be born seven times amongst men;' he afterwards somewhat modified its force as he said, 'but each birth shall be for the advantage of the world, and for the restoration of justice.' "

Of all the deities now reverenced in India, Vishnu in his many forms has perhaps the largest number of worshippers; and the account of his life and the praises presented to him occupy a very large portion of the later Hindu scriptures. This pre-eminence was certainly not recognized in the Vedic Age, as the following passage will show :

'May the gods preserve us from the place from which Vishnu strode over the seven regions of the earth. Vishnu strode over this [universe]; in three places he planted his step; [the world or his step] was enveloped in his dust. Vishnu, the unconquerable preserver, strode three steps.' In these verses there is probably the germ of the Dwarf Incarnation, and also of the attribute of Preserver.

Amongst the thousand names of Vishnu, the following, in addition to those already given, are most commonly known :

Madhusudana, the destroyer of Madhu; and Kaitabhajit, the conqueror of Kaitabha. These were two demons who issued from Vishnu's ear as he lay asleep on the serpent Sesha at the end of a Kalpa, and were about to destroy Brahma, as he sat on the lotus which sprang from Vishnu's navel, when this deity slew them, and hence obtained these names :

Vaikunthanath, "The Lord of Paradise."

Kesava, "He who has excellent hair."

Madhava, "Made of honey; or a descendant of Madhu."

Swayambhu, "The self-existent one."

Pitamvara, "He who wears yellow garments."

Janarddana, "He who causes the people to worship."

Vishvamvara, "The protector of the world."

Hari, "The saviour;" lit. he who takes possession of.

Ananta, "The endless."

Damodara, "Bound with a rope."

Mukunda, "The deliverer."

Purusha, "The man," or "The spirit."

Purushottama, "The supreme man or spirit."

Yajneswara, "The lord of sacrifice."

Lakshmi

Lakshmi, or very commonly, Sri, is the wife of Vishnu, and under various names appears in this relation in his various incarnations. The *Vishnu Purana* has this to say : "As the lord of the worlds, the god of gods, Janardana descends amongst mankind in various shapes; so does his coadjutor Sri. Thus, when Hari was born a dwarf, the son of Aditi, Lakshmi appeared from the lotus as Padma, or Kamala; when he was born as Rama (Parasurama) of the race of Bhrigu, she was Dharani; when he was Raghava (Ramachandra), she was Sita; and when he was Krishna, she was Rukmini. In the other descents of Vishnu she was his associate. If he takes a celestial form, she appears as divine; if a mortal, she becomes a mortal too, transforming her own person agreeably to whatever character it pleases Vishnu to assume."

The account of the churning of the ocean, to which frequent reference is made in the Hindu scriptures, is found in the Ramayana, and several of the Puranas; though there are some discrepancies, they agree in the main. The reason for this is that a saint named Durvaras, a portion of Siva, was travelling, when he met a celestial nymph with a sweet-smelling garland, which at his request she gave to him. Excited with the scent, he was dancing, when he met Indra, seated on his elephant. To please the mighty god, the saint presented him with the garland, who placed it upon his elephant's head. The elephant in his turn becoming excited, seized the garland with his trunk and threw it upon the ground. Durvaras, seeing his gift slighted, cursed the god in his anger, and told him that his kingdom should be overwhelmed with ruin. From that time Indra's power began to wange; for though he sought forgiveness, the saint's anger was not appeased. As the curse was experienced by the gods, they fled to Brahma for help. He told them he could not assist them; that Vishnu alone could do this. Brahma conducted them to Vishnu; and, having sufficiently lauded him, caused him to agree to their request. The *Vishnu Purana*, states :

> " The gods addressed the mighty Vishnu thus :
> 'Conquered in battle by the evil demons,
> We fly to thee for succour; soul of all,
> Pity and by thy might deliver us!'
> Hari, the lord, creator of the world,
> Thus by the gods implored, all graciously
> Replied, 'Your strength shall be restored, ye gods—
> Only accomplish what I now command :
> Unite yourselves in peaceful combination
> With these your foes; collect all plants and herbs
> Of diverse kinds from every quarter; cast them
> Into the sea of milk; take Mandara,
> The mountain, for a churning stick, and Vasuki,
> The serpent, for a rope; together churn
> I The ocean to produce the beverage—
> Source of all strength and immortality—
> Then reckon on mine aid : I will take care
> Your foes shall share your toil, but not partake
> In its reward, or drink the immortal draught.'
> Thus by the god of gods advised, the host
> United in alliance with the demons.
> Straightway they gathered various herbs, and cast them

Into the waters; then they took the mountain
To serve as churning-staff, and next the snake
To serve as cord, and in the ocean's midst
Hari himself, present in tortoise form,
Became a pivot for the churning-staff.
Then did they churn the sea of milk; and first
Out of the waters rose the sacred cow—
God-worshipped Surabhi—eternal fountain
Of milk and offerings of butter; next,
While holy Siddhas wondered at the sight,
With eyes all rolling, Varuni uprose—
Goddess of Wine. Then from the whirlpool sprang
Fair Parijata, tree of Paradise, delight
Of heavenly maidens, with its fragrant blossoms
Perfuming the whole world. The Apsarasas,
Troop of celestial nymphs, matchless in grace,
Perfect in loveliness, were next produced.
Then from the sea uprose the cool-rayed moon,
Which Mahadeva seized; terrific poison
Next issued from the waters—this the snake-gods
Claimed as their own. Then, seated on a lotus,
Beauty's bright goddess, peerless Sri, arose
Out of the waves; and with her, robed in white.
Came forth Dhanvantari, the gods' physician.
High in his hand he bore the cup of nectar—
Life-giving draught—longed for by gods and demons."

On Sri's appearance the sages were enraptured, the gandharvas sang her praises, and the celestial nymphs danced before her. Ganga and the other sacred streams followed her, and the heavenly elephants took up their pure waters in golden vessels and poured them upon her. The sea of milk presented her with a wreath of unfading flowers ; and the artist of the gods decorated her with lovely ornaments. Thus bathed, attired, and adorned, the goddess, in the presence of the gods, cast herself upon the breast of Hari. From the demons she turned away; hence they were miserable. Seeing the cup of nectar, they tried to seize it, when Vishnu, assuming the appearance of a beautiful woman, attracted their attention, whilst the gods quaffed the divine cup. The result was that in the conflict which followed the gods were successful.

Lakshmi, or Sri, is regarded as the goddess of Love, Beauty, and Prosperity. When a man is growing rich, it is said that Lakshmi has come to dwell with him; whilst those in adversity are spoken of as "forsaken of Lakshmi." In pictures she is painted as a lady of a bright golden colour, seated on a lotus, with two arms.

Lakshmi is known also by the following names :—

Haripriya, "The beloved of Hari."

Padma, "The Lotus," and Padmalaya, "She who dwells on a lotus."

Jaladhija, "The ocean-born."

Chanchala, "The fickle one."

Lokamata, "The mother of the world."

7

THE INCARNATIONS OR AVATARAS OF VISHNU

Matsya Avatara

The earliest account of what was afterwards regarded as an incarnation of Vishnu is found in the *Satapatha Brahmana*. It will be noticed that though in this passage a wonderful fish is described, it is not said to have been an incarnation of any of the gods. The *Mahabharata* says that Brahma assumed this form; whilst the Puranas teach that the fish here spoken of was Vishnu. This transfer of work from one deity to another is not a matter of much surprise, when we remember how frequently it is declared that all the various gods are but forms of one supreme being.

The *Satapatha Brahmana* says :—

"There lived in ancient time a holy man
Called Manu, who, by penances and prayers,
Had won the favour of the lord of heaven.
One day they brought him water for ablution;
Then, as he washed his hands, a little fish
Appeared, and spoke in human accents thus :
'Take care of me, and I will be thy saviour.'
'From what wilt thou preserve me ?'
Manu asked. The fish replied, 'A flood will sweep away
All creatures; I will rescue thee from that.'
'But how shall I preserve thee ?' Manu said.
The fish rejoined, 'So long as we are small,
We are in constant danger of destruction,
For fish eat fish; so keep me in a jar.

When I outgrow the jar, then dig a trench,
And place me there; when I outgrow the trench,
Then take me to the ocean—I shall then
Be out of reach of danger.' Having thus
Instructed Manu, straightway rapidly
The fish grew larger; then he spoke again :
'In such and such a year the flood will come;
Therefore construct a ship, and pay me homage.
When the flood rises, enter thou the ship,
And I will rescue thee.' So Manu did
As he was ordered, and preserved the fish,
Then carried it in safety to the ocean ;
And in the very year the fish enjoined
He built a ship, and paid the fish respect,
And there took refuge when the flood arose.
Soon near him swam the fish, and to its horn
Manu made fast the cable of his vessel.
Thus drawn along the waters, Manu passed
Beyond the northern mountain. Then the fish,
Addressing Manu, said, 'I have preserved thee,
Quickly attach the ship to yonder tree;
But, lest the waters sink from under thee,
As fast as they subside, so fast shalt thou
Descend the mountain gently after them.'
Thus he descended from the northern mountain.
The flood had swept away all living creatures;
Manu alone was left."

The typical Puranic account of this Avatara is that of the *Bhagavata Purana*. With this the accounts in the other Puranas agree in the main. All the Puranas agree in regarding the fish as an incarnation of Vishnu. Now follows the account from the *Bhagavata* :

"Desiring the preservation of herds, Brahmans, and virtuous men—of the Vedas, of law, and of precious things—the Lord of the Universe assumes many bodily shapes; but though he pervades, like the air, a variety of beings, yet he is himself unvaried, since he has no qualities subject to change. At the close of the last Kalpa there was a general destruction, occasioned by the sleeping Brahma, whence his creatures in different worlds were drowned in a vast ocean. Brahma being inclined to slumber, desiring response after a lapse of ages, the strong demon Hayagriva came near him, and stole the Vedas, which had flowed from his lips.

"When Hari, the preserver of the universe, discovered this deed of the prince of the Danavas, he took the shape of a minute fish, called Saphari. A holy king named Satyavrata then reigned—a servant of the spirit which moved on the waves; and so devout, that water was his only sustenance. He was the child of the Sun, and one day as he was making a libation in this river Kritamala, and held water in the palm of his hand, he perceived a small fish moving in it. The King immediately dropped the fish into the river, together with the water which he had taken from it; when the Saphari thus addressed the monarch : 'How canst thou, O king, who showest affection to the oppressed, leave me in this river water, where, I am too weak to resist the monsters of the stream?' He, not knowing who had assumed the form of a fish, applied his mind to the preservation of the Saphari, and having heard his very suppliant address, he placed it in a small vase full of water; but in a single night its bulk was so increased that it could not be contained in the jar, and thus again addressed the illustrious prince : 'I am not pleased with living miserably in this little vase; make me a large mansion, where I may dwell in comfort'. The king, removing it thence, placed it in the water of a cistern; but it grew three cubits in less than fifty minutes, and said, 'O king! it pleases me not to stay in this narrow cistern; since thou hast granted me an asylum, given me a spacious habitation.' He then removed it and placed it in a pool, where, having ample space around its body, it became a fish of considerable size. 'This abode, O king, is not convenient for me, who must swim at large in the waters; please remove me to a deep lake!' Thus addressed, the pious monarch threw the suppliant into a lake, and, when it grew of equal bulk with that piece of water, he cast the vast fish into the sea. When the fish was thrown into the waves, he thus again spoke to Satyavrata : 'Here the horned sharks and other monsters of great strength will devour me; thou shouldest not, O valiant man, leave me in this ocean.'

"Thus repeatedly deluded by the fish, who had addressed him with gentle words, the king said, 'Who art thou that beguilest me in that assumed shape? Never before have I seen or heard of so prodigious an inhabitant of the waters, who, like thee, has filled up in a single day a lake a hundred leagues in circumference. Surely thou art Bhagavat who appears before me; the great Hari, whose dwelling was on the waves.

"The lord of the universe intending to preserve the king from the sea of destruction caused by the depravity of the age, thus told him how he was to act : 'In seven days from the present time, the three worlds will be plunged in an ocean of death; but, in the midst of the destroying waves, a large vessel sent by me for thy use shall stand before thee. Then thou shalt take all medicinal herbs, all the varieties of seeds, and accompanied by seven saints, encircled by pairs of animals, thou shalt enter the spacious ark, and continue in it secure from the flood, on one immense ocean without light, except the radiance of the holy companions. When the ship shall be agitated with an impetuous wind, thou shalt fasten it with a large sea serpent on my horn; for I will be near thee, drawing the vessel, with thee and thy attendants."

"Hari, having thus directed the monarch, disappeared; and Satyavrata humbly waited for the time when the sea, overwhelming its shores, would deluge the whole earth. He saw the vessel advancing, and entered it having carried into it the medicinal plants, and conformed to the directions of Hari. The saints thus addressed him : 'O king, meditate on Kesava; who will surely deliver us from this danger, and grant us prosperity.' The god being invoked by the monarch, appeared again distinctly on the vast ocean in the form of a fish, blazing like gold, extending a million of leagues, with one stupendous horn; on which the king, as he had been commanded by Hari, tied the ship, and, happy in his preservation, stood praising the destroyer of Madhu. When the monarch had finished his hymn, the primeval male, Bhagavat, who watched for his safety on the greater expanse of water, spake aloud to his own divine essence, pronouncing a sacred Purana [the *Matsya Purana*], which contained the rules of the Sankhya philosophy. Then Hari, rising from the destructive deluge, which was now abated, slew the demon Hayagriva, and recovered the sacred books."

Kurma Avatara

This incarnation was necessitated by the fact that the gods were in danger of losing their authority over the demons. In their distress they applied to Vishnu for help, who told them to churn the sea of milk that they might procure the *Amrita*, or water of life, by which they would be made strong, and promised to become the tortoise on which the mountain

Mandara as a churning stick should rest. As a full account of this operation has been already given when describing Lakshmi, who was one of its chief products, there is no necessity to repeat it here. A few additional particulars will be found in the following extract from the *Vishnu Purana*.

"Hari having been entreated to help the gods, thus spoke : 'I will restore your strength. Do you act as I enjoin. Let all the gods and asuras cast all sorts of medicinal herbs into the sea of milk, and together churn the ocean for ambrosia, depending on my aid. To secure the assistance of the *daityas*, you must be at peace with them, and engage to give them an equal share of your associated toil; promising them that by drinking of the *amrita* ... they shall become mighty and immortal. I will take care that the enemies of the gods shall not partake of the precious draught; they shall only share in the labour."

The gods entered into an arrangement with the *asuras*, and together they made the necessary preparations. "The assembled gods were stationed by Krishna at the tail of the serpent Vasuki (the churning rope), and the *daityas* and *danavas* at its head and neck. Scorched by the flames emitted from his inflated hood, the demons were shorn of their glory; whilst the clouds, driven by his breath towards his tail, refreshed the gods by showers. In the midst of the milky sea, Hari himself, in the form of a tortoise, served as a pivot for the mountain, as it was whirled around. The holder of the mace and discus was present in other forms amongst the gods and demons, and assisted to drag the monarch of the serpent race; and in another vast body sat upon the summit of the mountain. With one portion of his energy, unseen by gods and demons, he sustained the serpent king; and with another infused vigour unto the gods."

Varaha Avatara

There are two accounts of this incarnation from two recensions of the Ramayana. In one, it is said that Brahma assumed the form of a boar; in the other, Vishnu *in the form of Brahma* is said to have accomplished this work. The alteration of the text is very noticeable. "All was water only, in which the earth was formed. Thence arose Brahma, the self-existent, with the deities. He then becoming a boar, raised up the earth, and created the whole world with the saints his sons." So far the probably older recension. In the later one we read, "All was water only, through which the earth was formed. Thence arose Brahma, the self-existent, the imperishable Vishnu. He then, becoming a boar, raised up this earth and created the whole world."

In the following account from the *Vishnu Purana* it will be noticed that, as in the last quotation from the Ramayana, it was Vishnu in the form of Brahma who became a boar. As the earlier writers had declared this to have been Brahma's work, it was necessary to identify Vishnu with him.

"Tell me how at the commencement of the present age, Narayana, who is named Brahma, created all existing things. At the close of the last age, the divine Brahma endowed with the quality of goodness, awoke from his night of sleep, and beheld the universal void. He, the supreme Narayana, ... invested with the form of Brahma, ... concluding that within the waters lay the earth, and being desirous to raise it up, created another form for that purpose. And as in the preceding ages he had assumed the shape of a fish, or a tortoise, so in this he took the form of a boar. Having adopted a form composed of the sacrifices of the Vedas for the preservation of the whole earth, the eternal, supreme, and universal soul plunged into the ocean."

The earth, bowing with devout adoration, addressed the boar, as he approached, in a hymn of great beauty, in which she reminds him that she sprang from him, and is dependent on him, as in fact are all things. Being thus praised, "the auspicious supporter of the world emitted a low murmuring sound, like the chanting of the Sama-Veda; and the mighty boar, whose eyes were like the lotus, whose body was vast as the Nila mountains, and of the dark colour of the lotus leaves, uplifted upon his ample tusks the earth from its lowest regions. As he reared up his head, the waters that rushed from his brow purified the great sages, Sanandana and others residing in the sphere of the saints. Through the indentations made by his hoofs, the waters rushed into the lower worlds with a thundering noise. Before his breadth, the pious denizens of Janaloka were scattered, and the Munis sought for shelter amongst the bristles upon the body of the boar, trembling as he rose up supporting the earth, and dripping with moisture. Then the great sages Sanandana and the rest, residing continually in the sphere of the saints, were inspired with delight, and bowing lowly, they praised the stern-eyed upholder of the earth."

"Triumph, lord of lords, supreme! Kesava, sovereign of the earth ... cause of production, destruction and existence. *Thou art*, O god! there is none other supreme condition than thou. Thou, lord, art the person of the sacrifice; thy feet are the Vedas; thy tusks are the stake to which the victim is bound; thy teeth are the offerings; thy mouth is the altar; thy tongue is the fire; and the hairs of thy body are the sacrificial grass. Thy eyes, O omnipotent! are day and night; thy head is the seat of all—the place of Brahma; thy name is all the hymns of the Vedas; thy nostrils are all oblations. O thou, whose snount is the ladle of oblation; whose deep voice is the chanting of the Sama-Veda; whose body is the hall of sacrifice; whose joints are the different ceremonies; and whose ears have the properties of both voluntary and obligatory rites; do thou, who art eternal, who art in size a mountain, be propitious . . . raise up this earth for the habitation of created beings!"

The supreme being thus eulogized, upholding the earth, raised it quickly, and placed it on the summit of the ocean, where it floats like a mighty vessel, and, on account of its expansive surface, does not sink beneath the waters.

Nrisingha Avatara

Hiranyakasipu, who, the *Vayu Purana* says, had obtained a boon from Brahma, that he should not be slain by any created being. When therefore his pride, fostered by his supposed immunity from danger, had led him to great excesses, so that his death was desired both by gods and men, Vishnu descended in the form of a living being, half-man and half-lion, and so neither man nor animal, and slew him. By the assumption of this form the *letter* of Brahma's promise was kept. The *Vishnu Purana* says :

"Hiranyakasipu, the son of Diti, had formerly brought the three worlds under his authority. He had usurped the sovereignty of Indra, and exercised himself the functions of the sun, of air, of the lord of waters, of fire, and of the moon. He himself was the god of riches; he was the judge of the dead; and he appropriated to himself without reserve all that was offered in sacrifice to the gods. The deities, therefore, flying from their seats in heaven, wandered, through fear of the *daitya,* upon the earth, disguised in mortal shapes. Having conquered the three worlds, he was inflated with pride, and, eulogized by the Gandharvas, enjoyed whatever he desired."

This demon had a son named Prahlada, who was a very devout worshipper of Vishnu, whom his father hated most intensely. "On one occasion Prahlada came, accompanied by his teacher, to the court of his father, and bowed himself before his feet as he was drinking. Hiranyakasipu desired his prostrate son to rise, and said to him, 'Repeat in substance and agreeably what during the period of your studies you have acquired.' Prahlada said, 'I have learned to admire him who is without beginning, middle, or end, increase or diminution; the imperishable lord of the world, the universal cause of causes.' On hearing these words, the sovereign of the *daityas,* his eyes red with wrath and his lips swollen with indignation, turned to the preceptor of his son, and said, 'Vile Brahman! what is this preposterous commendation of my foe that, in disrespect to me, you have taught this boy to utter ?' The preceptor denies the charge, and Prahlada himself replies,' Vishnu is the instructor of the whole world; what else should any one learn or teach, save him, the supreme spirit?' 'Blockhead!' exclaimed the king, 'who is this Vishnu, whose name you thus reiterate so impertinently before me, who am the sovereign of the three worlds ?' 'The glory of Vishnu,' replied Prahlada, 'is to be meditated upon by the devout; it cannot be described; he is the supreme lord, who is all things, and from whom all things proceed.' The king threatens death; but the son says,' Vishnu is the creator and protector not of me alone, but of all human beings, and even, father, of you.' The father can bear this no longer, so orders his son to return to his preceptor's house.

"Prahlada is taken away, but after a time is sent for again. When requested to recite some poetry, he commenced to sing the praises of Vishnu, which so exasperated the king, that he cried out, 'Kill the wretch! He is not fit to live who is a traitor to his own race.' Upon this the attendants rushed upon Prahlada with their weapons, and, though hundreds struck him, none could injure him. His father then entreated him to desist from praising Vishnu; but this the son would not do, as he said he had no fear, 'as long as his immortal guardian against all dangers was present in his mind.'

"The young prince" (by his father's orders) "was then assailed by the elephants of the skies, as vast as mountain peaks; cast down upon the earth, and trampled on and gored by their tusks; but, he continued to meditate on Govinda, and the tusks of the elephants were blunted against his breast.

"Failing in this, the king said, 'Let fire consume him; and do thou, deity of the winds, blow up the fire, that this wicked wretch may be consumed.' And the *danavas* piled a mighty heap of wood around the prince, and kindled a fire to burn him, as their master had commanded. But Prahlada cried, 'Father, this fire, though blown by the winds, burneth me not; and all around I behold the face of the skies, cool and fragrant with beds of lotus flowers.'

"The Brahmans now interceded with the king on the prince's behalf, promising either to teach him to recant his errors, or to find some means of accomplishing his death; but instead of profiting by their instructions, he spends his time in speaking to all about him of the glory of Vishnu and the happiness of his worshippers. They informed the king of their failure to bring the prince to a right state of mind; whereupon the cooks are ordered to mix poison with his food. But this expedient was futile, as the others had been. The Brahmans now reason with him, and try to show him that it is the chief duty of a son to honour his father; but their sophistry is unsuccessful. They remind him that they had promised to use incantations to accomplish his death. This menace he meets with these words : 'What living creature slays or is slain? What living creature preserves or is preserved? Each is his own destroyer or preserver as he follows evil or good.' Enraged by this reply, they now produce a magical female figure, enwreathed in a flame of fire, whose tread parched the earth, and who struck Prahlada upon the breast. Her blow fell harmless upon him; but turning towards the Brahmans, she slew them all, and disappeared. In answer to the prince's prayer, they were, however, restored to life, and, having blessed Prahlada, departed and told the king all that had happened.

"Having sent for his son, Hiranyakasipu inquired again, by what magical art he was able thus to protect himself. Prahlada said that it was not by magic at all, but simply by the indwelling of Vishnu that he was able to ward off evil; and further that the same power was within the reach of all who would trust him. The king, enraged at this avowal, commanded his attendants to cast his son from the summit of the palace where he was sitting, and which was many yojanas in height, upon the tops of the mountains, where his body would be dashed to pieces against the rocks. Accordingly the *daityas* hurled the boy down, but as he fell cherishing Hari in his heart, Earth, the nurse of all creatures, received him gently in her lap, thus entirely devoted to Kesava, the protector of the world."

Hiranyakasipu, seeing that this fall had not injured his son in any way, asks Samvara, the mightiest of enchanters, to try his hand; but though he puts forth all his skill, the boy remains unhurt. After this, the prince goes again to his preceptor's house, where he is instructed in politics. When his education in this science was completed, he is taken to the king for examination; but on being questioned as to his mode of government, he admits that though he has been instructed in these subjects, he does not approve of what his teachers had said, and again sings the praises of Vishnu. His father, burning with rage, exclaimed, 'Bind him with strong bands and cast him into the ocean. Death is the just retribution of the disobedient.' The *daityas* bound the prince with strong bands, as their lord had commanded, and threw him into the sea. As he floated on the waters, the ocean was convulsed throughout its whole extent, and rose in mighty indulations, threatening to submerge the earth. When Hiranyakasipu observed this, he commanded the *daityas* to hurl rocks into the sea, and pile them closely on one another, burying beneath their incumbent mass him whom fire could not burn. . . . 'Here, since he cannot die, let him live for thousands of years at the bottom of the ocean, overwhelmed by mountains.' This was done. But Prahlada was uninjured. His mind was filled with thoughts of Hari, and he came to recognize his real identity with Vishnu. As soon as Prahlada, through the force of contemplation, had become one with Vishnu, the bands with which he was bound burst instantly asunder. Prahlada, after hymning the praises of Vishnu, again returns to his father, who no sooner saw him, than he kissed him on the forehead, embraced him, and shed tears, and said, 'Dost thou live, my son?' "

For a time there was complete reconciliation between them. And only in a very cursory manner does the *Vishnu Purana* allude to the death of Hiranyakasipu. After speaking of the reconciliation between the father and son, without any intimation of further dispute, it goes on to say : "After his father had been put to death by Vishnu in the form of the man-lion, Prahlada became the sovereign of the *daityas*." In the *Bhagavat* we are told that Prahlada had said that Vishnu was in him, in his father; in fact, was everywhere. "Hiranyakasipu says, 'Why, if Vishnu is everywhere, is he not visible in this pillar ?' Being told that Vishnu, though unseen, was really present there, he struck the pillar, saying, 'Then I will kill him.' Immediately Vishnu, in the form of a being half-man and half-lion, came forth from the pillar, laid hold of Hiranyakasipu by the thighs with his teeth, and tore him up the middle. Brahma's boon to this *daitya* king, as a reward of his religious observances, was that no common animal should destroy him, that he should die neither in the day nor night, in earth or in heaven, by fire, by water, or by the sword. This promise was kept in the letter, for it was evening when Vishnu slew him; this is neither day nor night. It was done under the droppings of the thatch, and this, according to a Hindu proverb, is out of the earth, and he was not killed by a man or an ordinary animal."

The Vamana Avatara

The four Avataras that have already been, described are said to have occurred in the Satya-yuga, it was in the Treta-yuga, or second age, that this incarnation is supposed to have occurred.

This incarnation was undertaken to recover heaven for the gods. Bali, a demon, grandson of Prahlada whose story has just been given, was king over the three worlds—heaven, earth and sky. In the form of a Brahman dwarf, Vishnu appears, and asks, as a gift, all he could cross over in three steps. This the king grants. Immediately the pigmy becomes a giant, and with one step strides over heaven, and with the second over the earth, and thus fulfils his purpose. The *Skanda Purana* states :

"In the battle between the gods and asuras for the possession of the *amrita* produced at the churning of the ocean, the demons were defeated. Bali prepared a costly sacrifice in order that he might regain his power. As he presented his offerings to the sacred fire, he obtained from it a wondrous car drawn by four white horses, a banner displaying a lion, and celestial armour and weapons. The sacred rites being finished, he raised a large army, and in his newly-acquired chariot went and laid siege to Amravati, the capital of Indra's heaven. The gods in terror turned to their preceptor for advice. He told them that their enemies had been rendered invincible by penance. On hearing this, they were greatly alarmed, and Indra besought the preceptor, Brihaspati, to tell them what to do. He advised them to forsake Amravati, assume other forms, and find a home elsewhere. They obeyed; Indra became a peacock, Kubera a lizard, and the other gods, variously disguised, went to the hermitage of Kasyapa, to whom they related their misfortunes. On hearing their story, the sage desired his wife Aditi to perform a severe penance, in order to induce Vishnu to become her son, that through him the gods might be restored to heaven."

In the *Satapatha Brahmana,* is the following. "The gods and the *asuras,* who both sprung from Prajapati, strove together. Then the gods were worsted; and the *asuras* said, 'This world is now certainly ours! Let us divide the earth, and let us subsist thereon.' The gods heard of it and said, 'The *asuras* are dividing the earth : come, we will go to the spot where they are dividing it!' Placing at their head Vishnu, the sacrifice, they proceeded [thither], and said, 'Put us with yourselves in possession of this earth; let us have a share of it.' The *asuras* grudgingly said, 'We will give you as much as this Vishnu can lie upon.' Now Vishnu was a dwarf. The gods did not reject this offer. They placed Agni in the East, and thus they went on toiling and worshipping. By this means they acquired the whole earth."

The next form of the legend is that of the *Ramayana*. Visvamitra, a sage, addressing Rama, tells him the story. "Formerly Bali, the son of Virochana, after conquering the chief of the gods, enjoyed the empire of the three worlds, intoxicated with the increase of his power. When Bali was celebrating a sacrifice, Indra and the other gods addressed Vishnu saying, 'That mighty Bali is now performing sacrifice; he who grants the desire of all creatures; the prosperous lord of the *asuras*. Whatever suppliants wait upon him, he bestows on them whatever they wish. Do thou take the form of a dwarf, and bring about our highest welfare.' Thus addressed by the gods, Vishnu took the form of a dwarf, and, approaching the son of Virochana, begged three of his own paces. Having obtained three paces, Vishnu assumed a miraculous form, and with three paces took possession of the world. With one step he occupied the whole earth; with a second, the eternal atmosphere; and with a third, the sky. Having assigned to the *asura* Bali an abode in Patala (the infernal region), he gave the empire of the world to Indra."

The *Vishnu Purana* barely notices this event, but it is fully described in the *Bhagavata* is there asked, "Why did Hari, the lord of creatures, ask, like a poor man, three pieces of land from Bali ? And why, when he had obtained his object, did he bind him ? And why was an innocent being bound by the lord of sacrifice?" The answer given is as follows : After Bali had been killed by Indra, he was restored by the Brahmans of the race of Bhrigu, who consecrated him for supreme dominion, and performed a sacrifice to obtain it for him. He then sets out for Amravati, as before narrated; and Indra is told, when he applies to his preceptor for advice, that Bali had obtained this power "by virtue of the Brahman's sacrifice;" and that, save by Hari, he is unconquerable. "He now reaps the fruit of Brahmanical power; through contempt of these same Brahmans he shall perish with all his descendants."

The gods forsake their capital, which is occupied by Bali. Aditi, the mother of the gods, is distressed as she sees the condition of her children; and acting upon the advice of her husband, propitiates Vishnu, who says : "I shall with a portion of myself become thy son, and deliver thy children. Wait upon thy husband, the sinless Prajapati, virtuous female, meditating upon me, who in this form abide within him." Aditi followed the advice of the god; and Kasyapa knew by meditation that a portion of Hari had entered into him. In due time the son was born, and became a dwarfish Brahmanical student.

As the Bhrigus are performing a sacrifice for Bali on the banks of the Narmada river, this dwarf visits Bali at Indra's heaven. "Acquainted with his duty, Bali placed upon his head the auspicious water with which the Brahman's feet had been washed, and said, 'Welcome to thee, O Brahman! What can we do for thee ? Ask of me, student, whatever thou desirest. Son of a Brahman, I conclude thou art a suppliant; ask a cow, pure gold, an embellished house, food and drink, a Brahman's daughter, flourishing villages, horses, elephants, and carriages." The dwarf concludes a speech with the semblance of moderation as follows : "I ask from thee a small portion of ground, three paces measured step by step. I desire no more from thee. A wise man incurs no sin, when he asks [only] as much as he needs." The king, though astonished at the smallness of the request, takes a vessel of water in his hand, and is about to confirm the gift; when his preceptor, seeing through Vishnu's device, tries to dissuade his pupil. In a long speech he seeks to show that rather than be left homeless it would be better for him to break his word. But the king persists in fulfilling his promise; even though cursed by his preceptor for doing so. With two steps Vishnu strode over the universe; there was nowhere for him to take a third.

The gods congratulate Hari; Bali is bound by Garuda and then reproached by Vishnu for not fulfilling his promise. "*Asura,* three paces of ground were given to me by thee; with two paces the entire world has been traversed; find a place for the third. As thou hast not given what was promised, it is my pleasure that thou shouldst dwell in the infernal regions. That man falls downward who, after promising a Brahman, does not deliver to him what he had solicited. I have been deluded by thee." Bali offers his head as a place for Vishnu's foot, saying, "I fear not the infernal regions so much as a bad name." Bali goes to Patala, and is there visited by his grandfather Prahlada. First Vishnu's wife and then Brahma intercede with him on the demon's behalf, who, in reply, promises that Bali shall again become Indira; but that in the mean time he must dwell in Sutala, where "by my will, neither mental nor bodily pains, nor fatigue, nor weariness, nor discomfiture, nor diseases afflict the inhabitants." Bali gladly left Patala, and went to Sutala, to wait until the time came when, in accordance with the promise of Vishnu, he should again rule over gods and men.

Another legend teaches that Vishnu gave Bali the choice of going to heaven, taking with him five ignorant people, or of going to hell with five wise. He chose the latter, for there is no pleasure anywhere in the company of the ignorant; whilst a bad place with good company is enjoyable.

Parasurama Avatara

The incarnation of Parasurama, or Rama with axe, was undertaken by Vishnu for the purpose of exterminating the Kshattriya, or warrior caste which had tried to dominate. Twenty-one times Rama is said to have cleared the earth of these men, but by various means some few were preserved alive who were able to perpetuate the race.

The following legend of the birth of Parasurama is from the *Vishnu Purana*. A prince named Gadhi, who was himself an incarnation of Indra, had a daughter named Satyavati. Richika, a descendant of Bhrigu, demanded her in marriage. The king asked from the decrepit old Brahman a thousand white horses, each having one black ear, as a wedding present. These horses were obtaind, by the help of Varuna, and Richika got the hand of the princess.

In order of effect the birth of a son, Richika prepared a dish of rice, barley, and pulse, with butter and milk, for his wife to eat, and, at her request, consecrated a similar mixture for her mother, by partaking of which she hoped to give birth to a prince of martial prowess. Leaving both dishes with his wife, after carefully describing which was for herself and which for her mother, the sage went away into the forest. When the time for eating the food came, the mother said to Satyavati, "Daughter! all mothers wish their children to be possessed of excellent qualities, and would be mortified to see them surpassed by the merits of their brother. Give me, therefore, what your husband has set apart for you, and you eat that which was intended for me. The son which it is intended to procure for me, is destined to be the monarch of the whole world; whilst that which your dish will give you must be a Brahman, alike devoid of affluence, valour, and power." Satyavati consented to this proposal, and they exchanged the dishes.

On Richika's return, perceiving what had happened, he said to his wife, "Sinful woman! what hast thou done? Thou hast eaten of the consecrated food that was prepared for thy mother; thou hast done wrong. In that food I had infused the properties of power, and strength, and heroism; in thine, the qualities suited to a Brahman—gentleness, knowledge, and resignation. In consequence of having reversed my plans, thy son shall follow a warrior's propensities, and use weapons, and fight, and slay. Thy mother's son shall be born with the inclinations of a Brahman, and be addicted to peace and piety." Satyavati, hearing this, fell at her husband's feet, and asked that she might not have such a son as he had described; "but if such there must be, let it be my grandson and not my son." The Muni relented, and said, "So be it." Accordingly in due time she gave birth to a son named Jamadagni, who married Renuka, and had by her the destroyer of the Kshattriya race, Parasurama, who was a portion of Narayana, the spiritual guide of the universe.

This is all we find about Parasurama's work in the *Vishnu Purana.* The story of his exploits is told at length twice over in the *Mahabharata,* and is found in the *Bhagavata, Padma,* and *Agni Puranas.* The following account is from the Mahabharata.

Jamadagni, the son of Richika, having married Renuka, "conducted the princess to his hermitage, and she was contented to partake in his ascetic life. They had four sons, and then a fifth, who was Jamadagnya (Parasurama), the last, but not the least, of the brethren. Once when her sons were absent gathering the fruits on which they fed, Renuka, who was exact in the discharge of all her duties, went forth to bathe. On her way to the stream she beheld Chitraratha, the Prince of Mrittikavati, with a garland of lotuses on his neck, sporting with his queen in the water, and she felt envious of their felicity. Defiled by unworthy thoughts, wetted, but not purified by the stream, she returned disquieted to the hermitage. Beholding her fallen from her perfection, and shorn of the lustre of her sanctity, Jamadagni reproved her, and was exceeding wroth.

"Upon this, her sons came from the wood, and each as he entered was successively commended by his father to put his mother to death; but, neither of them made any reply. Lastly Rama returned to the hermitage, when the mighty and holy Jamadagni said to him, 'Kill thy mother, who has sinned; and do it without repining.' Rama accordingly took up his axe and struck off his mother's head; whereupon the wrath of Jamadagni was assuaged, and, pleased with his son, said : 'Since thou hast obeyed my commands, and done what was hard to be performed, demand from me whatever blessing thou wilt, and thy desires shall be fulfilled.' Rama begged these boons : the restoration of his mother to life, with forgetfulness of having been slain, and purification from all defilement; and for himself, invincibility in single combat. All these his father bestowed.

"It happened on one occasion that, during the absence of the Rishi's sons, the mighty monarch Karttavirya, the sovereign of the Haihaya tribe, endowed by the favour of Dattatreya with a thousand arms, and a golden chariot that went wheresoever he willed came to the hermitage of Jamadagni, where the wife of the sage received him with proper respect. This Kartavirya, by reason of his strength, had greatly oppressed the gods, Rishis, and all creatures. The gods and Rishis applied to Vishnu, who, with Indra, devised the means of destroying him. The king, inflated with the pride of valour, made no return for the hospitality of the Rishi's wife; but carried off with him the calf of the milch cow of the sacred oblation.

"When Rama returned, his father told him what had happened; and seeing the cow in distress, he was filled with wrath. Taking up his splendid bow, he assailed Karttavirya, and overthrew him in battle. With sharp arrows Rama cut off his thousand arms, and he perished. The sons of Karttavirya, to avenge their father's death, attacked the hermitage of Jamadagni when Rama was absent, and slew the pious and unresisting sage, who called repeatedly, but fruitlessly, upon his valiant son. Rama deeply lamented his father's death, performed the last obsequies, and lighted the funeral pile. He then made a vow that he would extirpate the whole Kshattriya race. In fulfilment of which, with remorseless and fatal rage, he destroyed the sons of Karttavirya; and, after them, whatever Kshattriyas he encountered. Thrice seven times did he clear the earth of the Kshattriya caste. After he had cleared the world of Kshattriyas, their widows came to the Brahmans, praying for offspring. The religious Brahmans, free from any impulse of lust, cohabited with these women, who, in consequence, brought forth valiant Kshattriya boys and girls."

In the *Ramayana* is an interesting legend in which Parasurama, himself an incarnation of Vishnu, is described as meeting with Rama, the next avatara of the same deity, and in which the superiority of Rama is declared. "As King Dasaratha was returning to his capital with Rama, he was alarmed by the ill-omened sounds uttered by certain birds. This indicated the arrival of Parasurama. He was fearful to behold, brilliant as fire, and bore his axe and a bow on his shoulder. Being received with honour, he preceeded to say to Rama, the son of Dasaratha, that he had heard of his prowess in breaking the bow produced by Janaka, and had brought another which he asked him to bend, and to fit an arrow on the string; and offered, if he succeeded in doing so, to engage with him in single combat. Parasurama went on to say that the bow Rama had broken was Siva's; but that the one he now brought was Vishnu's. *Parasurama* offered Vishnu's bow for his antagonist to try his strength on. Thus challenged, Rama snatches the bow, bends it, and fits an arrow to the string; and then tells his challenger that as he is a Brahman he will not slay him, but will either take away his superhuman capacity of movement, or deprive him of the blessed abodes he had gained by austerity. Parasurama entreats that his power of movement may not be taken away, but consents that his blissful abodes may be destroyed. 'By bending this bow,' he said, 'I recognize thee to be the imperishable slayer of Madhu, the great lord.' Rama shoots the arrow, and destroys Parasurama's abodes."

Rama Avatara

In Northern India this is perhaps the most popular of all the incarnations of Vishnu, and certainly the *Ramayana,* in which his history is found, contains some of the most beautiful legends in the whole of the sacred writings of the Hindus. The *Ramayana* is very largely occupied with the story of Rama's life, and the poets have found in its legends subjects for their most attractive poems.

Dasaratha, the King of Ayodha, being childless, determined to make an *asvamedh*, or horse sacrifice, to obtain a son. It was necessary, in order to make an acceptable offering, that the horse destined for sacrifice be allowed to wander at will for a whole year, as a sign that the authority of its owner was acknowledged by the neighbouring princes. The people loved their king, and during his reign were very prosperous; but, owing to the want of a son, the happiness of king and subjects was incomplete. The sacrifice therefore was determined on, the holy place fixed, the horse set free, and the king, encouraged by the Brahmans, invited the neighbouring princes to attend the great preparations made. At length the rite was satisfactorily accomplished and the presiding Brahman addressing Dasaratha said :—

"Four sons, O monarch, shall be thine,
Upholders of the royal line."

In due time the four sons of Dasaratha were born; and from infancy the strongest affection existed between Rama the firstborn and Lakshman, and between Bharat and Satrughna.

When Rama was about sixteen years of age, a Rishi named Visvamitra came to Dasaratha's court, asking his assistance against two demons, named Maricha and Suvahu, who were commanded by Ravana to annoy him, and prevent the completion of his sacrifices. At first the king pleaded the youthfulness of his son as an excuse for refusing to allow him to undertake a work so arduous; but at length his scruples were overcome, and Rama with the faithful Lakshman set out for the hermitage.

On their journey to the hermitage they visit several places of importance, and Visvamitra beguiles the time with numerous legends; he also bestows on Rama various arms and powers. On reaching the end of their journey, for six days and nights they have to watch for the demons; just as the sacrifice was about to end, these disturbers of the hermitage appear, are conquered by Rama, and their attendants by Lakshman.

Next morning the hermits tell Rama that King Janaka of Mithila had arranged for a sacrifice to which they are invited. Rama is asked to accompany them, and is induced to do so by the mention of a wonderful bow in possession of the king, which no one was able to bend. The bow was a gift from Siva, as a reward for sacrifice. On the way to Mithila they pass through a grove, in which, unseen by gods and men, Ahalya, the wife of Gautama the sage, had been undergoing penance for countless ages, on account of her adultery with Indra. Though the god came to her in the form of her husband, she saw through his disguise, yet did not resist his overtures. Her husband condemned her to live unknown in the forest until Rama should liberate her. Her hour of release had now come : Rama sees her, touches her feet, and the curse being at an end, her husband receives her back.

In due time they reach Mithila. The princes are introduced to the king, who gives them a hearty welcome, and narrates the history of the world-famed bow they have come to see. He tells them it was the bow with which Siva, when angry at not being invited to Daksha's sacrifice, wrought such havoc amongst the assembled gods.

One day, as Janaka was ploughing, an infant sprang from the ground, whom he named Sita (a furrow), on account of her secret birth. In the

Uttara Kanda is a legend, the object of which is to show that Sita is another form of Lakshmi, and that it was she who wished to accomplish the death of Ravana.

Regarding the child thus mysteriously found to be other than of mortal birth, to all suitors for her hand Janaka said that she was to be the wife of him who could bend the wonder-working bow. Many of the neighbouring princes had tried, but failed. And now Janaka says—

"This heavenly bow, exceeding bright,
These youths shall see, O anchorite.
Then if young Rama's hand can string
The bow that baffled lord and king,
To him I give, as I have sworn,
My Sita, not of woman born."

The bow is brought, and Rama invited to try his strength. He takes it up easily in his hand, and as he was drawing the string, it snapped in two, to the wonder and fright of the beholders. Rama thus becomes the successful suitor of Sita, and messengers are despatched to invite his father to the wedding. His two brothers also come; and not only Rama and Sita are united, but his three brothers are wedded to the three other daughters of Janaka. They then return home and live in happiness and prosperity.

After a time King Dasaratha wishes to abdicate in favour of Rama his firstborn. When he had fixed upon a suitable time, the old man sends for his son, and enjoins him to prepare himself for the great event, by passing the night in holy penances. The people hearing of the king's intention are delighted; the city is illuminated, and they spend the night in festivities. In the mean time a servant goes to Kaikeya, the mother of Bharata, and succeeds in exciting her jealousy of Rama to such an extent, that she secludes herself in the room of discontent in the palace. The king visits her, when she reminds him that on an occasion of great danger she alone had stood by him, and that he then promised her a boon. She now requested the fulfilment of that vow and concludes her address by asking that her son be installed as Prince Regent, and Rama be sent to live a hermit's life in the forest for fourteen years.

The king, almost mad with grief at this request, being bound by word and oath, is compelled to comply. The city is in tears that but yesterday was bright with joy; and the ceremony that was arranged for Rama is performed in favour of Bharata, much against his will. Rama tried to persuade Sita to allow him to proceed to the forest alone; but to this she will not for a moment consent.

At length Rama, Sita, and Lakshman depart, amidst the tears of the whole city. When they reach the forest Dandaka, they seek a quiet spot, and at last settle down at Chitrakuta.

Dasaratha dies of grief a short time after their departure, and the city is again flooded with tears. Bharata visits the exiles, with the intention of bringing his brother home to occupy the throne, but to this Rama will not consent. Bharata therefore continues to rule in his stead, but always regards him as the rightful king, and keeps a pair of his shoes, which are exposed to view on state occasions, to indicate that Bharata is acting only as Viceroy.

When ten years of his forest life were past, Rama sets off for the hermitage of Agastya, a man who had gained great merit by his austerities. There they build a cottage, but are not able to live in peace very long. As Rama and Sita are sitting together under a tree, a giantess named Suparnakha, the sister of Ravana, passes by, and falls madly in love with Rama.

The giantess questions Rama as to the reason of his being in the forest. After giving a full account of himself and Sita, he inquires who she may be. She says she is Ravana's sister, and openly avows her love.

Rama, smiling, told her that as he was married he could not accept her kind offer, but advised her to try his brother. She acts upon this advice; but Lakshman sends her back to Rama. Thinking that Sita was the obstacle to the attainment of her wishes, she was about to slay her; Rama prevented her from doing this, and Lakshman cut off her nose and ears. She fled to her brother Khara, whose anger she roused by the tale of her mutilation, who sent fourteen giants, giving them strict orders to kill Rama, Sita, and Lakshman. These giants are easily slain. Khara is terribly angry when he hears of their death; and, quickly raising an army of 14,000 warriors, goes against his foes. Rama, single-handed, destroyed them nearly all.

Hearing this Ravana decides to avenge his sister. Ravana orders his chariot, starts off alone to Maricha, and asks his assistance, who dissuades him from attempting to fight with Rama; but soon afterwards, when Suparnakha, with her mutilated face, appears before Ravana, she arouses his indignation.

The giantess retells her tale, exciting her brother's anger afresh. He immediately sets off again for the hermitage of the fiend Maricha, and asks him to assist in his exploit by assuming the form of a golden deer with silver spots, by which Sita's attention would be attracted.

Maricha, remembering the power of Rama when as a mere boy he went to assist the hermit Visvamitra, and how he himself was wounded by him, again tries to dissuade Ravana. But this time he cannot prevail, and there is not much choice left him, for Ravana declares that if Maricha does not do as he says he will kill him.

Maricha assumes the form of a deer, and, proceeding to the vicinity of the hermitage, attracts the attention of Sita, who becomes anxious to possess it. Rama, leaving Lakshman to guard the home, goes in pursuit, and shoots it. As the fiend was dying after assuming Rama's voice, he cried out loudly enough to be heard by the wife and brother, "Ho, Sita! Ho, Lakshman!" They imagining that some evil had come to Rama, Lakshman hurried towards the spot whence the cry proceeded; whilst Ravana, who was waiting near, seized the opportunity to carry off the defenceless Sita. Held in his magical car, they reached Lanka, where she was placed in one of Ravana's palaces. He tried both by kind words and fearful threatenings to win her love; but kindness and cruelty were equally ineffective.

Whilst this was happening at Lanka, Rama was almost mad with grief. When Lakshman came to him after the deer was slain, he feared some evil had happened; and on their return to the cottage, as Sita was not to be found, his anguish was intolerable. He wandered about calling upon the trees, mountains, and rivers to tell him what had happened to his loved one; but they were silent as the grave. A vulture at the point of death, who had fought with Ravana on Sita's behalf, informs him of her capture by the great fiend.

In their wanderings, the brothers meet with a giant named Kabandha, who, owing to a curse, had to wear the hideous form in which he appeared, until his arms should be cut off by Rama. As he was running away with the brothers on his shoulders, they fulfulled this condition, there being no other way of escape for them. On learning who they were, he was delighted, and asked them, as a favour, to burn his body in order that he might regain his proper form, and ascend to heaven. As the flames encircled him, he assumed a heavenly shape, and when in mid-air, told them where Sita was taken, and advised them to seek the help of Sugriva, the King of the Vanar (monkey) tribes, as only through his aid could they recover her. Acting upon this advice, they proceed to Pampa, Sugriva's home.

When Sugriva saw the brothers, imagining them to be friends of his brother Bali, by whom he had been deprived of his throne, he was greatly alarmed, and sent Hanuman, his commander-in-chief, to learn who they were, and why they had come. When Hanuman learns the object of their visit, thinking they might be induced to assist his master to regain his kingdom, he promises Sugriva's help, and, taking them upon his shoulders, hurries off with them into the presence of the Vanar king.

Sugriva produces a robe, bracelets, and anklets that fell from Sita as she was being carried off by Ravana; the anklets Rama recognizes at once, and is greatly comforted as Sugriva tells him that though at present unable to inform him where Sita has been taken, he will be able to obtain this information, and assist him in his attempt to rescue her. Sugriva then narrates the story of his quarrel with his brother, but, before believing that Rama can materially assist him, wished to test the wonderful bow of the hero. He was greatly astonished as he saw an arrow Rama discharged pierce seven palmtrees in line, pass through a hill behind them, and, after traversing six subterranean worlds, return to the quiver. The Vanar king, seeing he has secured no common ally, goes forth fearlessly against his brother; and in the fight, when Sugriva was getting worsted, Rama sends an arrow which slays his brother. This was regarded by the dying man as an act of gross injustice, because Rama slew him without informing him who he was; had he only known he would gladly have assisted him in his quest for Sita.

Sugriva, on the fall of his brother, re-ascends the throne, but is so fully occupied with the pleasures of his position as to forget the promise of help he had given Rama, by whose prowess his dominion had been regained. Hanuman, ever faithful to Rama's cause, reminds him of his duty.

But this reminder of his duty is insufficient to arouse the king from his selfish enjoyment; it was not until Rama sends a strong message by Lakshman that he takes action and collects a mighty army.

The king gave instructions to each leader of a division, as to the limits of the district he was to search for the lost princess; but as Ravana was believed to have gone towards the south, Hanuman's district, special instruction was given to him; and Rama entrusted him with a ring which, if successful in discovering Sita, he could show her as a proof that he was a messenger from her husband. For a long time the search was fruitless, and would have been given up as hopeless, but for Hanuman's perseverance. When they were about to relinquish the search, they met the vulture Sampati, brother of Jatayus, whom Ravana had slain as he attempted to prevent him from carrying off Sita. This bird was the first to put Rama on the right track for obtaining his wife. Sampati, hearing that Ravana had slain his brother, was most anxious to avenge his death, and willingly rendered all the assistance he could. He informs the seekers that Sita is at Lanka.

But here a difficulty occurred; there were a hundred leagues of water to be crossed; who could make the leap? Hanuman again comes to the front and declares that he can do so. According to his promise, Hanuman made the marvelous leap. After meeting with various adventures, at length he reaches the capital of Lanka, and, diminishing in size until he is no bigger than a cat, passes through the city unnoticed, and finally enters the Asoka grove where Sita was confined. He was just in time to witness an unsuccessful attempt of Ravana to induce his lovely captive to forget her husband, and become his bride.

When she is alone, Hanuman addresses her. At first, on hearing a monkey speak, she imagines herself dreaming; but the sight of her husband's ring convinces her that the strange messenger is a friend, and she is delighted to hear all he has to tell.

Though Hanuman had found Sita, and offered to carry her on his shoulders to her long-lost husband, a difficulty arose; she feared that in rising to the height which so long a leap necessitated, she might be giddy and find it necessary to lay hold of him; but of her own free will she would on no account so much as touch the limbs of living man except those of her husband. Instead, then, of availing herself of the monkey's offer, she prefers to remain where she is for the present, and simply sends back a kind message to Rama, with a gem to assure him that she has received his. Hanuman does not care to return without having effected some injury on his foe; he therefore destroys the grove and temple, and slays several of Ravana's heroes. At length he is made captive. When taken before Ravana, he confesses that he is a messenger from Rama to Sita, and earnestly advises her restoration. This so exasperates the giant that he would have slain him at once had he not been an envoy—and an envoy's life is sacred. Some of Ravana's people, however, set fire to his tail, and though he does not experience much pain, he manages to set fire to the city in several places.

When Hanuman had completed his work in Lanka, he made a return leap placed Sita's gem in Rama's hand, and told him all that had transpired in Ravana's capital. The prince was delighted to hear of his wife's constancy; but as the difficulty of transferring an army from the mainland over a hundred leagues of sea seemed impossible to surmount, he despaired of seeing her again. Sugriva, advises that a bridge can be built.

The army, which had remained some distance away, now marches to the seashore, and Rama is very curious to learn by what means so vast a bridge can be built. He in his anguish calls upon the sea to withdraw and allow his followers to march across as on dry land; but although the Ocean will not grant this prayer, he does assist with his advice, as he tells him to enlist the services of a tribe of *Dasyas* (servants), who, together with the monkey host, construct a bridge in five days. No sooner is this completed than the troops march across, Rama being carried by Hanuman, and Lakshman by Angad; and though Ravana hears of their approach, and his spies, terrified at the appearance of the invading army, counsel him to yield, he obstinately refuses, and at last the attack upon his city is made.

After fierce fighting, with considerable loss on both sides, Rama and Lakshman are dangerously wounded by Indrajit, a son of Ravana; but on some wonderful herbs being applied to them by Garuda, the marvellous bird of Vishnu, they are restored. A second time they fall, and are again restored by herbs which Hanuman fetched in an incredibly short space of time from the Himalayas. At last Rama and Ravana meet face to face. Rama's destructive arrows seem at first to have met with a foe as wonderful as themselves.

Acting on the advice of Matali, the charioteek sent by Indra, Rama, tired of this fruitless toil, launched an arrow " whose fire was kindled by the Almighty Sire," which pierced the giant's heart and laid him dead at his feet. Hanuman is despatched to assure Sita of the death of her captor, and in a few hours she is carefully sent in a palanquin by Vibhishan, the brother and successor of Ravana. This Rama causes to be opened, that the monkeys may see his wife's face, as he says—

"Ravana bore thee through the sky,
And fixed on thine his evil eye ;
About thy waist his arms he threw,
Close to his breast his captive drew ;
And kept thee, vassal of his power,
An inmate of his ladies' bower."

Hearing these cruel and unexpected words, Sita makes a most pathetic appeal, in which she vehemently asserts her innocence; but as there are no signs of relenting in her husband, she wishes to die, or to prove her innocence by the fire-ordeal, and asks Lakshman to prepare a funeral pile.

Lakshman performs this sad office; and when all is ready, she walks round it, and, before entering the fire, addresses Agni:

"As this fond heart, by virtue swayed,
From Raghu's son has never strayed,
So universal witness, Fire,
Protect my body on the pyre.
As Raghu's son has idly laid
This charge on Sita, hear and aid."

Having made this appeal to Agni to proclaim her innocence, she enters the fire. The gods, descending from heaven in their glory, address Rama, saying:

"Couldst thou, the Lord of all, couldst thou,
Creator of the worlds, allow
Thy queen, thy spouse to brave the fire,
And give her body to the pyre?
Dost thou not yet, Supremely Wise
Thy heavenly nature recognize?"

Rama frankly confesses that he believes himself to be only a mortal; Brahma tries to enlighten him, as he assures him that he is Vishnu incarnate for the purpose of slaying Ravana, and that Sita, whom his cruel conduct had driven into the fire, was no other than Lakshmi, his celestial spouse. In confirmation of this, Agni appears in the fire, and, taking Sita by the hand, conducts her to her husband, and declares her to be pure and spotless. Rama receives her with the greatest joy, and states that he was certain of her innocence all along, but that as others might have doubted her, he had caused her to pass through this ordeal.

Dasaratha, the father of Rama, now descends from heaven, and tells him that even in that happy place he had been sad to witness the sorrows of his beloved son. Indra next appears, and, at Rama's request, brings back to life the many Vanars who had perished in his cause; and then other gods thank Rama for the relief he has given them by the death of Ravana. When these congratulations are over, Rama, Sita, and Lakshman mount a magic car, lent him by Vibhishan, in which in a single day they travel from Lanka to his own city. On arriving near it, Hanuman is sent to inform Bharat of their return; and the joy this intelligence gives to the faithful Bharat, and to the citizens generally, is indescribable. Rama quickly assumes his position as king and the people enjoy unexampled prosperity.

This state of universal happiness does not continue for ever. People in the city have doubts regarding the purity of their queen, which at length reach the ears of Rama, who, taking advantage of a wish of Sita once again to see a hermitage, leaves her to live an ascetic life. When her twin sons, born in her forest home, come of age, she sends them to their father's court. The king on seeing them, deeply feels the injustice he had done their mother, and determines at any cost to reinstate her as his queen. On her arrival he asks her to assert her innocence before the assembled court; but even Sita could not bear this. She calls to the earth which gave her birth now to give her a home ; the earth opened and received her into her bosom. After this Rama grows tired of life, and Time comes to inform him that his work is done. Hearing this, the good king goes to the banks of the sacred stream, and forsaking his body ascends to his home in heaven.

Rama, to a vast number of Hindus, is not merely the King of Ayodha, whose history is told in the Ramayana; nor the benefactor of gods, as he slew their enemy, Ravana; but their saviour and friend. As the dead are carried to the river-side to be burned, the friends repeatedly cry, "Rama, Rama, Satya Nama," *i.e.* "Rama, Rama, the true name." Probably this is owing to the fact that in life his power of intercession for the dead was great; whilst his kindness to and care for his followers were such as to encourage men's trust.

Krishna Avatara

In the *Mahabharata*, Krishna—which literally means 'the black or dark one'—is sometimes represented as rendering homage to Siva, and therefore acknowledging his own inferiority to that deity, or as recommending the worship of Uma, the consort of Siva, and as receiving boons from both these deities. In some passages, again, he bears merely the character of a hero endowed with extraordinary powers, and in others his divine nature is even disputed or denied by adversaries, though they are eventually punished for this unbelief. As the intimate ally of Arjuna, he claims the rank of the supreme deity; but there are other passages, again, in the *Mahabharata* in which the same claim of Siva is admitted, and an attempt is made at compromising their rival claims, by declaring both deities one and the same.

In the "Prem Sagar," the Hindi version of the *Bhagavata Purana,* is the following account of the object of this incarnation. A king of Mathura, named Ugrasena, had a beautiful wife, who was barren. One day, when walking in a wood, she lost her companions; and when alone, a demon becoming enamoured of her assumed her husband's form, and as a result a son was born, who was named Kansa. When a mere child Kansa manifested a most cruel disposition—his great delight being to catch and kill children— and he grew up to be a source of sorrow to his father, family, and country. He advised his father to give up the worship of Rama, the god of his race, and to call in secret only on Mahadeva (Siva). His father replied with sorrow 'Rama is my lord, and the dispeller of my grief; if I do not worship him, how shall I as a sinful man cross over the sea of the world?" Kansa hearing this, dethroned his father, and having usurped his place issued a proclamation throughout his dominions forbidding men to worship Rama, and commanding them to reverence Siva; and his tyranny at length became so unbearable, that the Earth, assuming the form of a cow, went to Indra and, complaining of all this, said: "Evil spirits have begun to commit great crimes in the world; in dread of whom Religion and Justice have departed; and if you will permit me, I, too, will abandon the world, and descend into the lower regions." Indra hearing this went in company with the other gods to Brahma to see what redress could be afforded. Brahma conducted them to Siva, who, in his turn, conducted them to Vishnu; and reminding him of the deliverance he had afforded to gods and men in his previous manifestations, they induce him again to become a man for the destruction of Kansa. The gods and goddesses, delighted at this assurance of help, promise also to forsake their heavenly homes that they may be his companions during his earthly sojourn; and Vishnu himself arranges that Lakshman, who in the Rama incarnation had been his brother and constant and faithful companion, and Bharata also and Sutraghna, should accompany him; and that Sita, under the name of accompany him; and that Sita, under the name of Rukmini, should be his wife.

The *Vishnu Purana,* from which most of the following legends are taken, gives a somewhat different account of Vishnu's reply. Krishna was the incarnation of "a part of a part of the supreme being." When entreated to become incarnate, "the supreme lord plucked off two hairs, one white and one black, and said to the gods, 'These my hairs shall descend upon the earth, and shall relieve her of the burden of her distress!' The white hair was impersonated as Balarama, and the black as Krishna. "The *asuras* shall all be destroyed. This my black hair shall be impersonated in the eighth conception of Devaki, the wife of Vasudeva, who is like a goddess, and shall slay Kansa, who is the demon Kalanemi."

When Vasudeva and his wife Devaki were being driven by King Kansa in a chariot, "a voice in the sky, sounding loud and deep like thunder, addressing Kansa, said, 'Fool that you are, the eighth child of the damsel you are now driving shall take away your life!'" Kansa hearing this drew his sword, and was about to slay Devaki; but Vasudeva interposed, saying, "Kill not Devaki, great warrior ! Spare her life, and I will deliver to you every child she may bring forth." Kansa, appeased with this promise, spared the lady, but, to prevent any mistake, placed a guard by day and night over their apartments; and as child after child was born, it was given up to him and slain.

Kansa was under the impression that he had destroyed Devaki's children, but this was not the case. The children that were handed over to him were children of Hiranyakasipu, whom Vishnu slew as the Man-Lion, who were brought from the nether regions by *Yoganindra,* "the great illusory energy of Vishnu," and lodged in Devaki's womb in order that the cruel Kansa might be overreached. Vishnu said to this goddess: "Go, Nidra (Sleep), to the nether regions, and by my command conduct successively six of their princes to be conceived by Devaki. When these shall have been put to death by Kansa, the seventh conception shall be formed of a portion of Sesha (the serpent-deity), who is part of me; and this you shall transfer before the time of birth to Rohini, another wife of Vasudeva, who resides at Gokula." This child was Balarama. "The report shall run that Devaki miscarries. I will myself become incarnate in her eighth conception; and you shall take a similar character as the embryo offspring of Yasoda, the wife of a herdsman named Nanda. In the night of the eighth of the dark half of the month Nabhas I shall be born; and you will be born on the ninth. Impelled and aided by my power, Vasudeva shall bear me to the bed of Yasoda, and you to the bed of Devaki. Kansa shall take you and hold you up to dash you against a stone; but you shall escape into the sky, where Indra shall meet and do homage to you through reverence of me."

When Devaki gives birth to her eighth son, Vasudeva takes the child, and, eluding the vigilance of the guards, hurries through the city. On reaching the river Yaṃuna, which he has to cross, though ordinarily both wide and deep, it assists him in his flight, the water only rising to his knees. Just as he reaches Nanda's house, Yasoda had given birth to her child, which Vasudeva seizes, and leaving Devaki's child in its place, returns to his prison home, and manages to re-enter unobserved. Soon after this the cry of the new-born child being heard by the guard, Kansa is quickly informed of its birth, and, rushing into the room, seized and dashed it against a stone. But fate was too strong for him. Immediately the child touched the ground, "it rose into the sky, and, expanding into a gigantic figure, having eight arms, each wielding some formidable weapon, laughed and said to Kansa, 'What avails it thee to have hurled me to the ground? He is born that shall kill thee.'' Soon after this, as he feared nothing more from them, he released Vasudeva and Devaki from their confinement, and, in dread of meeting his great enemy, withdrew into the inner apartments of his house.

On regaining his liberty, Vasudeva speedily sought out Nanda, who of course was unaware of the change of children effected by Vasudeva, and, after congratulating him on the birth of a son, suggested the advisability of his returning home; as, having paid his taxes, there was nothing to detain him in the city. He feared lest the spies of Kansa should notice the peculiar excellences of the child, and destroy him according to Kansa's order. At the same time he took his other child by Rohini (Balarama), and placed him under the care of Nanda to be brought up as his own child. By this means, as Rama and Lakshman were inseparable companions in the previous incarnation, Krishna and Balarama were as intimately connected in this.

The herdsman Nanda and his family had not been long settled at Gokula before efforts were made to destroy the infant Krishna. A female fiend named Putana, the sucking of whose breast was instant death to an infant, came by night, and, taking the child in her arms, offered him her breast. Krishna seized it with both hands, and sucked with such violence that the hideous being roared with pain, and giving way in every joint fell down dead.

There are many legends connected with his boyhood, which speak of his extraordinary power. On one occasion, when a mere infant, lying under Nanda's wagon, he cried for the breast, and, being impatient because his mother did not come quickly, kicked the wagon over, to the great astonishment of the bystanders. He and Balarama played with and tormented the calves to such an extent, that Yasoda became angry; and to prevent its repetition, tied Krishna to a heavy; wooden mortar in which corn is threshed, and went on with her work. Krishna, trying to free himself from this, dragged it until it became wedged fast between two Arjuna trees, and with a strong pull the trees were uprooted. The people, astonished because the trees fell when no storm was blowing, thought the place must be unlucky, and moved away to Vrindavana. The *Bhagavata* says that these trees were two sons of Kuvera, the god of riches, who, owing to a curse of the sage Narada, were thus metamorphosed, and that it was for the purpose of liberating them that Krishna accomplished this feat. Krishna and Balarama, "the guardians of the world, were keepers of cattle in the cowpens of Vrindavana," until they were seven years of age, during which years, according to the *Bhagavata Purana,* boys were full of childish tricks : stealing butter from the the neighbouring cowherds appears to have been their favourite pastime.

In the *Bhagavata Purana* there are legends also of attempts being made by Kansa to rid himself of his dreaded foe. One day a demon was sent who hoped to surprise him when wandering with the cattle in the woods ; but the boy, seeing through his disguise, seized him by the foot, swung him round his head and dashed him so violently on the ground that he immediately died. The next day, another demon, assuming the form of an immense crane, seized Krishna with its bill; but he became so hot that the crane immediately released him: Krishna then crushed its beak under his foot. Yet another came as a great serpent, and swallowed Krishna and his companions, the cowherds, with their cows; but he was no sooner in the reptile's stomach than he expanded himself, and burst open his prison. Krishna was not always defending himself ; often he benefited his companions. When Brahma stole some calves, and carried off the boys who tended them, Krishna made other calves and other boys, so that the theft was never known by the cowherds.

We now return to the narrative of the *Vishnu Purana.* The river Yamuna was the home of the serpent Kaliya, who made its waters boil with the fires of passion, so that trees on its banks were blighted by its fumes, and birds were killed by its heat. Krishna, seeing how his friends at Vrindavana were inconvenienced by this, plunged into the stream, to the dismay of the cowherds, and, after challenging the serpent to fight, was about to slay him. Moved, however, by the intercession of the lady serpents, he allowed him to live on condition that he and his family forsook the Yamuna, and took up their abode in the sea.

The Gopis (wives of the cowherds) were madly in love with Krishna. As he and Balarama played the flute, they came to dance with them; but as all could not hold Krishna's hand as they danced, he multiplied himself into as many forms as there were women, each woman believing she held the hand of the true Krishna. On one occasion he watched the Gopis as they went to bathe in the Yamuna river, and, stealing their clothes, sat in a tree and refused to restore them until each came in the form of a suppliant with uplifted hands to fetch them. The *Bhagavata* teaches that these women, impelled though they were by passion to seek Krishna, obtained through him final emancipation from sin. "In whatever way a man may worship him he will obtain deliverance. Some knew and sought him as a son, some as a friend, some as an enemy, some as a lover, but in the end all obtained the blessing of deliverance and emancipation ."

Of all these women Krishna's favourite was Radha, the wife of Ayanagosha. Her sister-in -law told her brother of his wife's misconduct, and Radha was in fear lest he should murder her. When, however, she communicated her fears to Krishna, he easily reassured her. He told her that when her husband came, he (Krishna) would transform himself into Kali, and instead of finding her with a lover, he would see her engaged in worshipping a goddess. Her husband happening to pass that way soon after, noticed Radha bowing down, and joined in worshipping Krishna, whom he mistook for Kali. It is Radha whose name is ever associated with Krishna in hymns, songs, prayers, and pictures, Radha is worshipped along with Krishna.

After some years Kansa is informed of Krishna's existence, and, as we have noticed above, sent various demons to slay him; but as these efforts failed, the king determined on a grand scheme by which he hoped to rid himself of his dreaded foe. He accordingly sent Akrura, one of the few good men in his kingdom, with a most polite invitation to Krishna and Balarama to visit him at his capital, to witness some athletic sports.

Akrura, having told Krishna of the ill-feeling of Kansa and of the plots he had made against his life, was greatly encouraged with the assurance that in three days Kansa and his adherents would be slain. He took leave of the guests when they approached the city of Mathura. Entering the city unattended, and dressed as poor country people, they meet a washerman of Kansa at work, whom they first annoy by throwing his clothes on the ground, and, when he expostulates with them, kill him, and robe themselves in Kansa's garments. Seeing the gaily-dressed, strong, and good-looking young men, a flower-seller presents them with some of his choicest flowers; for his generosity Krishna bestows rich blessings upon him in this life and promises heaven after death. After this they meet a deformed girl named Kubja, carrying ointments and perfumes to the palace, some of which, at his request, she gives to Krishna. For her kindness her deformity is cured, she is made beautiful, and invites the brothers to her home.

The day following was fixed for the sports. Two fierce wrestlers were commanded by fair means or foul to slay Krishna and his brother; and in case they should fail to do this, an enormous elephant was in readiness to trample them to death. But wrestlers and elephant were themselves slain. Seeing his grand scheme signally fail, the king lost his temper and called out loudly to his guards to slay the youths; instead of this, however, Krishna rushed upon and slew the king in the midst of the assembly, and falling at the feet of his father and mother, Vasudeva and Devaki, placed Ugrasena, Kansa's father, upon the throne, and with his brother took up his abode at Mathura.

Amongst many others, Krishna fell in love with Rukmini, the daughter of Bhismaka, King of Vidharbha; but her brother Rukmin hated him, and refusing to give his consent, at the advice of Jarasandha, she was betrothed to Sisupala. This Sisupala was no other than Hiranyakasipu and Ravana, whom in previous incarnations Vishnu had slain. On the eve of the wedding Krishna carries off Rukmini, leaving Balarama and his friends to take care of themselves; and when Rukmin follows him with an immense army, Krishna easily destroys his companions, and, but for the intercession of Rukmini, would have killed his brother-in-law too. This Rukmini was none other than Lakshmi, Sita and others, who, in her earlier incarnations, had stood in a similar relationship to him.

Krishna was not without a rival. A man named Paundraka professed that he was the true incarnation of Vishnu, and that Vasudeva (son of Vasudeva) was a pretender. The King of Benares was induced to believe in this false Krishna, and at his request sent an order for the real Krishna to come and do him homage, and at the same time to bring with him his discuss and other insignia of office. Krishna did not hesitate. Setting off next day, he destroyed the army of his rival and addressing Paundraka himself said, "You desired me by your envoy to resign to you my insignia : I now deliver them to you. Here is my discus, here my mace, here is Garuda. The discuss did its work, the rival of Krishna was cut to pieces; but, as the Raja of Benares continued to fight, his head was cut off, and fell in the city.

When Krishna had finished his work, and had destroyed demons and wicked men, especially Kansa, the time came for him to return to heaven; but, before his departure, owing to a curse pronounced by angry Brahmans, it was necessary that the Yadava race from which he sprang should pass away. This curse was pronounced to avenge an insult offered by some Yadu boys to Narada and other Rishis when engaged with their devotions. These boys, as a joke, dressed up a son of Krishna, named Samba, in women's clothes, and taking him to the Rishis asked, "What child will this female give birth to?" The Rishis, greatly annoyed, said, "She will bring forth a club which shall crush the whole Yadava race." Accordingly a club came from Samba's body, which King Ugrasena ordered to be ground to powder and thrown into the sea. The dust that fell on the shore became rushes, but a small part of the club, like a lance head, could not be broken : this was thrown into the sea, was swallowed by a fish, which was caught by a fisherman, and made into an arrow point by a huntsman named Jara.

A messenger from the gods now visited Krishna, telling him that, as his work was done, he should ascend to his home. This he was quite willing to do; but, advised the Yadavas to forsake their city and go to Prabhasa. On reaching the seashore they indulged in liquor and began to fight violently amongst themselves, and for arms seized the rushes which sprang from the dust of the fatal club that came from Samba. Krishna and Balarama trying to make peace between the combatants only led to their swifter destruction, until at last the two brothers were left alone of their race. Whilst sitting and talking on the banks of a river, a serpent crawled out of Balarama's mouth—the serpent Sesha, of which he was an incarnation, and so his end was come. Krishna, left alone, sat meditating, with his foot upon his knee, when the hunter Jara, armed with the fatal arrow, passed by, and taking Krishna for a deer, shot him, and thus his death was unwittingly caused by the last part of the cursed club. Jara, seeing his mistake, fell at Krishna's feet and asked forgiveness, to whom Krishna said, "Fear not thou in the least. Go, hunter, through my favour to heaven, the abode of the gods." Immediately a celestial car appeared, in which the man ascended to heaven; and Krishna abandoned his mortal body.

Buddha Avatara

This incarnation of Vishnu is "originally foreign to the cycle of the Avataras of Vishnu, and therefore is only briefly alluded to in some of Puranas. Where this is done, the intention must have been to effect a compromise between Brahmanism and Buddhism, by trying to represent the latter religion as not irreconcilably antagonistic to the former."

In the *Bhagavata Purana* are only four short passages respecting him. "At the commencement of the Kali-yuga will Vishnu become incarnate in Kikata, under the name of Buddha, the son of Jina, for the purpose of deluding the enemies of the gods. The Undiscernible Being, having assumed a mortal form, preached heretical doctrines in the three cities founded by Maya (and in Kasi), for the purpose of destroying, by deluding them, the enemies of the gods, steadfast in the religion prescribed by the Vedas. Praise to the pure Buddha, the deluder of the Daityas and the Danavas. By his words, as Buddha, Vishnu deludes the heretics."

In the *Skanda Purana* the legend, of which the *Bhagavata* gives but the merest outline, is more fully given. There was a dire famine in the earth, owing to the failure of rains for six successive years. On this account Brahma in great distress visited a prince named Ripanjaya, and told him that if he would become king, the gods would serve him, and his name should be changed to Divodasa. On asking why he was chosen before all others, Brahma tells him, "All other kings are wicked, and the gods will not shower rain upon the earth unless you accept the government."

Divodasa accedes to Brahma's request on condition that that deity would assist him and that all the other gods would forsake the earth, so that he might reign without a rival, and be the only one who could confer happiness on men. Brahma, in fulfilling this condition, with some difficulty persuaded Siva to forsake Kasi (Benares), his favourite dwelling-place.

Divodasa fixed his throne at Kasi, where for 8000 years he ruled with the greatest benefit to men. The gods becoming jealous of his power went to Brihaspati, their preceptor, and, whilst they spoke well of the effects of the king's government, complained that he, and not the gods, was benefited by it. Siva especially was annoyed at this enforced absence from Kasi; for although he sent several times to make inquires about its inhabitants, his messengers were too happy on earth to return to their lord in heaven. Vishnu, accompanied by Lakshmi and Garuda, at Siva's request, "then proceeded to Kasi, a little to the north of which he formed by his divine power a pleasant abode named Dharmakshetra, and there, attended by his lovely spouse, did he reside under the form of Buddha, while Lakshmi became a female recluse of that sect. Garuda also appeared under the name of Panyakirti, as a pupil with a book in his hand, and attentively listening to the delusive instructions of his preceptor (Buddha), who with a low, sweet, and affectionate voice taught him various branches of natural and supernatural religion."

Vishnu, as Buddha, taught that "the universe was without a creator; it is false therefore to assert that there is one universal and Supreme Spirit, for Brahma, Vishnu, Rudra, and the rest are names of mere corporeal beings like ourselves. Death is a peaceful sleep : why fear it?" He further taught that "we should guard as our own life the life of another; that pleasure is the only heaven, and pain the only hell, and liberation from ignorance the sole beatitude. Sacrifices are acts of folly." Through the exertions of Panyakirti, these doctrines soon spread through the city; whilst Lakshmi deluded the women by teaching them to "place all happiness in sensual pleasures; as the body must decay, let us, before it becomes dust, enjoy the pleasures which it gives. The distinction of castes has been vainly imagined." As Lakshmi gave numerous boons to her disciples, her influence was great, and her teaching spread widely.

As a result of the dissemination of these doctrines in the city, Divodasa became dispirited. Vishnu in the form of a Brahman appeared to him, and hears an account of his troubles, and is delighted as he expresses a wish to resign his crown. The king mentions a number of cases in which virtuous men have had to suffer, owing to the power of the gods, and inquires how he can obtain final beatitude. Vishnu informs him that he has acted unwisely in compelling Siva to forsake Kasi, and advises him to consecrate an image of that god, by worshipping which he will obtain the fulfilment of his desires. Divodasa follows this counsel, inaugurates his son as king, and as he is worshipping the Linga he had set up, Siva appears and conducts him to Kailasa (Siva's heaven). It is the common belief of the people in the west of India, that when Vishnu had effected the apostasy of Divodasa, he was prevailed upon to terminate the propagation of his heretical opinions, and disappeared in a deep well at Gaya.

The following legend from the *Siva Purana* gives another reason for the rise of Buddhism. A famous Rishi named Gautama, with his virtuous wife named Ahalya, performed during a thousand years a severe *tapas* (penance) in the southern country near the mountain Brahmadri. During this time there was a severe drought, to remove which, Gautama worshipped Varuna for six months with great fervour, when the deity promised to grant any boon that should be asked. Gautama asked for rain, but Varuna said, "How can I transgress the divine command? Ask some boon which it is in my power to grant." Gautama then desired Varuna to cause a surpassingly beautiful hermitage to appear, shaded from the sun by fragrant and fruit-bearing trees, where holy men and women by meditation shall be liberated from pain, sorrow, and anxiety; and as thou art lord of water, let it enjoy a perennial fountain. Varuna granted this request, and the hermitage of Gautama became the loveliest on the terrestrial orb.

One day as the disciples of Gautama went to the fountain, some Brahman women tried to prevent them drawing water until they had filled their own pots. Ahalya herself was subjected daily to the same annoyance: the Brahman women would not allow her to draw water before they had themselves obtained all they required. These women, not satisfied with annoying the ascetics, complained to their husbands of the unkind treatment they alleged they had received from Ahalya. Their husbands resorted to Ganesa for advice, who being pleased with their devotion promised a boon; they asked that Gautama might be made to leave his hermitage without their incurring the sin of driving him away. To this Ganesa reluctantly consented; and in order to effect this object he transformed himself into a poor debilitated cow, and walked into a field of rice where Gautama was standing, and began to eat the grain. The sage, knowing nothing of this disguise, took up a straw and tried to drive the cow away; no sooner did he touch it than it fell down dead. Having incurred the enormous guilt of killing a cow, the poor man had to leave the neighbourhood.

Gautama and his wife moved to a distance; but until he had expiated his sin they could not perform acceptable worship. Gautama seeks the Brahmans, and asking how he can be free from his crime, is told to walk round the mountain of Brahma a hundred times; bathe in the Ganges, and consecrate and worship ten million images of Siva. As he is propitiating him, Siva, delighted with his earnestness, appears, informs him of the trick by which Ganesa had driven him from the hermitage, and brings the Ganges so near that he can bathe in it easily. Tradition says that Gautama was so disgusted with the conduct of the Brahmans that he separated himself from their communion, and established a new system of religion, which for a time eclipsed Brahmanism.

The following extracts, giving an account of Buddha, are from the *Lalita-Vistara* a Buddhist work which says : Buddha was born at Kapilavastu, the capital of a kingdom of that name, situated at the foot of the mountains of Nepal, north of the present Oudh. His father, the King of Kapilavastu, was of the family of the Sakyas, and belonged to the clan of the Gautamas. His mother was Mayadevi, daughter of King Suprabuddha, and need we say that she was beautiful, as he was powerful and just? Buddha was therefore by birth a Kshattriya and took the name of Sakya from his family, and that of Gautama from his clan. His mother died seven days after his birth, and the father confided the child to the care of his deceased wife's sister, who, however, had been his wife even before the mother's death. The child grew up a most beautiful and most accomplished boy, who soon knew more than his masters could teach him. He refused to take part in the games of his playmates, and never felt so happy as when he could sit alone, lost in meditation in the deep shadows of the forest. It was there that his father found him when he had thought him lost; and, in order to prevent the young prince from becoming a dreamer, the king determined to marry him at once. When the subject was mentioned by the aged ministers to the future heir to the throne, he demanded seven days for reflection, and, convinced at last that not even marriage could disturb the calm of his mind, he allowed the ministers to look out for a princess. The princess selected was the beautiful Gopa, the daughter of Dandapani. Though her father objected at first to her marrying a young prince who was represented to him as deficient in manliness and intellect, he gladly gave his consent when he saw the royal suitor distancing all his rivals in feats of arms and power of mind. Their marriage proved one of the happiest, but the prince remained absorbed in meditations on the problems of life and death. 'Nothing is stable on earth,' he used to say; 'nothing is real. Like is like the spark produced by the friction of wood. It is lighted and is extinguished—we know not whence it came, or whither it goes. It is like the sound of a lyre, and the wise man asks in vain from whence it came and whither it goes. There must be some supreme intelligence where we can find rest. If I attained it I could bring light to man; if I were free myself, I could deliver the world.' The king, who perceived the melancholy mood of the young prince, tried everything to divert him from his speculations; but all was in vain. Three of the most ordinary events that could happen to any man proved of the utmost importance in the career of Buddha.

One day, when the prince with a large retinue was driving through the Eastern gate of the city on the way to one of his parks, he met on the road an old man, broken and decrepit. One could see the veins and muscles over the whole of his body; his teeth chattered, he was covered with wrinkles, bald, and hardly able to utter hollow and unmelodious sounds. He was bent on his stick, and all his limbs and joints trembled. 'Who is this man?' said the prince to his coachman. 'He is small and weak, he is hardly able to walk. Is there something peculiar in his family, or is this the common lot of all created beings ?'

" 'Sir,' replied the coachman, 'that man is sinking under old age, his senses have become obscure, suffering has destroyed his strength, and he is despised by his relations. But this is not peculiar to his family. In every creature youth is defeated by old age.

" 'Alas!' replied the prince, 'are creatures so ignorant, as to be proud of the youth by which they are intoxicated, not seeing the old age which awaits them? Coachman, turn my chariot quickly for what have I to do with pleasure?' and the young prince returned to the city without going to the park.

Another time the prince was driving through the Southern gate to his pleasure-garden, when he perceived in the road a man suffering from illness, hardly able to breathe, and frightened at the approach of death. Having questioned his coachman, and received from him the answer which he expected, the young prince said : 'Alas! health is but the sport of a dream, and the fear of suffering must take this frightful form. Where is the wise man, who, after having seen what he is, could any longer think of joy and pleasure?' The prince turned his chariot, and returned to the city.

A third time he was driving to his pleasure-garden through the Western gate, when he saw a dead body on the road, lying on a bier and covered with a cloth. The friends stood about crying. The prince, again calling his coachman to witness this painful scene, exclaimed : 'Oh, woe to youth, which must be destroyed by old age! Woe to health, which must be destroyed by so many diseases! Woe to this life, where a man must remain for so short a time!' Then, the young prince said, 'Let us turn back; I must think how to accomplish deliverance.'

A last meeting put an end to his meditation. He was driving through the Northern gate on the way to his pleasure-gardens, when he saw a mendicant who outwardly calm, subdued, looking downwards, wearing with an air of dignity his religious vestment and carrying an alms-bowl.

'Who is this man?' asked the prince.

'Sir,' replied the coachman, 'this man is one of those who are called *bhikshus* or mendicants. He has renounced all pleasures, all desires, and leads a life of austerity. He tries to conquer himself. He has become a devotee. Without passion, without envy, he walks about asking for alms.'

'This is good and well said,' replied the prince. 'The life of a devotee has always been praised by the wise. It will be my refuge, and the refuge of all other creatures. It will lead us to a real life, to happiness and immortality.' With these words, the young prince turned his chariot and returned to the city.

After having declared to his father and his wife his intention of retiring from the world, Buddha left his palace one night when all the guards were asleep. After travelling the whole night, he gave his horse and his ornaments to his groom, and sent him back to Kapilavastu.

Buddha first went to Vaisali, and became the pupil of a famous Brahman, who had gathered round him 300 disciples. Having learnt all that the Brahman could teach him, Buddha went away diappointed. He had not found the road to salvation. He then tried another Brahman at Rajagriha, the capital of Magadha who had 700 disciples, and there, too, he looked in vain for the means of deliverance. He left him, followed by five of his fellow-students, and for six years retired into solitude, near a village named Uruvilas, subjecting himself to the most severe penances. At the end of this period, however, he arrived at the conviction that asceticism, far from giving peace of mind and preparing the way to salvation, was a snare and a stumbling-block. He gave up his exercises, and was at once deserted by his five disciples. Left to himself, he now began to elaborate his own system. He had learned that neither the doctrines nor the austerities of the Brahmans were of any avail for accomplishing the deliverance of man, and for freeing him from the fear of old age, disease, and death. After long meditations and ecstatic visions, he at last arrived at that true knowledge which discloses the cause, and thereby destroys the fear, of all the changes inherent in life. It was from the moment when he arrived at this knowledge that he claimed the name of Buddha the enlightened.

The further history of the new teacher is very simple. He proceeded to Benares, which at all times has been the principal seat of learning in India, and the first converts he made were the five fellow-students who had left him when he threw off the yoke of the Brahmanical observances. Many others followed, but as the *Lalita-Vistara* breakes off at Buddha's arrival at Benares there is further consecutive account of the rapid progress of his doctrine. From what can be gathered from the Buddhist canon, he was invited by the King of Magadha, Bimbisara, to his capital, Rajagriha. Many of his lectures were delivered at the monastery of Kalavataka, with which the king or some rich merchant had presented him; others on the Vulture Peak, one of the five hills which surround the ancient capital.

Three of his most famous disciples—Sariputra, Katyayana, and Maudgalyayana—joined him during his stay in Magadha, where he enjoyed for many years the friendship of the king. The king was afterwards assassinated by his son Ajatasatru, and then Buddha settled for a time at Sravasti, north of the Ganges. Most of Buddha's lectures were delivered at Sravasti, the capital of Kosala, and the King of Kosala himself, Prasenagit, became a convert to his doctrine. After an absence of twelve years, we are told that Buddha visited his father at Kapilavastu, on which occasion he performed several miracles, and converted all the Sakyas to his faith. His own wife became one of his followers, and, with his aunt, offer the first instance of female Buddhist devotees in India.

We have fuller particulars again of the last days of Buddha's life. He had attained the good age of three score years and ten, and had been on a visit to Rajagriha, where the king, Ajatasatru, the former enemy of Buddha and the assassin of his own father, had joined the congregation, after making a public confession of his crimes. On his return he was followed by a large number of disciples, and when on the point of crossing the Ganges, he stood on a square stone, and, turning his eyes back towards Rajagriha, he said, full of emotion, 'This is the last time that I shall see that city.' He likewise visited Vaisali, and, after taking leave of it, he had nearly reached the city of Kusinagara, when his strength began to fail. He halted in a forest, and, while sitting under a Sal tree, he gave up the ghost, or, as a Buddhist would say, entered into Nirvana.

Buddhism, the religion taught by Buddha, starts with the doctrine common to it and Hinduism of transmigration. It then goes on to say that pain and pleasure are simply the result of Karma (works), no notice whatever being taken of the existence or non-existence of God. It assumes that existence is and must be miserable; and that the highest conceivable good is to obtain entire exemption from existence. Death does not necessarily bring this exemption; it may be but an entrance into a worse form of it than is at present endured. Buddha's four Sublime truths, containing the germ of his system, are as follows : The first is that pain exists; the second, that desire is the cause of pain; the third, that pain can be ended by Nirvana, or exemption from existence, the fourth shows the way that leads to Nirvana. The great thing is to get rid of desire, and when this is accomplished, the soul is ready for complete Nirvana, and a man dying in this state will not again be born. He taught the evil of caste distinctions, and all who embraced his tenets became members of a great brotherhood. Instead of the painful mortifications and costly sacrifices by which the Hindus were compelled to make expiation for sin, he taught that confession and promise of amendment were all that was necessary. Its moral code is one of the most perfect in the world : the spring of all virtue is Maitri, which can only be translated as charity or love.

There is one peculiarity of the followers of Buddha as compared with the Hindus, *viz.* the preservation of and veneration for relics of their founder. With the exception of legend stating that Krishna's bones were placed in the image of Jagannath, and another teaching that Vishnu cut the dead body of Sati into fifty-one parts, each of which is now enshrined in a temple, we have no record of relics being preserved by the Hindus. But the Buddhists profess to have carefully preserved parts of their great leader, and enshrine them in Dagobas. One of the most celebrated of these is in Sri Lanka. A tooth of Buddha is believed to be kept in it; in others a single hair is most religiously guarded. These Dagobas are not temples, though in some cases they form part of buildings that are, or have been, used for workship.

Kalki Avatara

This incarnation, unlike those already described, has yet to come. It is the hope of the Hindus, that he who has so frequently visited the earth to restore order and happiness will come yet again to inaugurate a reign of universal goodness, peace, and prosperity. When Vishnu in the form of Krishna reascended to heaven, the Fourth or Kali Yuga commenced, which, as its name implies, is an age of strife and dissension. In the *Vishnu Purana* the character of this age is vividly described in words that seem prophetic. At its termination Vishnu is expected to come again, bearing the name Kalki, to put an end to wickedness, and establish a kingdom of righteousness similar to the First or Krita Yuga—the age of Truth. These four ages, in the same order and with similar characteristics, will again and again be experienced until the final end of all things shall come. The following extract from the *Vishnu Purana* will give an idea of the evils of the present age, which Kalki is to remove.

In Magadha a sovereign named Viswasphatika will extirpate the Kshattriya race, elevate fishermen, barbarians, Brahmans, and other castes to power; whilst Sudras, outcasts and barbarians will be masters of the Indus, Darvika, Chandrabhaga, and Kashmir. "The kings will be of churlish spirit, violent temper, and ever addicted to falsehood and wickedness. They will inflict death on women, children, and cows; they will seize the property of subjects, be of limited power, and will, for the most part, rapidly rise and fall; their lives will be short, their desires insatiable, and they will display but little piety. The people of various countries intermingling with them will follow their example; and the barbarians being powerful in the patronage of princes, whilst purer tribes are neglected, the people will perish. Wealth and piety will decrease day by day, until the world shall be wholly depraved. Property alone will confer rank, wealth will be the only source of devotion, passion will be the sole bond of union between the sexes, falsehood will be the only means of success in litigation and women will be the objects merely of sensual gratification. Earth will be venerated only for its mineral treasures (*i.e.* no spot will be peculiarly sacred); the Brahmanical thread will constitute a Brahman; external types will be the only distinctions of the several orders of life, dishonesty will be the universal means of subsistence, weakness will be the cause of dependence, menace and presumption will be the subterfuge for learning, liberality will be devotion, simple ablution will be purification (*i.e.* gifts will be made from the impulse of ordinary feeling, not in connection with religious rites or as an act of devotion, and ablution will be performed for pleasure or comfort, not religiously with prescribed ceremonies and payers). Mutual assent will be marriage, fine clothes will be dignity, and water afar off will be esteemed a holy spring. The people, unable to bear the heavy burdens imposed upon them by their avaricious sovereigns, will take refuge among the valleys, and be glad to feed upon wild honey, herbs, roots, fruits, flowers, and leaves; their only covering will be the bark of trees, and they will be exposed to cold and wind, and sun and rain. No man's life will exceed three-and-twenty years. Thus in the Kali Age shall decay flourish, until the human race approaches annihilation."

"When the practices taught by the Vedas and the institutes of law shall nearly have ceased, and the close of the Kali Age shall be nigh, a portion of that divine being who exists of his own spiritual nature in the character of Brahma, and who is the beginning and the end, and who comprehends all things, shall descend upon the earth. He will be born in the family of Vishnuyasas, an eminent Brahman of Sambhal village, as Kalki, endowed with the eight superhuman faculties. By his irresistible might he will destroy all the Mlechchhas (outcasts), thieves, and all whose minds are devoted to iniquity. He will then re-establish righteousness upon earth; and the minds of those who live at the end of the Kali Age shall be awakened and be made pellucid as crystal. The men who are changed in virtue of that particular time shall be as the seeds of human beings, and shall give birth to a race who shall follow the laws of the Krita Age, or Age of Purity."

In the descriptions of Kalki, and in pictures, he is represented as a white man riding upon or bowing down before a white horse, and with a sword in his hand : he is the purifier of the present degenerate age, and the restorer of purity and goodness.

Jagannath

This deity is not reckoned as one of the Avataras of Vishnu in the Puranas. Tradition declares him to be, and common belief accepts him as, an appearance of Vishnu himself, and not the incarnation of a portion of his essence. There are several legends professing to account for the form in which he is worshipped, and for the peculiar sanctity of Puri, the chief place of his worship. There is a peculiarity in the phraseology employed by the people who visit his shrine : they speak of going to *see* Jagannath, not to worship him as is the case with other gods; and it is the sight of the image in the temple, or as it is being bathed, or drawn in its ponderous car, that is so eagerly desired as a means by which sin in the worshipper is destroyed.

According to the *Ain-i-Akbari*, a king desirous of founding a city sent a learned Brahman to select a proper site. The Brahman after a long search reached the seashore and there saw a crow diving into the water, and having washed its body, made obeisance to the sea. Understanding the language of birds, he learned from the crow that if he remained there a short time, he would comprehend the wonders of the land. The king, apprised of this occurrence, built a large city and temple on the spot near where the crow had appeared. One night the Raja in a dream heard a voice saying to him : "On a certain day cast thine eyes on the seashore, when there will arise from the water a piece of wood 52 in. long and 18 in. broad : this is the true form of the deity; take it up and keep it hidden in thine house seven days, and in whatever shape it shall then appear, place it in the temple and worship it." The Raja acted upon the advice given in his dream; and, when he had set up the image received from the sea, called it Jagannath, the Lord of the World, and it became the object of worship of all ranks of people.

According to a Bengali version : Narayana (Vishnu) and his wife having taken up their abode in the blue mountains of Orissa, where he was known by the name of Nilmadhava, was visited by great numbers of gods and men, and the neighbourhood obtained the name of Mokshyakhettra (the field of emancipation from births). A king named Indradhumna, a son of the Sun, a devout worshipper of Vishnu, being anxious to pay a visit to Nilmadhava, before starting, sent Vidyapati, the brother of his family priest, to learn the way to Orissa, that he might act as guide. On his return he gave such an account of all he had seen, that the king was more anxious to go than ever. Having made his arrangements, taking his family with him, the king went under the guidance of Vidyapati, but, on his arrival there, was most grievously disappointed to learn that the god had withdrawn himself from the public gaze. As he cried with sorrow and vexation, a voice from the sky reached his ear : "As you cannot see Nilmadhava, make a wooden image and worship that; Narayana will inhabit it, and by the sight of the image you and others will obtain final emancipation." The king followed this advice. As he was preparing to make the image, Narayana himself, in the form of an old Brahman named Visvakarma, came and offered to form the image in fifteen days. The offer was accepted, and within the specified time the image of Jagannath, with those of his brother and sister, was made.

The peculiarity of the worship of Jagannath is that his image is not only worshipped in its proper temple but on three days of the year is exposed to public view. On the first of these days, called the Snan Jattra (Bathing Festival), the idol is taken from its shrine, and on a lofty platform, in sight of vast multitudes, bathed by the priests. This exposure is supposed to be productive of a cold; so that, ten days after, the Rath Jattra (Car Festival) is held; at this time the image is placed on an immense car made expressly for the purpose, and taken to the temple of another god for a change of air. The car is drawn by the excited crowd; the people believing it to be a meritorious act. After remaining for a few days, the third festival (the Return) is held, at which, with somewhat diminished fervour, the idol is dragged back to its home. Puri is the place where it is believed the deity is seen with greater benefit to the worshipplers; but it is considered that there is considerable religious merit obtained by seeing, and assisting to draw, his car in places nearer home. Every town and almost every large village has its festival of this god; and with the promises of salvation from sin is a great wish to see him.

Chaitanya

Chaitanya is believed by his followers to have been an incarnation of Vishnu; and as he lived in historical times, about 300 years ago, it is interesting to notice how a human being came to be regarded as divine. He is worshipped in Nadiya in Bengal, and it is a singular fact, that, at his shrine, there is a very small image of Krishna, of whom he was a disciple and apostle, whilst the image of Chaitanya is large and conspicuous. The Hindus who acknowledge this god say that, amongst the many incarnations of Vishnu, four are most important. The first, in the Satya-yuga, called the Suklavarna (the white), was Ananta; the second, in the Treta-yuga, called the Raktavarna (the red), was that of Kapiladeva; the third, in the Dwapara-yuga, called the Krishnavarna (the black), was Krishna; and the last, in the Kali-yuga, called the Pitavarna (the yellow), was Chaitanya.

The founder of the sect, of which Chaitanya was the most illustrious member, was a Brahman named Adaitya, who lived at Santipore in Bengal. Another leader, named Nityananda, was born at Nadiya a short time before Chaitanya.Chaitanya's father was a Brahman, named Jagannath Misra; his mother's name was Suchi ; their first son, Visvambhara, was a religious mendicant. When their renowned son was born, his mother was rather old; and as the child seemed weak, in accordance with a custom which prevailed in those times, he was hung in a basket on a tree to die.Adaitya happening to pass by the house at the time, imagining that the child thus exposed might be the incarnation of the deity he was expecting, and which he had foretold, wrote with his foot on the soft earth the incantation employed at the initiation of a disciple into the mysteries of the worship of Krishna. The mother, impressed by this act, lifted the child from the tree, who immediately took kindly to his food, which he had before neglected, and showed signs of strength and vigour.

Chaitanya made great progress in learning. At sixteen he married Vishnupriya, with whom he lived until he was forty-four years of age, when he was persuaded by Adaitya and other mendicants to renounce his *poita* (Brahmanical thread) and join them in their religious life. This was to lose his high position as a Brahman. Leaving home, parents and wife, he removed to Benares, and many thought him guilty of a great crime in forsaking a large family that was dependent upon him for support. On his arrival at that city he began to teach the doctrines of his sect and gathered many disciples. He called them Vaishnavas—worshippers of Vishnu—and although his teaching was diametrically opposed in many important matters to orthodox Hinduism he was eminently successful. Many who had formerly chiefly worshipped Siva and other deities, adopting his teaching, made Krishna the supreme. The main tenets of his teaching were these: That men should renounce a secular life, and spend their time in visiting shrines; that they abandon the distinctions of caste, and eat freely with all who joined their sect, whatever their caste might be; and that they honour the name of Vishnu, and exercise *bhakti* in that god as the means of salvation. He allowed widows to remarry; forbade the eating of flesh and fish, and the worshipping of those deities to whom animal sacrifices were offered ; and further, that his disciples should not hold fellowship with those who offered such sacrifices. It is a curious coincidence that about the same time that Luther was preaching salvation by faith, in Europe, Chaitanya in India was giving prominence to the doctrine that salvation was to be obtained through faith *(bhakti)* in Krishna.

From Benares Chaitanya went to Puri, the great shrine of Jagannath, where he proclaimed his doctrines to the many pilgrims he met there; and whilst there it is said that he obtained four additional arms. Adaitya and Nityananda, who had induced him to assume the position of leader, remained for some years in Benares doing similar work; but though they afterwards returned to the secular state, their descendants are greatly respected by the members of this sect. It is reckoned that about one-fifth of the Hindus of Bengal are followers of this teacher. Immoral women generally profess to be his disciples. By their conduct they have excommunicated themselves from orthodox Hindu society, and being outcasts cannot secure the proper performance of their funeral rites. As members of this casteless sect these rites are not refused them.

Kamadeva

Kamadeva, the god of love, is generally regarded as the son of Vishnu and Lakshmi, under the forms of Krishna and Rukmini, but he is also described in some places as a son of Brahma. The latter account of his origin arises probably from the following. In the *Rig-Veda*, Kama is described as the first movement that arose in the *One,* after it had come into life through the power of fervour or abstraction. In the *Atharva-Veda* this Kama or desire, not of sexual enjoyment, but of good in general, is celebrated as a great power superior to all the gods, and is supplicated for deliverance from enemies. According to one hymn in the *Rig-Veda*, Kama is worshipped and said to be unequalled by the gods; according to another, he is the god of sexual love. In the latter aspect he is thus addressed: "May Kama, having well directed the arrow, which is winged with pain, barbed with longing, and has desire for its shaft, pierce thee in the heart." It is in this character that he appears in the Puranas.

Kama is known in Hindu mythology as a victim of Siva's anger. A demon named Taraka, having greatly distressed the gods, they wished to destroy him. But only a son of Siva could accomplish this. In consequence of his intense grief at the loss of his wife Sati, Siva had unfortunately become insensible to love. The gods therefore instigated Kama to assist by wounding him with his arrows. At last he was successful, just as Parvati (Sati in a new form) was near, who at once captivated the stricken deity. Angry with Kama for his presumption, he caused a flame to issue from his third eye, which consumed the god who had interrupted his devotions. In the *Vamana Purana* is a lengthy account of the effect of Kama's arrows. The wounded god could find no rest. He threw himself in the Kalindi river, but "the waters were dried up and changed into blackness; and ever since, its dark stream, though holy, has flown through the forest like the string that binds a maiden's hair." As he wandered about from place to place seeking relief, the wives of the saints in the forest of Daruvanam forsook their homes and followed him.

This led their husbands to curse Siva, who, being enraged at the evil Kama had done to him, consumed him.

The *Bhagavata* continues the story as follows:—Rati, the wife of Kama, being almost mad with grief at the loss of her husband, entreated Parvati to intercede with Siva that he might restore him to life. Parvati encourages her by showing how her wish will be gratified. "He will be born as the son of Sri Krishna, and his name will be Pradyumna. A demon named Sambara will carry him off and cast him into the sea. Having entered the body of a fish, he will re-appear in the food of Sambara. Go, take up your abode in the house of Sambara, and when your husband arrives, take him and bring him up; eventually he will slay Sambara and will live happily with you." Acting on this advice, Rati became a servant in the house of the demon.

The *Vishnu Purana* completes the story: When Pradyumna was but six days old, he was stolen from the lying-in chamber by Sambara, terrible as death; for the demon knew (having been told by the sage Narada) that Pradyumna, if he lived, would be his destroyer. Sambara cast him into the sea, where a large fish swallowed him, and he was born again from his body: for the fish was caught by fishermen and by them delivered to the great asura, Sambara. His wife Mayadevi, the mistress of his household, superintended the operations of the cooks, and, when the fish was cut open, saw a beautiful child.

Whilst wondering who this could be, and how it came there, Narada appeared to satisfy her curiosity, and said to her: "This is the son of him by whom the whole world is created and destroyed; the son of Vishnu, who was stolen by Sambara from the lying-in chamber, and tossed by him into the sea, where he was swallowed by the fish. He is now in thy power; do thou, beautiful woman, tenderly rear the jewel of mankind." Thus counselled by Narada, Mayadevi took charge of the boy, and carefully reared him from childhood, being fascinated by the beauty of his person. The affection became still more impassioned when he was decorated with the bloom of adolescence. The gracefully-moving Mayadevi, then fixing her heart and eyes upon the high-minded Pradyumna, gave him, whom she regarded as herself, all her magic and illustrative arts.

"Observing these marks of passionate affection, the son of Krishna said to the lotus-eyed Mayadevi: "Why do you indulge in feelings so unbecoming the character of a mother ?" To which she replied: 'Thou art not a son of mine; thou art the son of Vishnu, whom Kala Sambara carried away and threw into the sea; thou wast swallowed by a fish, but wast rescued by me from its belly. Thy fond mother is still weeping for thee.' When the valiant Pradyumna heard this, he was filled with wrath, and defied Sambara to battle. In the conflict the son of Madhava slew the hosts of Sambara. Seven times he foiled the delusions of the enchanter, and, making himself master of the eighth, turned it against Sambara and killed him. By the same faculty he ascended into the air, and proceeded to his father's house, where he alighted, along with Mayavati, in the inner apartments. When the women beheld Pradyumna, they thought it was Krishna himself. Rukmini, her eyes dimmed with tears, spoke tenderly to him, and said: 'Happy is she who has a son like this, in the bloom of youth. Such would be the 'age of my Pradyumna, if he were alive. Who is the fortunate mother adorned by thee? And yet from thy appearance, and from the affection I feel for thee, thou art assuredly the son of Hari.'

"At this moment Krishna and Narada arrived; and the latter said to Rukmini: 'This is thine own son, who has come hither after killing Sambara, by whom when an infant he was stolen. This is the virtuous Mayavati, his wife, and not the wife of Sambara. Hear the reason. When Manmatha (Kama), the deity of love, perished, the goddess of beauty, desirous to secure his revival, assumed a delusive form, and by her charms fascinated the demon Sambara, and exhibited herself to him in various illusory enjoyments. This thy son is Kama; and this is the goddess Rati, his wife.'"

Kama is usually represented as a beautiful youth, holding in his hands a bow and arrows of flowers. He travels about through the three worlds accompanied by his wife Rati, the cuckoo, the humming-bee, spring personified, and gentle breezes. Although in Bengal no images are made to represent him, he is worshipped at the time of marriage, and happiness in the married state, and offspring, are sought from him.

Kama has many names indicative of the influence he is supposed to exert amongst men. Amongst others may be mentioned:—

Madan, "He who intoxicates with love."

Manmatha, "He who agitates the mind."

Mara, "He who wounds."

Pradyumna, "He who conquers all."

Ananga, "He who is without a body."

Kushumesu, "He whose arrows are flowers."

8

SIVA

Siva is the third person of the Hindu Triad. As Brahma was Creator, Vishnu Preserver, in order to complete the system, as all things are subject to decay, a Destroyer was necessary; and destruction is regarded as the peculiar work of Siva. This seems scarcely in harmony with the form by which he is usually represented. It must be remembered, however, that, according to the teaching of Hinduism, death is not death in the sense of passing into non-existence, but simply a change into a new form of life. He who destroys, therefore, causes beings to assume new phases of existence—the Destroyer is really a re-Creator; hence the name Siva, the Bright or Happy One, is given to him, which would not have been the case had he been regarded as the destroyer in the ordinary meaning of that term.

In the later Hinduism, as taught in the Epics and Puranas, Siva plays a most important part, several books having been written for the purpose of celebrating his praise; yet his name as that of a god does not occur in the Vedas. In order, therefore, to gain greater reverence for him amongst men, he is declared to be the Rudra of the Vedras. In some passages in the Vedras, Rudra is identified with Agni; yet the distinctive epithets applied to him in the Rig-Veda appear sufficiently to prove that he was generally discriminated from Agni by his early worshippers.

Between the texts from the Brahmanas relative to Rudra, and the earliest descriptions of the same deity in the Epic poems, a wide chasm intervenes. The Rudra of the Mahabharata is not very different from the god of the same name who is portrayed in the Satarudriya, but in the later literature his importance is immensely increased, his attributes are more clearly defined. Instead of remaining a deity, as he was in the Vedic Age, Rudra has thrown Agni, Vayu, Surya, Mitra, and Varuna completely into the shade; and although Indra still occupies a prominent place in the Epic legends, he has sunk down into a subordinate position, and is quite unable to compete in power and dignity with Rudra, who, together with Vishnu, now engrosses the almost exclusive worship of the devotees.

There is no connected account of his life. His career was not clearly defined like an Avatara of Vishnu, of which we have a history of his birth, life, and death. Though he often appeared on earth in human form, and frequently dwelt at his favourite city, Benares, his heavenly home was at Kailasa on the Himalayas. All that can be done is to give a few out of the many legends found in the sacred books in which his character and works are described. From these we get some idea respecting Siva.

Rudra, according to the Ramayana, married Uma, the daughter of Daksha, who reappears in various stages of the life of Siva as Parvati, Durga, Kali, etc. Fearing that the children of such parents would be dangerous to live with, the gods entreated Siva and Uma to live a life of chastity: to this they consented. The request, however, came too late to prevent the birth of Kartikeya. Uma declared that the wives of the other gods should also be childless. Siva took a prominent position at the churning of the ocean; he drank the poison, as nectar, that was produced before the *amrita,* which caused his neck to become dark-coloured—hence one of his names is Nilkanta, " the blue-necked."

As Uma was sitting with her husband in their home on Mount Kailasa, seeing the gods driving by in their chariots, she was told that they were proceeding, at her father's invitation, to take part in a great sacrifice he was about to make. As Siva had offended him, Daksha had not invited him. The *Bhagavata Purana* gives the cause of this slight upon Siva: "On one occasion the gods and Rishis were assembled at a sacrifice celebrated by the Prajapatis. On Daksha's entrance, all rose to salute him excepting his father Brahma and Mahadeva (Siva). Daksha, after making his obeisance to Brahma, sat down by his command, but was offended at the treatment he received from Siva. Seeing him seated, Daksha did not brook this want of respect; but looking at him obliquely with his eyes, as if consuming him, thus spake: 'Hear me, ye Rishis, with the gods and the Agnis, while I, neither from ignorance nor passion, describe what is the practice of virtuous persons. But this shameless being (Siva) detracts from the reputation of the guardians of the world—he by whom, stubborn as he is, the course pursued by the good is transgressed. He assumed the position of my disciple, inasmuch as, like a virtuous person, in the face of Brahmans and of fire, he took the hand of my daughter who resembled Savitri. This monkey-eyed god after having taken the hand of my fawn-eyed daughter has not even by word shown suitable respect to me, whom he ought to have risen and saluted. Though unwilling, I yet gave my daughter to this impure and proud abolisher of rites and demolisher of barriers. He roams about in dreadful cemeteries, attended by hosts of ghosts and spirits, like a madman, naked, with dishevelled hair, wearing a garland of dead men's skulls and ornaments of human bones, pretending to be Siva (auspicious), but in reality Asiva (inauspicious), insane, beloved by the insane, the lord of Bhutas (spirits), beings whose nature is darkness. To this wicked-hearted lord of the infuriate, whose purity has perished, I have, alas! given my virtuous daughter, at the instigation of Brahma.' Having thus reviled Siva, who did not oppose him, Daksha, having touched water, incensed, began to curse him: 'Let this Bhava (Siva), lowest of the gods, never at the worship of the gods receive any portion along with the gods Indra, Upendra (Vishnu), and others.'

"Daksha then left the assembly. After his departure a follower of Mahadeva pronounced a curse upon him, and the Brahmans who sympathized with him: 'Let Daksha, brutal, be excessively devoted to women, and have speedily the head of a goat. Let this stupid being continue to exist in this world in ceremonial ignorance!' Upon this, Bhrigu (a brother of Daksha, and a Rishi) launched a counter-curse upon the followers of Siva: 'Let those who practise the rites of Bhava be heretics and opponents of the true scriptures. Having lost their purity, deluded in understanding, wearing matted hair and ashes and bones, let them undergo the initiation of Siva, in which spirituous liquors are the deity.' Hearing this imprecation, Siva and his followers left the assembly, while Daksha and the other Prajapatis celebrated for a thousand years the sacrifice in which Vishnu was the object of veneration."

The enmity thus commenced between Siva and Daksha continued; and in consequence, at the great sacrifice made when his father-in-law was appointed chief of the Prajapatis, Siva was not invited. Uma was greatly grieved, as her husband told her, "The former practice of the gods has been that in all sacrifices no portion should be divided to me. By custom, the gods lawfully allot me no share in the sacrifice." According to the *Mahabharata,* he then sets off for the assembly and with his attendants puts an end to the sacrifice, which, taking the form of a deer, is followed by Siva into the sky. A drop of perspiration falls from his forehead, from which a fire proceeds, out of which issues a dreadful being

Jvara (Fever), which burns up the other things prepared for the sacrifice, and even puts to flight the gods. Brahma now appears to Siva, promises that the gods shall hence-forth give him a share in the sacrifices, and proposes that Jvara shall be allowed to range over the earth.

The *Bhagavata* gives a more lengthy and somewhat different account of the termination of Daksha's ceremony. Sati (Uma) was most anxious to attend it. Though her husband tries to dissuade her, she disregards his warning and goes; but, being slighted by her father, reproaches him for his hostility to her husband, and threatens to abandon her physical body by which she was connected with her parent. She then voluntarily gives up the ghost. Seeing this, Siva's attendants, who had followed, rush on Daksha to slay him: This, however, is prevented, and Siva's followers, are put to flight. When Siva heard of his wife's death, he was greatly angered, and from a lock of his hair a gigantic demon arose (named Virabhadra), whom he commanded to destroy Daksha and his sacrifice. This was accomplished. He plucked out Bhrigu's beard, tore out Bhaga's eyes, knocked out Pushan's teeth, and cut off Daksha's head. In their distress, the gods are advised to propitiate Siva. For this purpose they resort to Kailasa, where they see Siva carrying ashes, a staff, a tuft of hair, an antelope's skin, and a digit of the moon, his body shining like an evening cloud. Siva in part relents, and allows Daksha to have a goat's head. Daksha worships Siva, and Uma, who had voluntarily given up herself to the flames, and thus become a *Sati* was re-born as Parvati, being then the daughter of Himavat, the god of the Himalayas and Mena.

Siva adopted the garb, and lived the life of an ascetic. Though generally worshipped under the form of the linga, he is represented in human form, living in the Himalayas along with Parvati, sometimes in the act of trampling on or destroying demons, wearing round his blue neck a serpent, and a necklace of skulls, and furnished with a whole apparatus of external emblems, such as a white bull on which he rides, a trident, tiger's skin, elephant's skin, rattle, noose, etc. He has three eyes, one being in his forehead, in allusion either to the three Vedas, or time past, present and future. He has a crescent on his forehead, the moon having been given to him as his share of the churning of the ocean. Again, Mahadeva, or the great deity Siva, is sometimes connected with humanity in another personification very different from that just noted, viz, that of an austere ascetic, with matted hair, living in a forest and teaching men by his own example, first, the power to be obtained by penance (*tapas*), mortification of the body and suppression of the passions; and, secondly, the great virtue of abstract meditation, as leading to the loftiest spiritual knowledge, and ultimately to union, or actual identification with the great spirit of the universe.

The following legend from the *Vamana Purana*, describes the ordinary life of Siva as an ascetic. Devi (Parvati), oppressed with violent heat, thus addressed her lord : "O Isha! the heat increases in violence; hast thou no house to which we might repair, and there abide, protected from the wind, the heat, the cold?" Sankara replied: "I am, O lovely one; without a shelter, a constant wanderer in forests." Having thus spoken, Sankara with Sati remained during the hot season under the shade of trees, and when it was passed, the rainy season with its dark clouds succeeded. On beholding which, Sati said to Siva, "Heart-agitating winds do blow, O Maheshwara, and rushing torrents roar; let me entreat thee to build a house on Kailasa, where I may abide with thee in comfort." Siva replied, "O my beloved, I have no riches for the erection of a house, nor am I possessor of aught else than an elephant's skin for a garment, and serpents for my ornaments." The consort of Siva, having heard these harsh words, seemingly true, but devoid of truth, looking on the ground with anger said, "Then say, O Sambhu, how can we pass in comfort the rainy season under the shade of trees?" Siva replied, "With our bodies covered with a cloud, O lovely one, shall the rainy season pass without any rain falling on thy tender frame." Having thus spoken, Siva stopped a cloud, and with the daughter of Daksha, fixed his abode within it, and hence has he since been celebrated in heaven under the name of *Jimula-Kitu* (he whose banner is a cloud). When the rains were over, they took up their abode in Mount Mandara.

The home life of Siva and his spouse does not appear to have been of the happiest. As they could each bestow gifts upon their worshippers, it sometimes happened that the one wanted to bless those whom the other wished to curse. In the *Ramayana* and *Mahabharata* is an account of a dispute between them in connection with the struggle between Rama and Ravana. In the earlier part of the contest, Rama being unable to overthrow his enemy because of the assistance afforded him by Siva, the gods whom Ravana had oppressed went, with Rama at their head, to ask him to withdraw his help. Siva consented to accompany them on the seventh day of the conflict to witness the destruction of their foe. Durga (Parvati) severely reproached her husband, asking how he could witness the destruction of his own worshipper, a worshipper who had stood praying to him surrounded by four fires; who had continued his devotions in the chilling cold, standing in water; and had persevered standing on his head, amid torrents of rain. She then poured forth a torrent of abuse, calling him a withered old man, who smoked intoxicating herbs, lived in cemeteries and covered himself with ashes. Siva now gets angry, and reminds his wife that she was only a woman and therefore could know nothing; and further that she too wandered about from place to place, engaged in war, killed giants, drank their blood and hung their skulls around her neck. Durga became so enraged at these reproaches, that the gods were frightened. They entreated Rama to join them in supplication to her, or Ravana would never be destroyed. He did so; she then became propitious and consented to the destruction of the demon. Durga is represented in the *Sivopakhyana* as being exceedingly jealous because her husband, in his begging excursions, visited the houses of women of ill-fame, and in the Ramayana is an account of a terrible quarrel between them because Parasurama beat her sons Kartikeya and Ganesa.

In the *Vamana Purana* is a legend explaining why Siva adopted the dress and habits of a religious mendicant. Formerly, when all things had been destroyed, and naught remained but one vast ocean, that lord who is incomprehensible (Brahma) reposed in slumber for a thousand years. When the night had passed, desirous of creating the three worlds, the skilled in the Vedas, investing himself with the quality of impurity, assumed a corporeal form with five heads (Brahma). Then also was produced from the quality of darkness another form with three eyes, and twisted locks, and bearing a rosary and a trident. Brahma next created Ahankara (consciousness of individual existence), which immediately pervaded the nature of both gods; and under its influence Rudra said to Brahma, "Say, O lord! how camest thou hither, and by whom wert thou created ?" Brahma asks in return, "And where have you come from ?" The result is a terrible quarrel, in which Siva, inflamed with anger, cut off the fifth head of Brahma, which had uttered the boastful words. But when Siva tried to throw the head to the ground it would not fall, but remained in his hand. Brahma then created a giant to slay Siva in his weakened state, which was caused by the sin of injuring Brahma, the father of Brahmans. To escape from him Siva fled to Benares. The peculiar sanctity of Benares arises from the fact that it was there Siva became absolved from his great sin, and was freed from the head of Brahma, which, as a penance, he was doomed to carry with him wherever he went. It was his attempts to get free from the sin of Brahmanicide that made Siva a wandering mendicant.

The ordinary name by which Siva is known as Mahadeva, the great god; the origin of this is taught in the *Mahabharata*. The *asuras* had a boon bestowed by Brahma, that they should possess three castles which could be destroyed only by one who was able to overthrow them by a single arrow? Owing to this defence, they became hateful to the other gods, who went to Brahma, and he again conducts them to Mahadeva. Siva tells them that he alone cannot destroy these castles, but that with the aid of half his strength, they themselves would be able to accomplish this. They answered that as they could not sustain half his strength, they proposed that he should undertake the work aided by half their strength. Mahadeva consented to this, and thus became stronger than all the gods, and was thenceforward called Mahadeva. Notwithstanding this, in the account of Parasurama a legend is given in which Vishnu's superiority to Siva is shown; whilst in the Puranas devoted to Siva's praise it is distinctly affirmed that Brahma and Vishnu are inferior to him.

The unity of the various gods is stated in the following legend. As Lakshmi and Durga were sitting together in the presence of Siva, Lakshmi contended that her husband (Vishnu) was greater than Siva, because Siva had worshipped him. As they were conversing, Vishnu himself appeared, and, in order to convince his wife that he and Siva were equal, entered his body, and they became one. Another form of this story is found in the *Skanda Purana*. Siva asked Vishnu on one occasion to assume the form of a beautiful woman, such as he did at the churning of the ocean to attract the attention of the asuras whilst the gods drank the amrita. Vishnu consenting, Siva became excited and sought to embrace her. As Vishnu ran away, Siva followed him, and though Vishnu resumed his proper form, Siva clasped him so tightly that their bodies became one, and a name Har-Hari, is given to the deities thus united.

Siva is always represented as having a third eye situated in the middle of his forehead; the reason is given in the *Mahabharata*. As he was seated on the Himalayas, where he had been engaged in austerities, Uma, attended by her companions, and dressed as an ascetic, came behind him and playfully put her hands over his eyes. The effect was tremendous. Suddenly the world became dark, lifeless and destitute. The gloom, however, is as suddenly dispelled. A great flame burst from Mahadeva's forehead, in which a third eye, luminous as the sun, was formed. By fire from this eye the mountain was scorched, and everything upon it consumed. Uma then stands in a submissive attitude before her husband, and in a moment, the Himalaya, her father, is restored to his former condition.

Each god is represented as having special fondness for some bird or animal, on which he is supposed to travel, and which therefore is called his Vahan or vehicle. The bull is Siva's; and the image of his favourite bull, Nandi, is seen in front of many of the shrines sacred to Mahadeva. Owing probably to this circumstance, a custom prevails, where at the death of a worshipper of Siva, bullock is set loose, and allow it to wander at will. By the Hindus generally it is considered a meritorious act to feed these sacred bulls, and a sin to injure them.

As Siva himself lived the life of an ascetic, and practised severe penance, a similar life is supposed to be pleasing to him; hence many of the Saivites, or worshippers of Siva, practise great austerities, and resort to these as a means of gaining his favour. Wandering through the country are tens of thousands of Sanyasis, or pilgrims, who subsist upon charity, and expose themselves to cold and heat and many discomforts, in the belief that their life is pleasing to this deity. Some of them inflict upon themselves great physical pain by retaining their arms or legs in one posture for years, until it has become impossible to move them; others allow the thumb nail to grow through their finger; others gaze into the sun until they become blind; others again impose upon themselves a vow of silence, until at length they cannot speak.

The following extract from the *Bhagavata*, descriptive of Siva's appearance and conduct, countenances much that now forms part of his worship. Understanding that one of his worshippers was in distress, Siva assumed half the body of Parvati, fastened up his matted hair, rubbed his body over with ashes, ate a large quantity of hemp, swallow-wort and thorn-apple; and wearing a Brahmanical thread composed of white snakes, clad in an elephant's hide, with a necklace of beads, and a garland of skulls, riding upon Nandi, accompanied by ghosts, goblins, spectres, witches, imps, spirites and evil spirits, Bholanath came forth. On his forehead was the moon; he placed the Ganges on his head, and his eyes were very red. His most destructive weapon was a trident: with this he slew the foe who was obnoxious to his follower.

Though Siva's appearance is repeatedly described with considerable minuteness in the Puranas, and in pictures he is usually represented in the human form, it is in the form of the Linga that he is almost universally worshipped. This image does not suggest anything offensive to those unacquainted with its symbolic meaning, and some writers speak of its being innocuous to the Hindus themselves. But it is impossible for any one acquainted with the legends which account for its being the symbol of Siva, to see and worship it without impure thoughts being suggested. It is intended to represent the male and female reproductive organs.

Several legends are given to explain how it came to be the representative of Siva. The *Padma Purana* teaches that it was the result of a curse pronounced by Bhrigu. When that Sage was sent to discover which of the three gods was the greatest, he came to Siva's abode, but was prevented from entering immediately he arrived by a doorkeeper, who informed him that his master was with Devi his wife. After waiting for some time, Bhrigu's patience being exhausted, he said, "Since thou, O Sankara! hast treated me with contempt, in preferring the embraces of Parvati, your forms of worship shall be the Linga and Yoni."

The *Vamana* makes it the result of a curse pronounced by a number of Sages. When Sati died at Daksha's sacrifice, Siva wandered from place to place like a madman, mourning her absence. He travelled from hermitage to hermitage, but could find no rest. When the hermits' wives saw him they fell desperately in love with him and followed him from place to place. Their husbands, incensed at this, cursed the god, and deprived him of his manhood. A great commotion followed. Brahma and Vishnu interceded on his behalf with the hermits, who consented to withdraw their curse on condition that the offender should be represented by the Linga; and thus it became an object of worship to gods and men.

As a specimen of the legends by which the worship of Siva under this form is inculcated, the following is from the *Siva Purana.* A Rakshas named Bhima, have obtained invincible might as a boon from Rama, commenced exerting his newly acquired power by attacking the king of Kamrupa. Having conquered the king, and seized his kingdom and riches, he placed him in chains in a solitary prison. The king, being eminently pious, notwithstanding his confinement, continued daily to make clay figures of the Linga, and to worship Siva with all the prescribed rites and ceremonies. Meanwhile the Rakshas continued his conquests, and everywhere abolished religious observances, and the worship enjoined in the Vedas. The gods being reduced by his power to great distress, appealed to Siva for help, and propitiated him by the worship of clay

Lingas. Sambhu assured them that he would effect the destruction of their enemy. At this very moment the prisoner was engaged in profound meditation before a Linga, when one of the guards, seeing him thus occupied, went and informed the Rakshas that his captive was performing some improper ceremonies. Hearing this, the monster, enraged, seized his sword and hastening to the prison, thus addressed the king: "Speak the truth, and tell me who it is that thou worshippest, and I will not slay thee; otherwise I will instantly put thee to death!"

The king, placing firm reliance on the protection of Siva, undauntedly replied, "In truth, I worship Sankara; do then what thou pleasest!" The Rakshas asked, "What can Sankara do to me? I know him well, that he was once obliged to become the servant of my uncle (Ravana). However, until you show me thy lord, and convince me of his might, I will not believe in his divinity!" The king replied, "Vile as I am, what power have I over the god? But mighty as he is, I know he will never forsake me!" To which the Rakshas said, "How can that delighter in *ganja,* and inebriation, that wandering mendicant, protect his worshippers? Let but thy lord appear, and I will immediately engage with him in battle." He then ordered the attendance of his army; and reviling the king, the mighty Rakshas smiting the Linga with his sword, said, laughing, "Now, behold the power of thy lord! Scarcely had his sword touched the Linga than Hara issued from it, and exclaimed, "Behold I am Iswara (god), who appears for the protection of his worshipper, on whom he always bestows safety and happiness; now learn to dread my might!" Siva then attacked the Rakshas, and with the glory which issued from his third eye, reduced him and his army to ashes.

Siva is said to have a thousand names; in addition to those already mentioned the following are most common:—

Maheswara, "The great god."

Ishwar, "The glorious."

Chandrashekara, "He who wears a half-moon on his forehead."

Bhuteswara, "Lord of Bhuts, or goblins."

Mritunjaya, "He who conquers death."

Sri Kanta, "He whose neck is beautiful."

Smarahara, "The destroyer of Smara or Kamdeva."

Gangadhara, "He who holds Ganga (the Ganges) in his hair."

Sthanu, "The everlasting."

Girisha, "The lord of the hills."

Digambara, "He who is clothed with space."

Bhagavat, "The lord."

Isana, "The ruler."

Mahakala, "The great time."

"Tryambaka, "The three-eyed."

Nataraja, "The cosmic dancer."

Panchanana

This is a form of Siva in which he is represented, as his name teaches, with five faces; the appearance of his body and the ascetic's dress being the same as in his ordinary forms. It is under this name that prayers for recovery from sickness are addressed to him as the physician or healer. In places where there is no temple, and no image of this deity, worship is offered to him before a shapeless stone, painted red, placed under a tree. This is a very common form of worship in the villages of Bengal. Some shrines of Panchanana have acquired considerable celebrity, to which women resort to obtain the gift of children as well as other blessings. In times of sickness offerings are made to this deity even if the sufferer is not ordinarily a worshipper of Siva. In cases of epilepsy it is the common belief that the victim is possessed by Panchanana, and offerings are made to induce him to depart; recovery is believed to be the result of the god's departure.

9

UMA

Uma

Uma is the name by which the consort of Siva is known. In the sacred books she appears in many forms, and is known by many names; but as there are legends giving the circumstances connected with the names and forms more generally known, these will be given as far as possible in chronological order.

When Devi (the goddess) appears as Uma, she is said to be the daughter of Daksha, a son of Brahma. Her father was at first very unwilling that his daughter should marry a mendicant, but his scruples were overcome by the persuasion of Brahma. As Siva is styled Mahadeva, Uma is frequently called simply Devi. At this period of her existence she is also called Sati, in allusion to the fact that when her father slighted her husband by not inviting him to the great sacrifice he made, she voluntarily entered the sacrificial fire and was burned to death in the presence of the gods, or, according to another account, was, under the same circumstances, consumed by her own power. The name Sati means " the true, or virtuous woman, and is given to those widows who ascend the funeral pile of their husbands, and undergo a voluntary death by being burned with his corpse. Ambika, another name of Uma, in one of the earliest books, is said to be the sister of Rudra; and yet in the later ones she is declared to be his wife.

The earliest work in which the name of Uma appears, is the Talavakara, or *Kena Upanishad*. In the third section of that treatise it is mentioned that on one occasion Brahma gained a victory for the gods. As, however, they were disposed to ascribe the credit of their success to themselves, Brahman appeared for the purpose of disabusing them of their mistake. The gods did not know him, and commissioned first Agni and then Vayu, to ascertain what this apparition was. When, in answer to Brahma's inquiry, these two gods represented themselves, the one as having power to burn, and the other to blow away anything whatever, he desired them respectively to burn and blow away a blade of grass; but they were unable to do this, and returned without ascertaining who he was. Indra was then commissioned to ascertain who this apparition was. 'So be it', he replied, and approached that being, who vanished from him. In the sky he came to a woman, who was very resplendent, Uma Haimavati. To her he said: 'What is this apparition?' She said, 'It is Brahman; in this victory of Brahman exult.' By this he knew that it was Brahman. The commentators on this passage declare that Uma means 'knowledge' and speak of Uma as the impersonation of 'divine knowledge'.

As in Siva, first of all two gods, Agni and Rudra are combined, so too his wife is to be regarded as a compound of several divine forms; and this becomes quite evident as we look over the mass of her epithets. While one set of these as Uma, Ambika, Parvati, Haimavati, belong to the wife of Rudra, others as Kali carry us back to the wife of Agni; while Gauri and others perhaps refer to Nirriti the goddess of all evil. The most remarkable instance of this is to be found in the Mahabharata in the hymn of Yudhishthira to Durga, where he calls her Yasoda Krishna,'born in the cowherd family of Nanda', 'sister of Vasudeva,' 'enemy of Kansa and as 'having the same features as Sankarshana.' Some such explanation is certainly necessary when we see that Kali is said to be the same with Uma, the embodiment of 'heavenly wisdom'.

In the following passage from the *Ramayana*, Uma is said to be the daughter of Himavat and Mena; the two forms of Uma and Parvati being considered as one. To Himavat, the chief of mountains, two daughters were born in beauty unequalled upon earth. The daughter of Meru, Mena by name, the pleasing and beloved wife of Himavat, was their slender-waisted mother. Of her was born Ganga, the eldest daughter of Himavat, and his second daughter was Uma, who, rich in austere observances, fulfilled a course of severe austerity. This daughter Uma, distinguished by severe austerity, adored by the worlds, the chief of the mountains gave to the matchless Rudra. These were the two daughters of the King of the Mountains: Ganga, the most eminent of rivers, and Uma the most excellent of goddesses.

Several of the names under which Uma is now known and worshipped are to be found in the older writings, though at that time they did not refer to Siva's wife. Uma, as we have already seen, was "Wisdom;" Ambika was a sister of Rudra; Durga "in a hymn of the

Taittiriya Aranyaka is an epithet of the sacrificial flame; and Kali, a word which occurs in the *Mundaka Upanishad,* is the name of one of the seven flickering tongues of Agni, the god of fire."

Uma is called the mother of Kartikeya, and in a certain sense of Ganesa too; but it is not at all clear whether it was really as Uma or in her succeeding birth as Parvati that she had these children.

The *Kurma Purana* has an account of Uma's creation which takes us back, a stage anterior to her birth as a daughter of Daksha. When Brahma was angry with his sons for adopting an ascetic life [and refusing to perpetuate the human race], a form half male and half female was produced from that anger, to whom Brahma said, 'Divide thyself' and then disappeared. The male half became Rudra, and the female, at the command of Brahma, became the daughter of Daksha under the name of Sati, and was given in marriage to Rudra, and when she subsequently gave up her life on being treated with disrespect by her father, she was born a second time as the daughter of Himavat and Menu, and named Parvati.

It should be noticed that although Uma is called the *wife* of Siva, it is understood that she represents the energy or active power of that deity; she assumed a body in order that she might be united to him in due form; in like manner Vishnu's energy became incarnate in Lakshmi, Sita, etc.

Parvati

The goddess in this form is the constant companion of her husband, but few independent actions are ascribed to her. In the Puranas, Siva and Parvati are generally represented as engaged in making love to each other, or as seated on Mount Kailasa discussing the most abstruse questions of Hindu philosophy. Occasionally, however, quarrels arose between them, and on one occasion Siva reproached, her for the blackness of her skin. This taunt so grieved her that she left him for a time, and, repairing to a deep forest performed most severe austerities, until Brahma granted her as a boon that her complexion should be golden, and from then on she is known as Gauri.

The following legend from the *Varaha Purana* describes her origin. Brahma when on a visit to Siva on Mount Kailasa, is thus addressed by him: "Say quickly, O Brahma, what has induced you to come to me?" Brahma replies, "There is a mighty asura named Andhaka (Darkness), by whom all the gods, having been distressed, came for protection, and I have hastened to inform you of their complaints." Brahma then looked intently at Siva, who by thought summoned Vishnu into their presence. As the three deities looked at each other, "from their three refulgent glances sprang into being a virgin of celestial loveliness, of hue like the petals of a blue lotus, and adorned with gems, who bashfully bowed before Brahma, Vishnu, and Siva. On their asking her who she was, and why she was distinguished by the three colours black, white, and red, she said, " From your glances was I produced; do you not know your own omnipotent energies ?" Brahma then praising her, said, "Thou shalt be named the goddess of three times (past, present and future), the preserver of the universe, and under various appellations shalt thou be worshipped, as thou shalt be the cause of accomplishing the desires of thy votaries. But, O goddess, divide thyself into three forms, according to the colours by which thou art distinguished." She then divided herself into three parts; one white, one red, and one black. The white was "Sarasvati, of a lovely, felicitous form, and the co-operator with Brahma in creation; the red was Lakshmi, the beloved of Vishnu, who with him preserves the universe; the black was Parvati, endowed with many qualities and the energy of Siva." In the preceding legend it was narrated how Parvati, originally black, became golden-coloured.

The *Vaivarta Purana* relates the circumstance which led to the re-appearance on earth of Uma, who had sacrificed herself and became a Sati, under the form of Parvati. Siva, hearing of the death of his wife, was overcome with grief; on his recovery he hastened to the banks of the river of heaven, where he beheld "the body of his beloved Sati arrayed in white garments, holding a rosary in her hand and glowing with splendour bright as burnished gold. No sooner did he see the lifeless form of his spouse, than, through grief for her loss, his senses forsook him." When he revived, gazing on her beautiful countenance, with tears in his eyes and sorrow in his voice, he thus addressed her: "Arise, arise, O my beloved Sati! I am Sankara, thy lord; look therefore on me, who have approached thee. With thee I am almighty, the framer of all things, and the giver of every bliss; but without thee, my energy! I am like a corpse, powerless and incapable of action: how then, my beloved, can thou forsake me? With smiles and glances of thine eyes, say something sweet as *amrita,* and with the rain of they genetic words sprinkle my heart, which is scorched with grief. Formerly, when thou didst see me from a distance, thou wouldst greet me with the fondest accents; why then to-day art thou angry, and wilt not speak to me? O mother of the universe, arise! Dost thou not see me here weeping? O beauteous one! thou can not have expired. Then, O my faithful spouse! why dost thou not honour me as usual?"

Siva, having thus spoken, raised the lifeless body, and in the anguish of separation pressed it to his bosom. Like a man deprived of his senses, the preceptor of the universe wandered over the seven *dwipas*, until, exhausted by fatigue and anguish, he fell down in a swoon at the foot of a banyan tree. The gods, seeing Siva in this state, were greatly astonished, and, accompanied by Brahma and Vishnu, hastened to the spot where he lay. Vishnu placed the head of the fainting Siva on his bosom and wept aloud; after a little time he encouraged his friend by saying, 'O Siva! recover thy senses, and listen to what I say. Thou wilt certainly regain Sati, since Siva and Sati are as inseparable as cold from water, heat from fire, smell from earth, or radiance from the sun!

Hearing these words, Siva opened his eyes, bedewed with tears, and said: 'O form of splendour! Who art thou? Who are these that accompany thee? Who am I, and where are my attendants?' As Vishnu heard these words he wept, and his tears, uniting with those of Siva, formed a lake, which hence became a famous place of pilgrimage. Vishnu at length calmed Siva, who, delighted with his words, beheld Sati, seated before him in a gem-adorned car, accompanied by numerous attendants, arrayed in costly garments, resplendent with ornaments, her placid face being irradiated with a gentle smile. The anguish of separation ceased, and joy filled his soul as Sati thus addressed him: 'Be firm, O Mahadeva. In whatever state of my being I may exist, I shall never be separated from my lord; and now have I been born the daughter of Himavat in order to become again thy wife; therefore no longer grieve on account of our separation.' Having thus consoled Siva, Sati disappeared.

In another chapter of the same Purana we have an account of their reunion. Sati soon obtained another birth in the womb of Himavat's wife; and Siva, collecting the bones and ashes from her funeral pile, made a necklace of the bones and covered his body with the ashes, and thus preserved them as memorials of his beloved. Not long after this, Sati was born as the daughter of Mena, excelling in beauty and virtue all created beings, and she grew up in her mountain home like the young moon increasing to its full splendour. Whilst still a girl, she heard a voice from heaven saying, 'Perform a severe course of austerity, in order to obtain

Siva for a husband, as he cannot otherwise be obtained.' Parvati, proud of her youth, smiling disdainfully at this instruction, thought within herself, 'Will he who, on account of the grief he felt for may having formerly consumed myself, not accept me as his spouse? And how can disjunction exist between those who have been predestined from their first being to be husband and wife?' Confident in her youth, loveliness, and numerous attractions, and persuaded that on the first mention of her name Siva would be anxious to espouse her, Parvati did not seek to gain him by the performance of austerity, but night and day gave herself to joyous sports with her companions." Her hopes, however, were disappointed. She had to perform most severe penance before she was reunited to her husband; and it was only by the assistance of Kamadeva, who, at the instigation of the gods, wounded him with his arrows as he was engaged in meditation, whilst Parvati was seated in front of him, that her wish was gratified. Siva at first was anything but grateful for this interference; and as before narrated he rewarded Kama by destroying him with a flame that issued from his third eye.

In a Bengali account of Durga, a legend is given from a later work than the Purana. It is the following : When Siva raised the dead body of Sati in his arms he began to dance in a frantic manner. The earth trembled beneath the weight of such a load; and Vishnu, fearing there would be an utter destruction of the universe if this were allowed to continue, let fly his discus, and cut the body into fifty-one pieces. These fell in different places, a leg here, a hand there; but wherever a part touched the earth, the spot became sacred, an image of the goddess was set up, and a temple rose—in some places it is said they *grew* to her honour—which pilgrims still visit as shrines. The renowned temple at Kali Ghat, near Calcutta, is said to possess the big toe of her left foot; and the other principal shrines of Parvati profess to contain a relic of her body.

Parvati is represented in pictures as a fair and beautiful woman, with no superfluity of limbs. Few miraculous deeds are claimed for her. It is when she appears as Durga, Kali, etc., that she manifests divine powers, and exhibits a very different spirit from that which appears in her as Parvati.

Durga

The consort of Siva now assumes a very different character from that in which she has so far been represented. In those .incarnations, though the wife of Siva, she acted as an ordinary woman, and manifested womanly virtues: as Durga she was a most powerful warrior, and appeared on earth, under many names, for the destruction of demons.

She obtained the name Durga because she slew an asura named Durga, the name of the goddess being the feminine form of the demon's name. The *Skanda Purana* gives the following account. Kartikeya, being asked by Agastya, the sage, why his mother was called Durga, says: "A giant named Durga, the sun of Ruru, having performed penance to get favour of Brahma, obtained his blessing, and grew so mighty that he conquered the three worlds, and dethroned Indra and the other gods. He compelled the wives of the Rishis to sing his praise, and sent the gods from heaven to dwell in the forests. He abolished religious ceremonies; Brahmans through fear of him gave up the reading of the Vedas; rivers changed their course; fire lost its energy, and the terrified stars retired from sight. He assumed the shape of the clouds, and gave rain whenever he pleased; the earth, through fear, yielded an abundant harvest, and the trees flowered and gave fruit out of the proper season."

The gods in their distress appealed to Siva. Indra, their king, said, "He has dethroned me!" Surya said, " He has taken my kingdom!" Siva, pitying them, desired Parvati to go and destroy this giant. She, accepting the commission willingly, calmed the fears of the gods, and first sent Kalaratri (Dark Night), a female whose beauty bewitched the inhabitants of the three worlds, to order the demon to restore things to their ancient order. He, however, full of fury, sent his soldiers to lay hold of Kalaratri; but by the breath of her mouth she reduced them to ashes. Durga then sent 30,000 other giants, who were such monsters in size that they covered the surface of the earth. At the sight of these giants, Kalaratri fled to Parvati, followed by the giants. Durga, with 100,000,000 chariots, 120,000,000,000 elephants, 10,000,000 swift-footed horses, and innumerable soldiers, went to fight Parvati, on the Vindhya mountain. As soon as he drew near, Parvati assumed 1000 arms, called to her assistance different beings, and produced a number of weapons from her body (a long list of these is given in the Purana). The troops of the giant poured their arrows on Parvati as she sat on the mountain Vindhya, thick as the drops of rain in a storm ; they even tore up trees, mountains, etc., and hurled them at her; in return she threw a weapon which carried away the arms of many of the giants. Durga himself then hurled a flaming dart at the goddess, which she turned aside; another being sent, she stopped it by a hundred arrows. He next aimed an arrow at Parvati's breast; this too she repelled, and two other weapons, a club and a pike. At last coming to close quarters, Parvati seized Durga and set her left foot on his breast, but he, managing to disengage himself, renewed the fight.

Parvati then caused a number of helpers to issue from her body, which destroyed the soldiers of the giants. In return, Durga sent a dreadful shower of hail, the effect of which Parvati counteracted. The demon now assumed the shape of an elephant as large as a mountain, and approached the goddess; but she tied his legs, and, with her nails, which were like scimitars, tore him to pieces. He rose again in the form of a buffalo, and with his horns cast stones, trees, and mountains, tearing up the trees by the breath of his nostrils. Parvati then pierced him with her trident; he reeled to and fro, and, renouncing the form of a buffalo, assumed his original body as a giant, with a thousand arms, having a weapon in each. Approaching Parvati, she seized him by his arms, and carried him into the air, whence she threw him to the ground with fearful force. Seeing that the fall had not destroyed him, she pierced him in the breast with an arrow, whereupon blood issued from his mouth in streams, and he died. The gods were delighted at the result, and soon regained their former splendour.

Still another account of the origin of Durga is found in the *Chandi*, a part of the *Markandeya Purana*. Mahisha, king of the giants, at one time overcame the gods in war, and reduced them to such a state of want that they wandered on the earth as beggars. Indra first conducted them to Brahma and then the Siva; but as these gods could render no assistance, they turned to Vishnu, who was so grieved at the sight of their wretchedness, that streams of glory issued from his face, whence came a female figure named Mahamaya (another name of Durga). Streams of light issued from the faces of the other gods also, which in like manner entered Mahamaya; in consequence of which she became like a mountain of fire. The gods then handed their weapons to her with a frightful scream ascended into the air, slew the giant, and gave redress to the gods.

The account, as found in the *Vamana Purana,* differs in some details. When the gods had sought Vishnu in their distress, he, and at his command Sankara (Siva), Brahma, and the other gods, emitted such flames from their eyes and countenances that a mountain of effulgence was formed, from which became manifest Katyayini, refulgent as a thousand suns, having three eyes, black hair, and eighteen arms. Siva gave her his trident, Vishnu a discus, Varuna a conch-shell, Agni a dart, Vayu a bow, Surya a quiver full of arrows, Indra a thunderbolt, Kubera a mace, Brahma a rosary and water-pot, Kala a shield and sword, Visvakarma a battle-axe and other weapons. Thus armed, and adored by the gods, Katyayini proceeded to the Vindhya hills. Whilst there, the asuras Chanda and Munda saw her, and being captivated by her beauty they so described her to Mahisha, their king, that he was anxious to obtain her. On asking for her hand, she told him she must be won in fight. He came, and fought; at length Durga dismounted from her lion, and sprang upon the back of Mahisha, who was in the form of a baffalo, and with her tender feet so smote him on the head that he fell to the ground senseless, when she cut off his head with her sword.

In pictures and images Durga is represented as a golden-coloured woman, with a gentle and beautiful countenance. She has ten arms ; in one hand she holds a spear, with which she is piercing the giant Mahisha; with one of her left hands she holds the tail of a serpent, with another the hair of the giant whose breast the snake is biting; her other hand are filled with various weapons. Her lion leans against her right leg, and the giant against her left. The images of Lakshmi, Sarasvati, Kartikeya, and Ganesa are frequently made and worshipped with that of Durga.

In Bengal the worship of this goddess forms the most popular of all the Hindu festivals; it continues for three days, and is the great holiday of the year. At this season, the members of the family whom business detains from home during the year return; and with the worship of Durga is associated all that is bright and cheerful. Sacrifices of buffaloes and goats are made to her; feasting, singing, and dancing are continued through the greater part of the night. Though her chief festival is in the autumn, she is also worshipped, though not so generally, in the spring. The reason of this as taught in a Bengali account is as follows:—Ravana was a devout worshipper of Durga, and had the *Chandi* (an extract from one of the Puranas) read daily. When, therefore, Rama attacked him, the goddess assisted her servant. It was in the spring that Ravana observed her festival. Rama, seeing the help his enemy received from this goddess, began himself to worship her. This was in the autumn. Durga was delighted with the devotion of Rama, and at once transferred her aid to him.

Durga is said to have assumed ten forms for the destruction of two giants, Sumbha and Nisumbha; the *Markandeya Purana* describes these incarnations in the following order:—(1) As Durga she received the message of the giants; (2) As Dasabhuja (the ten-armed) she slew part of their army; (3) As Singhvahini (seated on a lion) she fought with Raktabija; (4) As Mahishamardini (destroyer of a buffalo) she slew Sumbha in the form of a buffalo; (5) As Jagaddhatri (the mother of the world) she overcame the army of the giants; (6) As Kali (the black woman) she slew Raktabija; (7) As Muktakesi (with flowing hair) she overcame another of the armies of the giants; (8) As Tara (the saviour) she slew Sumbha in his own proper shape; (9) As Chinnamustaka (the headless) she killed Nisumbha; (10) As Jagadgauri (the golden-coloured lady renowned through the world) she received the praises and thanks of the gods .

The great conflict for success in which Durga assumed so many forms, is described as follows in the *Markandeya Purana.* At the close of the Treta Age, two danavas named Sumbha and Nisumbha, performed religious austerities for 10,000 years, the merit of which brought Siva from heaven, who discovered that by this extra-ordinary devotion, they sought to obtain the blessing of immortality. He reasoned long with them, and vainly endeavoured to persuade them to ask for any other gift. Being denied what they specially wanted, they entered upon still more severe austerities, for another thousand years, when Siva again appeared, but still refused to grant what they asked. They now suspended themselves with their heads downwards over a slow fire, till the blood streamed from their necks : they continued thus for 800 years. The gods began to tremble, lest, by performing such rigid acts of holiness, these demons should supplant them on their thrones. The king of the gods thereupon called a council, and imparted to them his fears. They admitted that there was ground for anxiety, but asked what was the remedy.

Acting upon the advice of Indra, Kandarpa (the god of love), with Rambha and Tilatama, the most beautiful of the celestial nymphs, were sent to fill minds with sensual desires. Kandarpa with his arrow wounded both; upon which, awaking from their absorption, and seeing two beautiful women, they were taken in the snare, and abandoned their devotions. With these women they lived for 5000 years; after which they saw the folly of renouncing their hopes of immortality for the sake of sensual gratifications. They suspected this snare must have been a contrivance of Indra; so, driving back the nymphs to heaven, they renewed their devotions, cutting the flesh off their bones, and making burnt offerings of it to Siva. They continued in this way for 1000 years, till at last they became mere skeletons; Siva again appeared and bestowed upon them his blessing—that in riches and strength they should excel the gods.

Being exalted above the gods, they began to make war upon them. After various successes on both sides, the *danavas* became everywhere victorious; when Indra and the gods, reduced to a most deplorable state of wretchedness, solicited the interference of Brahma and Vishnu. They referred them to Siva, who declared that he could do nothing for them. When, however, they reminded him that it was through his blessing they had been ruined, he advised them to perform religious austerities to Durga. They did so ; and after some time the goddess appeared, and gave them her blessing; then disguising herself as a common female carrying a pitcher of water, she passed through the assembly of the gods. She then assumed her proper form, and said, 'They are celebrating my praise.'

This new goddess now ascended Mount Himalaya, where Chanda and Munda, two of Sumbha and Nisumbha's messengers, resided. As these demons wandered over the mountain, they saw the goddess; and being exceedingly struck with her charms, which they described to their masters, advised them to gain her affections.

Sumbha sent Sugriva as messenger to the goddess, to inform her that the riches of the three worlds were in his palace; that all the offerings which used to be presented to the gods were now offered to him, and that all these offerings, riches, etc., would be hers, if she would come to him. The goddess replied that the offer was very liberal, but that she had resolved that the person she married must first conquer her in war, and destroy her pride. Sugriva, unwilling to return unsuccessful, pressed for a favourable answer, promising that he would conquer her in war, and subdue her pride; and asked in an authoritative strain: 'Did she know his master, before whom none of the inhabitants of the worlds had been able to stand, whether gods, demons, or men? How then could she, a female, think of resisting his offers? If his master had ordered him, he would have compelled her to go into his presence immediately.' She agreed that this was very correct, but that she had taken her resolution, and exhorted him, therefore, to persuade his master to come and try his strength with her.

The messenger went and related what he had heard. On hearing his account, Sumbha was filled with rage, and, without making any reply, called for Dhumlochana his commander-in-chief, and gave him orders to go to Himalaya and seize the goddess and bring her to him, and, if any attempted a rescue, utterly to destroy them.

The commander went to Himalaya, and acquainted the goddess with his master's orders. She, smiling invited him to execute them. On the approach of this hero, she set up a dreadful roar, by which he was reduced to ashes. After which she destroyed the army leaving only a few fugitives to communicate the tidings. Sumbha and Nisumbha, infuriated, sent Chanda and Munda, who, on ascending the mountain, perceived a female sitting on an ass, laughing. On seeing them she became enraged, and drew to her ten, twenty, or thirty of their army at a time, devouring them like fruit. She next seized Munda by the hair, cut off his head, and holding it over her mouth, drank the blood. Chanda, on seeing the other commander slain in this manner, himself came to close quarters with the goddess. But she, mounted on a lion, sprang on him, and, despatching him as she had done Munda, devoured part of his army, and drank the blood of the slain.

The *danavas* no sooner heard this alarming news than they resolved to go themselves, and collecting their forces, marched to Himalaya. The gods looked down with astonishment on this vast army, and the goddesses descended to help Mahamaya (Durga), who, however, soon destroyed her foes. Raktabija, the principal commander under Sumbha, and Nisumbha, seeing all his men destroyed, encountered the goddess in person. But though she covered him with wounds, from every drop of blood which fell to the ground a thousand *danavas* arose equal in strength to Raktabija himself. Hence innumerable enemies surrounded Durga, and the gods were filled with alarm at the amazing sight. At length Chandi, a goddess who had assisted Kali (Durga) in the engagement, promised that if she would drink the giant's blood before it fell to the ground, she (Chandi) would engage him and destroy the whole of his strangely-formed offspring. Kali consented, and the commander and his army were soon finished.

Sumbha and Nisumbha, in a state of desperation, next engaged the goddess in single combat, Sumbha making the first onset. The battle was inconceivably dreadful on both sides, till at last both the giants were slain, and Kali sat down to feed on the carnage she had made. The gods and goddesses chanted the praises of the celestial heroine, who in return bestowed a blessing on them.

In the following hymn of Arjuna to Durga in the *Mahabharatá*, her many names are mentioned: "Reverence be to thee, Siddha-Senani (generaless of the Siddhas), the noble, the dweller on Mandara, Kumari (Princess), Kali, Kapali, Kapila, Krishnapingala. Reverence to thee, Bhadrakali; reverence to thee, Maha Kali, Chandi, Chanda, Tarini (deliveress), Varavarini (beautiful-coloured). O fortunate Kalyayani, O Karali, O Vijaya, O Jaya (victory), younger sister of the chief of cowherds (Krishna), delighting always in Mahisha's blood! O Uma, Sakambhari, thou white one, thou black one! O destroyer of Kaitabha! Of sciences, thou art the science of Brahma (or of the Vedas), the great sleep of embodied beings. O mother of Skanda (Kartikeya), divine Durga, dweller in wildernesses. Thou, great goddess, art praised with a pure heart. By thy favour let me ever be victorious in battle." In another verse of this same book she is said to dwell perpetually in the Vindhya hills, and "to delight in spirituous liquors, flesh, and sacrificial victims."

The statement that Durga was the younger sister of Krishna refers to the fact that it was she who took Krishna's place in Devaki's womb after Vasudeva had carried the infant Krishna to Nanda, and whom Kansa attempted to destroy by dashing her against a stone immediately after her birth. Krishna promised, if she would take his place as Devaki's child, she would be assimilated to him in glory, would obtain an eternal place in the sky, be installed by Indra amongst the gods, obtain a perpetual abode on the Vindhya mountains, where meditating upon him (Vishnu) she would kill two demons, Sumbha and Nisumbha, and would be worshipped.

Chief forms of Durga

Durga received Chanda and Munda, the messengers of the giants; they, struck with her beauty, spoke so rapturously of her to their lords that Sumbha sent her an offer of marriage by Sugriva.

Dasabhuja, the ten-handed, destroyed Sumbha's army under the commander-in-chief Dhumlochana. Of these troops only a few fugitives escaped to carry the news of their defeat to their master.

Singhavahini (riding on a lion) fought with Chanda and Manda, and has four arms only. She drank the blood of the leaders, and devoured a large part of their troops.

Mahishamardini (the slayer of Mahisha) slew Sumbha as he attacked her in the form of a buffalo. She had eight or, according to other accounts, ten arms. There is little to distinguish the account of this form from that of Durga.

Jagaddhatri (the mother of the world) destroyed another army of the giants; is dressed in red garments, and is seated on a lion. She, too, has four arms only, and is very similar to Singhavahini; the difference being in the weapons she wields. As Singhavahini, she carries a sword and spear, and with two hands is encouraging her worshippers; as Jagaddhatri, she carries a conch-shell, discus, bow and arrow. In all the above forms she is represented as fair, beautiful, gentle-looking.

Kali (the black woman), or, as she is more commonly called, Kali Ma, the black mother, with the aid of Chandi, slew Raktabija, the principal leader of the giant's army. Seeing his men fall, he attacked the goddess in person; when from every drop of blood that fell from his body a thousand giants equal in power to himself arose. At this crisis another form of the goddess, named Chandi, came to the rescue. As Kali drank the giant's blood and prevented the formation of new giants, Chandi slew the monster herself.

Kali is represented as a black woman with four arms ; in one hand she has a sword, in another the head of the giant she has slain, with the other two she is encouraging her worshippers. For earrings she has two dead bodies; wears a necklace of skulls; her only clothing is a girdle made of dead men's hands, and her tongue protrudes from her mouth. Her eyes are red as those of a drunkard, and her face and breasts are besmeared with blood. She stands with one foot on the thigh, and another on the breast of her husband. This position of Kali is accounted for by the fact that, when her victory over the giants was won, she danced for joy so furiously that the earth trembled beneath her weight. At the request of the gods Siva asked her to desist, but as, owing to her excitement, she did not notice him, he lay down amongst the slain. She continued dancing until she caught sight of her husband under her feet; immediately she thrust out her tongue with shame at the disrespect she had shown him.

In the *Adhyatma Ramayana* is a legend giving quite a different origin of Kali; the object of the writer evidently being to enhance the glory of Sita, by showing that Kali was but a form that she had assumed. On Rama's return from the destruction of Ravana, he was boasting of his prowess, when Sita smiled and said, "You rejoice because you have slain Ravana with ten heads, but what would you say to a Ravana with a thousand ?" "Destroy him too" said Rama. Sita advised him to remain at home; but he collected his army of monkeys, and with his wife and brothers set off for Satadwipa to meet this new Ravana. Hanuman was despatched to discover the residence of the monster, and to gather all the information he could about him, and on his return Rama went to the attack. The giant regarded the army of his assailant as so many children. He shot three arrows. One of these sent all the monkeys to their home at Kiskindha; a second drove the demons to Lanka; whilst the third despatched the soldiers to Ayodha, Rama's capital. Rama was thunderstruck as he found himself alone, and, imagining that all his forces were destroyed, began to weep. Sita, laughing at her husband, assumed the terrific form of Kali, and furiously attacked the thousand-headed Ravana. The conflict lasted ten years, but at length she slew the giant, drank his blood, and began to dance and toss about the limbs of his lifeless body. Her dancing shook the earth to its centre ; but not until Siva lay on the ground, and her attention was called to the disrespect she was showing him, could she be prevailed upon to desist. Thus Siva saved the universe; and Sita, assuming her proper form, went home with Rama and his brothers.

The *Skanda Purana* explains that Chandi, who came to the rescue and assisted Kali in the destruction of Raktabija, was a form of Devi, assumed on another occasion for the destruction of Chanda. It is interesting to see that these leaders of Sumbha's army reappear, although they were slain, and their blood was drunk by Singhavahini. Two asuras, named Chanda and Munda, through a boon received from the divine mothers, became so powerful as to subdue the three worlds. The gods besought Devi, who appeared to them under the form of Chandi, to deliver them; she replied, "that she could do nothing for them until she had propitiated Siva." To accomplish this she retired to a forest, and, whilst engaged in worship, Siva first appeared, under the form of a vast Linga, and then, in answer to Chandi's prayer, revealed himself, and in answer to her praises thus addressed her: "O goddess! Thou art celebrated in the three worlds as Parasakti (the energy of the supreme being). Wherever thou art, there am I; and wherever I am, there is Chandika. There is no difference between us. What shall I do for you?" Chandi replies: "Formerly 1 slew Chanda and Manda in battle; but they have been born again as mighty asuras, and have oppressed the three worlds.

It is therefore to be enabled to destroy them that I seek thy protection." Siva promises his help, and sends her in the guise of a messenger to challenge them to fight. They accept the challenge, and are slain by Siva.

The *Linga Purana* seems to teach that Kali, though produced by Durga, was yet distinct from her. Formerly a female asura named Daruka had through devotion obtained such power that she consumed like fire the gods and Brahmans. But as she was attended by a host of female asuras, Vishnu and the gods feared to attack her, lest they should be guilty of the great sin of slaying a woman. Siva is then appealed to, who, addressing Devi, said, " Let me request, O lovely one! that thou wouldst effect the destruction of this Daruka." Parvati, having heard these words, created from her own substance a maiden of black colour, with matted locks, having an eye in her forehead, bearing in her hand a trident and a skull; she was of aspect terrible to behold, was arrayed in celestial garments, and adorned with all kinds of ornaments. On beholding this terrific form of darkness, the gods retreated in alarm. Parvati then created innumerable ghosts, goblins, and demons; attended by these, Kali, in obedience to her order, attacked and destroyed Daruka.

Muktakesi (having flowing hair) destroyed another part of the *danava's* forces. In appearance there is little to distinguish her from Kali: she has four arms; holds a sword and a helmet in her left hands, and with her right she is bestowing a blessing and dispelling fear. She, too, is standing upon the body of her husband.

Tara (the saviour) slew Sumbha, and holds his head in one hand and a sword in another. Her appearance, too, is similar to that of Kali. She must not be confounded with Tara, the wife of Brihaspati; or Tara, the wife of Bali, the asura king.

Chinnamustaka (the beheaded) slew Nisumbha. It is evident from her appearance that she found her task rather difficult, for her head is half-severed from her body. She is painted as a fair woman, naked, and wearing a garland of skulls, standing upon the body of her husband.

Jagadgauri (the yellow woman [renowned] through the world) received the thanks and praises of the gods and men for the deliverance she wrought; in her four hands she holds a conch-shell, a discus, a club, and a lotus.

Images are made of Durga at different seasons of the year in nearly all of these forms, and various blessings are sought from her by her worshippers. In addition to these she is worshipped under other names; some of the more generally known will now be given.

It should be mentioned that the Hindus who worship Durga in any of her forms, and the other female deities, when they represent the Sakti, or energy of their husbands, are called Saktas. An exception, however, must be made in respect to Sarasvati, Lakshmi, and the autumnal worship of Durga; this particular form of worship being common to almost all.

Pratyangira (the well-proportioned one). Of this form of Durga no images are made, but at night the officiating priest, wearing red clothes, offers red flowers, liquors, and sacrifices.

Annapurna (she who fills with food) is represented as a fair woman, standing on a lotus, or as sitting on a throne. In one hand she holds a rice bowl, and in the other a spoon used for stirring rice when it is being boiled. It is in connection with this form of Durga that the *Linga Purana* gives a legend explaining an image called Ardhanarishwara, which represents Siva and Durga as together forming one body. Siva as a mendicant supported his wife and children by begging; but on one occasion, owing to his use of intoxicating herbs, he was unable to go his rounds. Durga told him there was nothing in the house to eat; half the previous day's contributions they had eaten; Ganesa's rat and Kartikeya's peacock having finished the rest. Siva then went out to beg, and Durga started for her father's house with the children, but was met by Narada, who advised her, as Annapurna, to lay an embargo on the food of the houses where Siva asked for alms. The result was no one would give him anything. Narada meeting him advised him to go home; Annapurna met him at the door, and so pleased him by giving him food, that he pressed her to his breast with such force that they became one body.

Ganesajanani (the mother of Ganesa) is worshipped with her infant in her arms.

Krishnakrora (she who holds Krishna on her breast). When Krishna fought with the serpent Kaliya in the river Yamuna, he was bitten, and in pain called upon Durga for help. She heard his cry, and, by suckling him from her breast, restored him to health.

10

GODDESSES AS SAKTI

The Saktis

Although a full account of the three chief goddesses, Sarasvati, Lakshmi, and Parvati, has already been given, there still remains something to be said in order to indicate the position they occupy in the Pantheon. By far the greater part of the Hindus in Bengal, and a considerable number elsewhere, devote their chief, almost their exclusive worship to the wives of the gods rather than to their husbands; and by these people they are declared to be the source and support of all things. Of the three, Parvati, is by far the most popular. Comparatively few assign to the other two a similarly exalted position.

All the Hindus acknowledge the consorts of the gods in a general way, and on the days commonly devoted to their worship are careful to present the customary offerings. But the sects now under consideration are not content with this. As the goddesses fill their field of vision, their husbands are almost entirely neglected. Originally the term Sakti signified the energy, or power of a deity. In process of time this energy was supposed to dwell in the wife, and as a result the devotion of the worshippers was transferred to her. And for many centuries a special name has been given to those who pay their supreme worship to the energy of the gods that are, so to speak, incarnated in their wives. These are known as Saktas, just as those who make Siva their chief object of adoration are Saivites; or those who regard Vishnu as the supreme are Vaishnavas.

There is a respectable and recognized cult of Sakti worship, known as the right-handed; and there is one that is quite the opposite, known as the left-handed. The rites and ceremonies in the one case are openly performed, and do not greatly differ from those in common with other Hindu sects. But amongst the left-handed sects the greatest care is taken to keep secret, from the uninitiated, the doctrines and practices that regulate and form their worship. The goddesses, and especially Devi, or Durga, the wife of Siva, are the supreme objects of worship amongst the Saktas; and they are worshipped as the incarnation of the energy or force of their divine husbands. The authority for this form of Hinduism are the Tantras, not the Puranas. As in the case of the more modern deities an attempt is made to identify them with the older, so expressions in the more ancient books are caught up and explained in such a way as to make it apear that the Tantric teaching is in harmony with, or a legitimate development of them.

The description of Goddesses as such follows :

Lakshmi

The goddess Sri, who is also commonly known by the name Lakshmi, has been known in the Hindu tradition since pre-Buddhist times. She is one of the most popular goddesses in the Hindu pantheon. She has a considerable body of mythology and is widely worshipped by Hindus of all castes throughout India to this day. Since the late epic period she has been particularly associated with the god Vishnu as his wife or consort. In this role she plays the part of a model Hindu wife, obediently serving her husband as lord. Throughout her history Sri has been associated with prosperity, well-being, royal power, and illustriousness. In many respects she is the embodiment of these qualities, and it is commonly understood that when these qualities are evident, Sri herself is present of reveals herself.

The most detailed picture of Lakshmi in Vedic literature is found in the *Sri-sukta*, a hymn in praise of Sri which is part of an appendix to the *Rig-veda* and which is probably pre-Buddhist in date. This is surely one of the earliest hymns to Sri and associates her with certain symbols and qualities that persist throughout her history in the Hindu tradition.

The hymn to Sri also mentions two objects that come to be consistently associated with Sri throughout her history: the lotus and the elephant. She is seated on a lotus, is the color of a lotus, appears like a lotus, is covered with lotuses, and wears a garland of lotuses. Throughout her history, in fact, Sri (Lakshmi) is often called Padma and Kamala, "lotus."

As expressive of Lakshmi's nature two general meanings seem apparent. First, the lotus is a symbol of fertility and life which is rooted in and takes its strength from the primordial waters. The lotus growing from the navel of Vishnu marks the beginning of a new cosmic creation. The lotus suggests a growing, expanding world imbued with vigorous fertile power. It is this power that is revealed in Laksmi. She is the nectar (the *rasa*) of creation which lends to creation its distinctive flavor and beauty.

The second meaning of the lotus in relation to Lakshmi refers to purity and spiritual power. Rooted in the mud but blossoming above the water, completely uncontaminated by the mud, the lotus represents spiritual perfection and authority. A common motif in Hindu and Buddhist iconography is the lotus seat. The gods and goddesses, the budhas and bodhisattvas, typically sit or stand upon a lotus, which suggests their spiritual authority to be seated upon or to be otherwise associated with the lotus suggests that the being in question—god, budha, or human being—has transcended the limitations of the finite world (the mud of existence, as it were) and floats freely in a sphere of purity and spirituality.

One of the most popular and enduring representations of Sri-Laksmi shows her flanked by two elephants in the so-called Gaja-Lakshmi images. The elephants shower her with water from their trunks or empty pots of water over her. The elephants seem to have two related meanings. First, they most likely represent fertilizing rains. An ancient Hindu tradition says that the first elephants had wings and flew about the sky. In fact, they were clouds and showered the earth with rain wherever they went. These sky elephants, however, were cursed by a sage when they landed on a three under which he was meditating and broke his concentration. Stripped of their wings, they henceforth had to remain earth-bound. But these earth elephants are still regarded as cousins of clouds, and their presence is supposed to attract their "white cousins," who bring fertilizing rains with them.

Second, elephants suggest royal authority. Kings in ancient India kept stables of elephants, which formed their heavy artillery in military campaigns. Kings often traveled on elephants in ceremonial processions, and in general elephants were considered an important indication of royal authority.

An ancient Indian tradition asserts that creation proceeds from an infinite body of primordial water, that the world or the multitude of universes of later Hinduism ultimately arises from and rests upon this limitless expanse of waters. In its unrefined state this watery world is chaotic, or at least formless and overwhelming. Creation, or ordered existence, only takes place when this watery mass is somehow agitated, processed, or refined in such a way that form and growth take place. Within the watery formlessness resides the potency or essence of life, *rasa, amrta,* or *soma*. When this potency is released by the primordial waters, creation can proceed.

The role or place Lakshmi in this myth of creation seems fairly clear. Although the nectar of immortality is described as a separate entity that arises from the churning of the ocean, Lakshmi has many and obvious associations with the sap of existence that underlies or pervades all plant and animal life. She herself represents the miraculous transformation of the formless waters into organic life.

Most variants of the myth say that Lakshmi's association with Vishnu took place at the churning of the ocean. The relationship of Lakshmi and Vishnu seems appropriate in the context of the myth and at a general symbolic level in several ways. During her early history Sri's attraction to powerful rulers among the gods (and demons) was firmly established. In the churning-of-the-ocean myth Vishnu is clearly the dominant god. He oversees the entire operation and actually makes the churning possible by providing two indispensable participants: Vasuki, the cosmic serpent who is used as the churning rope, and the cosmic tortoise, upon which the churning stick rests. Furthermore, both Vasuki and the tortoise are actually forms of Vishnu himself. When Sri comes forth from the ocean, she is naturally attracted to Vishnu, the god who is obviously superior to the others. Conversely, Vishnu, as the divine overseer of the event, is the natural recipient of the treasures that result from the churning. As the master of ceremonies, Vishnu is entitled to the lovely goddess who emerges as a result of the efforts of the gods and demons.

As the great cosmic king's queen she is depicted as a model Hindu wife, loyal and submissive to her husband. One of her most popular iconographic depictions shows her kneeling before Vishnu to massage his feet. When Vishnu assumes his various *avataras* in order to uphold dharma, she incarnates herself as his helpmate, assuming an appropriate form as his spouse or consort. She thus assists and accompanies him in his world-maintaining role. The *Vishnu Purana* says:

"... as Hari descends in the world in various shapes—so does his consort Sri. Thus when Hari was born as a dwarf, as a son of Aditi, Lakshmi appeared from a lotus; ... when he was Raghava, she was Sita, and when he was Krisna, she became Rukmini. In the other descents of Vishnu, she is his associate. If he takes a celestial form, she appears as divine; if a mortal, she becomes a mortal too, transforming her own person agreably to whatever character it pleases Vishnu to put on."

Reflecting her increasing association with social order, several texts locate Lakshmi's presence in righteous behavior, orderly conduct, and correct social observance. She is said, for example, to live with those who tell the truth and are generous. She dwells with those who have clean bodies and are well dressed who eat with moderation, who have intercourse with their wives on a regular basis (something prescribed in the Hindu law books), and who cover themselves when asleep. In the *Mahabharata* she says: "I dwell in truth, gift, vow, austerity, strength and virtue."

The Worship of Lakshmi

Lakshmi is today one of the most popular and widely venerated deities of the Hindu pantheon. Her auspicious nature and her reputation for granting fertility, luck, wealth, and well-being seem to attract devotees in every Indian village. All of India's back country is the dominion of Lakshmi, the goddess of the lotus. Her likenesses are omnipresent on the walls and pillars, lintels and niches of sanctuaries, regardless of the deity of their specific dedication.

The most important festival in which Lakshmi is worshipped today (except in Bengal) is Dipavali (Divali), which is held in the late autumn. Three important and interrelated themes are seen in this festival: Lakhsmi's association with wealth and prosperity, her association with fertility and abundant crops, and her association with good fortune in the coming year. Perhaps the most obvious indication that Lakshmi is identified with prosperity is her popularity among merchants. During this festival it is customary for people, especially businessmen, to worship their account books. It seems to be clearly understood by merchants that wealth will not arise without Lakshmi's blessing or presence.

Parvati

Rivaling Lakshmi in popularity in the Hindu tradition is the goddess Parvati. Unlike Lakshmi, Parvati has hardly any independent history of her own. Her identity and nature and nearly all her nythological deeds are defined or acted out vis-a-vis her consort/husband, the great ascetic god Siva. Since epic times, when Parvati first appeared as a significant deity, she has been identified as a reincarnation of the goddess Sati, Siva's first wife, who committed suicide because of an insult to her husband.

So closely associated is Parvati with Sati that the two goddesses are usually treated as one, and their mythologies eventually come to sound very much alike. Both are defined in terms of their courtship and marriage with Siva, and Parvati's mythology is almost always treated as the ongoing story of Sati.

In classical Hindu mythology the raison detre of Parvati's (and Sati's) birth is to lure Siva into marriage and thus into the wider circle of worldly life from which he is aloof as a lone ascetic living in the mountains. This goddess (in both persons, as Sati and Parvati) represents the complementary pole to the ascetic, world-denying pole in the Hindu tradition. In her role as maiden, wife, and later mother (as Parvati) she extends Siva's circle of activity into the realm of the householder.

As is the case with Lakshmi, Parvati comes to represent certain philosophic absolutes in her association with Siva. As his *sakti*, or embodied power, she becomes identified with the creative force of the cosmos and the underlying potency of things. In some schools of Saivism Parvati also assumes the role of ideal devotee.

In general terms the underlying theme or meaning of this myth seems fairly clear. The theme of Siva's alternation between the poles of asceticism and eroticism and the creative (sometimes destructive) tension that results from this alternation pervades the entire corpus of Siva mythology. Underlying the mythology seems to be the assumption that Siva's stored-up potency, which accumulates during asceticism, should be released into the world to invigorate or enliven creation. In the logic of this mythology Sati plays the role of luring Siva from ascetic isolation into creative participation in the world. This theme is further developed and embellished in the Parvati cycle of myths in which Siva actually becomes involved in an ongoing family situation and becomes a divine householder.

Sati's devotion to Siva and her outrage at the way he is treated eventually bring him within the sacrificial arena. He is indifferent to the doings of Daksa until Sati kills herself because of the insult to her husband. Sati comes from the realm of established religion, the order of *dharma,* and marries into the realm of asceticism, thus combining in herself the two opposing worlds. When she kills herself she precipitates a clash between these two worlds, between Daksa and Siva, which is initially destructive but ultimately beneficial and creative. Satis's role is as a mediating influence between the two religious poles, both affirmed to be central, in the Hindu tradition. Her ability to involve Siva in the sacrifice makes Siva, previously aloof from the world, accessible in the sacrificial cult, the primary point of which is to maintain and nourish the creation.

Sati performs a similar feat when her body is cut to pieces and falls to earth. By following her to earth and embedding himself in her yoni, Siva is literally brought down to earth.Where previously he dwelled in the mountains and engaged in austerities, indifferent to the ongoing creation, he now is fully engaged in the creation as symbolized by the conjunction of the yoni and linga. Sati, in her role as mediator, has succeeded in involving the great ascetic god in the creation. Again, her role has been primarily that of making Siva accessible to the world. While Siva may continue to perform heroic asceticism in his mountain retreat in one of his several forms, he continues to be accessible to the world in the form of the linga.

The establishment of centers of worship on earth where pieces of Sati's body fell repeats the theme of making the divine accessible vis-a-vis Sati herself. In this myth the earth is sacralized (the earth being understood primarily as the Indian subcontinent). The earth itself is seen as the body of the goddess Sati. She becomes the earth and as such is made accessible to her devotees or to those who seek her powers.

Sati's death is thus transformative. Through her death she provokes Siva into a direct conflict with the sacrificial cult and then an accommodation with it. In this way Siva is brought within the circle of *dharma,* within the order of established religion. Similarly, Sati's corpse, or pieces of her corpse, sacralize the earth. In dying she gives herself up to be accessible on earth to those who need her power or blessing. In transplanting or transforming herself into the earth, she also brings into the sphere of human society the invigorating power of Siva in the form of the linga.

Mythology of Parvati

Parvati's name, which means "she who dwells in the mountains" or "she who is of the mountain," and her many epithets, such as Sailasuta (daughter of the mountain peaks), Giriputri (daughter of the mountains), Girirajaputri (daughter of the king of the mountains), Girisa (mistress of the mountains), identify her with mountainous regions. It is quite possible that Parvati's early history and origin may lie with a goddess who dwelled in the mountains. Such a goddess would be an appropriate mate for Siva, himself a deity who dwells in mountainous regions and on the fringes of society. Indeed, Parvati herself is described as a female forester in the company of Siva, who is also described as a forester in the *Mahabharata.*

Parvati's mythology is almost entirely dominated by her association with Siva. Her nature, too, develops or is characterized by her relationship with Siva. Although in certain Sakta texts she is said to transcend Siva and to subsume within herself all male deities or in other texts is identified with certain philosophic absolutes, for the most part these are late embellishments on her mythology and character and are the result of a theological effort on the part of devotees partial to various goddesses (the Saktas) to assert the underlying unity of all goddess Parvati is primarily the goddess who is Siva's wife, she who won him as her husband after heroic efforts and who persuaded or provoked him into creating a child, who was necessary for the preservation of the world.

Most renditions of Parvati's mythology explain the goddess's birth as necessary for producing a child of Siva. The demon Taraka has been granted the boon of being invincible to any creature except a child of Siva. As Siva is an ascetic, the gods have to find a woman or goddess capable of luring Siva into marriage. Parvati is usually understood to be a reincarnation of Sati and sometimes is described as consenting to be reborn for the help of the gods when she is petitioned by them. In some versions Parvati (and Sati) are understood to be manifestations of the supreme reality in the universe, the Mahadevi (great goddess), who condescends to incarnate herself for much the same reason that Vishnu does in his *avataras*, to maintain the balance between *dharma* and *adharma*.

Parvati, then, is born to Himavat and Mena. She is usually described as dark and in some versions is given the name Kali, "the dark one," because of her complexion. She is also described as very beautiful. She shows a keen interest in Siva from the outset, repeating his name to herself and taking delight in hearing about his appearance and deeds. While she is a child a sage comes to her home and after examining the marks on her body predicts that she will marry a naked yogi.

Parvati persists in her quest to win Siva as her husband by setting out to perform austerities. One of the most effective ways to achieve what a person wants in traditional Hinduism is to perform *tapas,* "ascetic austerities." If one is persistent and heroic enough, one will generate so much heat (also called *tapas*) that the gods will be forced to grant the ascetic a wish in order to save themselves and the world from being scorched. Parvati's method of winning Siva is thus a common approach to fulfilling one's desires. It is also appropriate, however, in terms of demonstrating to Siva that she can compete with him in his own realm, that she has the inner resources, control, and fortitude to cut herself off from the world and completely master her physical needs. By performing *tapas* Parvati abandons the world of the householder and enters the realm of the world renouncer, Siva's world. Most versions of the myth describe her as outdoing all the great sages in her austerities.

In some versions of the myth Parvati is tempted by an agent of Siva, or by Siva himself in disguise. She is told that Siva's appearance is terrible and that his habits are uncivilized and inauspicious. She is urged to desist from her desire to marry such a distasteful character. Parvati is never dissuaded from her purpose by these temptations, and as a result of her steadfastness Siva agrees to marry her.

After the two are married they depart to Mount Kailasa, Siva's favorite dwelling place, and immerse themselves completely in sexual dalliance, which continues uninterruptedly for long periods of time. Their lovemaking is so intense that it shakes the cosmos, and the gods become frightened. They fear the child's extraordinary powers. The gods interrupt Siva and Parvati's lovemaking. As a result Siva spills his semen outside Parvati. The potent seed, which is extremely fiery and hot, passes from one container to another, until it is finally contained in a suitable place, often the Ganges River, where it is incubated and born as the child Karttikeya. Karttikeya eventually finds his way back to his father and mother and by defeating the demon Taraka rescues the world.

A second child completes the divine family of Siva and Parvati when Ganesa is born. Parvati, desiring privacy, wishes to have a child of her own who will protect her from unwanted intrusions. She creates Ganesa from the dirt and sweat of her body and commands him to guard the entrance to her house against any intruder. When Siva himself tries to enter her apartments, Ganesa refuses to admit him. Siva becomes angry and decapitates the boy. Parvati is furious and demands that Ganesa be restored to life. Siva duly restores him to life by replacing his human head with an elephant head and puts him in charge of all his troops and heavenly attendants.

The main theme of the Parvati cycle of myths is clear. The association between Parvati and Siva represents the perennial tension in Hinduism between the ascetic ideal and the householder ideal. Parvati, for the most part, represents the householder. Her mission in almost all renditions of the myth is to lure Siva into the world of marriage, sex, and children, to tempt him away from asceticism, yoga, and otherworldly preoccupations. In this role Parvati is cast as a figure who upholds the order of *dharma*, who enhances life in the world, who represents the beauty and attraction of worldly, sexual life, who cherishes the house and society rather than the forest, the mountains, or the ascetic life. In this role she repeats the feat of Sati in luring Siva into an erotic relationship, which this time eventually brings him within the sacrificial, priestly order permanently. Parvati civilizes Siva with her presence; indeed, she domesticates him.

The tension between Parvati and Siva as representatives of the main types of religiosity in Hinduism is stated in various ways in the myths. Siva is always said to have no family, no lineage, and no interest in progeny, which is one of the central concerns of the order of *dharma* and the householder's religion. Parvati, on the contrary, is born into an established family and longs for marriage, children, and a home. Siva is associated with fire, which dries up or burns up the juices of life.In one of the most famous of his myths he burns the god of lust to ashes with the fire from his middle eye. Parvati is associated with Soma, the deity or substance associated with the life essence of all plants. In the most general terms, Siva as Agni is the fire that destroys the world at the end of each cosmic age. Parvati as Soma, in contrast, is the cosmic waters from which the world is inevitably reborn.

Throughout Hindu mythology it is well known that one of Siva's principal functions is the destruction of the cosmos. In fact, Siva has about him a wild, unpredictable, destructive aspect that is often mentioned. As the great cosmic dancer he periodically performs the *tandava*, an especially violent dance. Wielding a broken battle-ax, he dances so wildly that the cosmos is destroyed completely. In descriptions of this dance Siva's whirling arms and flying locks are said to crash into the heavenly bodies, knocking them off course or destroying them utterly. The mountains shake and the oceans heave as the world is destroyed by his violent dancing. Parvati, in contrast, is portrayed as a patient builder, one who follows Siva about, trying to soften the violent effects of her husband. She is a great force for preservation and reconstruction in the world and as such offsets the violence of Siva.

Parvati's goal in her relationship with Siva is nothing less than the domestication of the lone, ascetic god whose behavior borders on madness. Siva is indifferent to social propriety, does not care about offspring, declares women to be a hindrance to the spiritual life, and is disdainful of the trappings of the householder's life. Parvati tries to involve him in the worldly life of the householder by arguing that he should observe conventions if he loves her and wants her. She persuades him, for example, to marry her according to the proper rituals, to observe custom, instead of simply running off with her. She is less successful, however, in getting him to change his attire and ascetic habits.

The theme of the conflict, tension, or opposition between the way of the ascetic and the way of the householder in the mythology of Parvati and Siva yields to a vision of reconciliation, interdependence, and symbiotic harmony in a series of images that combine the two deities. Three such images or themes are central to the mythology, iconography, and philosophy of Parvati: (1) the theme of Siva-*sakti*, (2) the image of Siva as Ardhanarisvara (the Lord who is half woman), and (3) the image of the linga and yoni.

The idea that the great male gods all possess an inherent power by which or through which they undertake creative activity is assumed in Hindu mythology. When this power, or *sakti*, is personified it is always in the form of a goddess. Parvati, quite naturally, assumes the identity of Siva's *sakti* in many myths and in some philosophic systems. In the role of Siva's *sakti*, Parvati performs functions, or assumes meanings, which imply an underlying harmony or interdependent relationship between herself and Siva. She is often identified with the force underlying and impelling creation. While Siva remains more or less aloof in the creation of the world, Parvati as *sakti* is active, pervading the creation as its underlying strength and power understood that Parvati either must be set in motion by Siva or must act according to his will, wish, or design. Through Parvati, Siva (the Absolute) is able to express himself in the creation. Without her he would remain inert, aloof, inactive. Just as in the mythology Parvati is necessary for involving Siva in creation, so as his *sakti* she is necessary for his self-expression in creation. It is only in association with her that Siva is able to realize or manifest his full potential. Without Parvati Siva's great power does not, or cannot, manifest itself in creation. Parvati as *sakti* not only complements Siva, she completes him.

The meaning of the Ardhanarisvara form of Siva is similar. The image shows a half-male, half-female figure. The right side is Siva and is adorned with his ornaments; the left side is Parvati and adorned with her ornaments. In the *Siva-purana* the god Brahma is unable to continue his task of creation because the creatures that he has produced do not multiply. He propitiates Siva and requests him to come to his aid. Siva then appears in his half-male, half-female form. The hermaphrodite form splits into Siva and Parvati, and Parvati, at Brahma's request, pervades the creation with her female nature, which duly awakens the male aspect of creation into fertile activity. To an even greater extent than the Siva-*sakti* idea, image of Siva and Parvati emphasizes that the two deities are absolutely necessary to each other, and only in union can they fulfill themselves. In this form, God is both male and female, both father and mother, both aloof and active, both fearsome and gentle, both destructive and constructive, and so on.

Another important facet of Parvati is her role as a model of devotion to Siva, as the devotee of the Lord *par excellence*. At several points in her mythology Parvati is described as devoted to Siva, as unswerving in her attachment to him, and as incapable of being dissuaded from doting on him despite the most outrageous reports concerning his uncivilized, bizarre habits. Her remarkably steadfast, indeed, stubborn, devotion to him is most obvious during her long period of asceticism when she undertakes heroic bodily mortifications in order either to be granted the boon of having Siva for her husband or to attract the attention of Siva himself. In these scenes Parvati is portrayed as a devotee who seeks Siva's attention and blessing.

Another facet of Parvati is evident in Tamil Saivism. Parvati tends to have a calming, civilizing effect on Siva. Under her influence or in her presence, Siva is often tamed, distracted from his wild, rude, mad behaviour. In her presence, it seems, such behavior is inappropriate, and Siva almost always behaves in properly domestic ways when she is present. Becalmed, Siva is more attentive to the needs of his devotees (and to the needs and desires of his spouse) and more prone to grant them blessings.

Saraswati

Sarasvati is one of the few important goddesses in the *Vedas* who remain significant in later Hinduism. In the *Vedas* her character and attributes are clearly associated with the mighty Sarasvati River. She is the earliest example of a goddess who is associated with a river in the Indian tradition. As a river goddess she is praised for her ability both to cleanse and to fertilize. Later Vedic literature (the *Brahmanas)* consistently associates her, even equates her, with the goddess of speech, *Vak*. Increasingly in her later history her association with a river is deemphasized and her association with speech, poetry, music, and culture in general is affirmed. In classical and medieval Hinduism Sarasvati is primarily a goddess of poetic inspiration and learning. She becomes associated with the creator god Brahma and in this role she is creative sound, which lends to reality a peculiar and distinctive human dimension. She becomes identified with the dimension of reality that is best described as coherent intelligibility. Sarasvati to this day is worshipped throughout India and on her special day is worshipped by school children as the patron goddess of learning.

As early as the *Brahmanas* Sarasvati is consistently identified with Vagdevi, the goddess of speech. It is not at all clear what intrinsic connection between Sarasvati and Vagdevi led to this association. Perhaps the centrality of sacred speech in Vedic cult and the importance of Vedic rituals being performed on the banks of the Sarasvati River led to the identification of the two goddesses. In any case, Sarasvati increasingly becomes a goddess associated with speech, learning, culture, and wisdom; most post-Vedic references to her do not even hint that at one time she was identified with a river.

Far more characteristic of the later Sarasvatl is her association with speech. Even in the *Rig-veda* she is called impeller of true and sweet speech and awakener of happy and noble thoughts. Such epithets as Vagdevi (goddess of speech), Jihvagravasini (dwelling in the front of the tongue), Kavijihvagravasini (she who dwells on the tongues of poets), Sabdavasini (she who dwells in sound), Vagisa (mistress of speech), and Mahavani (possessing great speech) are often used for Sarasvati. Her mythological identification with the tongues of Brahma, Krishna, and Vishnu also underlines her identification with speech or creative sound.

The importance of speech in Hinduism is both ancient and central. The entire creative process is held to be distilled in the syllable *om*, and the idea of creation proceeding from *sabda-brahman* (ultimate reality in the form of sound) is often mentioned in Hindu texts. The potency of speech and sound is also seen in the centrality of *mantras* in Hinduism. A *mantra,* which may consist of words or of sounds alone, is held to possess great power. There resides in sound a potent quality, and this quality is embodied in the goddess Sarasvati.

Sarasvati is also identified with thought and intellect. Not only is she speech in the form of coherent sound, she is that which underlies or makes speech possible, namely, intelligence and thought. This association is indicated in such epithets for her as Smrtisakti (the power of memory), Jnanasakti (the power of knowledge), Buddhisaktisvarupini (whose form is the power of intellect), Kalpanasakti (who is the power of forming ideas), and Pratibha (intelligence, or she who is intelligence).

Sarasvati's association with science, learning, and knowledge further reinforces her nature as the goddess of speech and thought. She is called, for example, Vedagarbha (the womb or source of the Vedas, or knowledge), Sarvavidyasvarupini (whose form is all the sciences), Sarvasastravasini (who dwells in all books), Granthakarini (who causes books to be made), and many other such names. As mind, intellect, and thought, she inspires the arts and sciences. She is also the accumulated products of human thought. She is the sum of the human intellectual tradition as preserved in the sciences.

Sarasvati is also said to underlie, inspire, or embody the arts. She is said to provide inspiration to poets and to be present wherever artistic excellence is evident. Poets often praise her assistance or ask for her help. She is said to be associated with the Gandharvas, a supernatural race that excels at dancing, and she is often associated with music, both instrumental and vocal. In short, Sarasvati is manifest wherever human culture exists. Inspiring and embodying both the arts and sciences in human culture, she represents the greatness of human civilization in all its richness and diversity.

The predominant themes in Sarasvati's appearance are purity and transcendence. She is almost always said to be pure white like snow, the moon, or the *kunda* flower or to shine brilliantly and whitely like innumerable moons. Her garments are said to be fiery in their purity, or they are described as white and she is sometimes said to be smeared with sandalwood paste. Sarasvati's gleaming white body and garments express well her purity and transcendence, and these themes are in keeping with her typical association with the *sattva guna,* the pure, spiritual thread of *prakrti.*

Sarasvati's transcendent nature, which removes her from the impurities of the natural world and its rhythms of growth and fertility, is also suggested in her vehicle, the swan. The swan is a symbol of spiritual transcendence and perfection in Hinduism. Spiritual masters and heroes are sometimes called supreme swans *(paramahamsa)* in that they have completely transcended the limitations and imperfections of the phenomenal world.

Sarasvati is also typically shown seated on a lotus. Like the swan, the lotus seat of the goddess suggests her transcendence of the physical world. She floats above the muddy imperfections of the physical world, unsullied, pure, beautiful. Although rooted in the mud (like man rooted in the physical world), the lotus perfects itself is a blossom that has transcended the mud. Sarasvati inspires people to live in such a way that they may transcend their physical limitations through the ongoing creation of culture.

The benefits to be derived from the worship of Sarasvati, of the blessings that she is expected to bestow on her devotees, usually relate to the themes that we have noted as central to her character. She gives eloquence, wisdom, poetic inspiration, and artistic skill. She removes speech defects and dumbness and grants charming speech and a musical voice. Although she is sometimes said to grant wealth, long life, worldly enjoyments, and final salvation, she is primarily the goddess of wisdom and learning and specializes in promoting success among philosophers, scholars, and artists, who are her special devotees.

Throughout North India today Sarasvati's special *puja* is celebrated in early spring. On this day images of the goddess are established in schools and universities, and special cultural programs take place. This is also the day when books, pens, musical instruments, and gurus are formally worshiped.

Durga

One of the most impressive and formidable goddesses of the Hindu pantheon—and one of the most popular—is the goddess Durga. Her primary mythological function is to combat demons who threaten the stability of the cosmos. In this role she is depicted as a great battle queen with many arms, each of which wields a weapon. She rides a fierce lion and is described as irresistible in battle. The demon she is most famous for defeating is Mahisa, the buffalo demon. Her most popular epithet is Mahisa-mardini, the slayer of Mahisa, and her most common iconographic representation shows her defeating Mahisa.

At a certain point in her history Durga becomes associated with the god Siva as his wife, in this role Durga assumes domestic characteristics and is often identified with the goddess Parvati. She also takes on the role of mother in her later history. At her most important festival, Durga Puja, she is shown flanked by four deities identified as her children: Karttikeya, Ganesa, Sarasvati, and Lakshmi.

Around the fourth century A.D. images of Durga slaying a buffalo begin to become common throughout India. By the medieval period (after the sixth century) Durga has become a well-known and popularly worshiped deity. Her mythological deeds come to be told in many texts, and descriptions of and injunctions to undertake her autumnal worship are common in several late *Upa-puranas*.

Hindu mythology includes several accounts of Durga's origin. She is sometimes said to arise from Vishnu as the power that makes him sleep or as his magical, creative power. In the *Devi-mahatmya* she comes to the aid of the god Brahma and ultimately of Vishnu himself when Brahma invokes her to leave the slumbering Vishnu so that Vishnu will awaken and fight the demons Madhu and Kaitabha. The *Skanda-purana* relates that once upon a time a demon named Durga threatened the world. Siva requested Parvati to slay the demon. Parvati then assumed the form of a warrior goddess and defeated the demon, who took the form of a buffalo. Thereafter, Parvati was known by the name Durga. A similar account of her origin occurs in myths relating her defeat of the demons Sumbha and Nisumbha. Durga emerges from Parvati in these accounts when Parvati sheds her outer sheath, which takes on an identity of its own as a warrior goddess.

The best-known account of Durga's origin, however, is told in connection with her defeat of the demon Mahisa. After performing heroic austerities, Mahisa was granted the boon that he would be invincible to all opponents except a woman. He subsequently defeated the gods in battle and usurped their positions. The gods then assembled and, angry at the thought of Mahisa's triumph and their apparent inability to do anything about it, emitted their fiery energies. This great mass of light and strength congealed into the body of a beautiful woman, whose splendour spread through the universe. The parts of her body were formed from the male gods.

The creation of the goddess Durga thus takes place in the context of a cosmic crisis precipitated by a demon whom the male gods are unable to subdue. She is created because the situation calls for a woman, a superior warrior, a peculiar power possessed by the goddess with which the demon may be deluded, or a combination of all three. Invariably

Durga defeats the demon handily, demonstrating both superior martial ability and superior power. On the battlefield she often creates female helpers from herself. The most famous of these are the goddess Kali and a group of ferocious deities known as the Matrikas (mothers), who usually number seven.

Durga's distinctive nature, and to a great extent probably her appeal, comes from the combination of world-supportive qualities and characteristics that associate her with the periphery of civilized order. In many respects Durga violates the model of the Hindu woman. She is not submissive, she is not subordinated to a male deity, she does not fulfill household duties, and she excels at what is traditionally a male function, fighting in battle. As an independent warrior who can hold her own against any male on the battlefield, she reverses the normal role for females and therefore stands outside normal society. Unlike the normal female, Durga does not lend her power or *sakti* to a male consort but rather *takes* power from the male gods in order to perform her own heroic exploits. They give up their inner strength, fire, and heat to create her and in so doing surrender their potency to her.

Because Durga is unprotected by a male deity, Mahisa assumes that she is helpless, which is the way that women are portrayed in the *Dharma-sastras.* There women are said to be incapable of handling their own affairs and to be socially inconsequential without relationships with men. They are significant primarily as sisters, daughters, and mothers of males and as wives. Nearly all forms of Durga's mythical exploits portray her as independent from male support and relationships yet irresistibly powerful. She is beautiful and seductive in appearance, but her beauty does not serve its normal function, which is to attract a husband. It serves to entice her victims into fatal battle.

In short, this beautiful young woman who slays demons seeking to be her lovers and who exists independent from male protection or guidance represents a vision of the feminine that challenges the stereotyped view of women found in traditional Hindu law books.

Durga's nature is evident in her favorite habitats and in some of her favorite habits. Nearly all of Durga's myths associate her with mountains, usually the Himalayas or the Vindhyas. One of her common epithets is Vindhyavasini, "she who dwells in the Vindhya Mountains." These mountainous regions are areas considered geographically peripheral to civilized society and inaccessible except through heroic efforts.

Counterbalancing Durga's liminal, peripheral nature, which at times seems to threaten dharmic stability and to inhibit the spiritual quest for *moksa,* is her role as protectress of the cosmos. Dominating her mythology is her role as the destroyer of demons who have usurped the position of the gods. As a great warrior she is created by the gods and acts on their behalf. While she is often said to transcend the male gods who create her and to excel them on the battlefield, she acts for their welfare. In doing this she acts to maintain or restore cosmic harmony and balance.

The theology underlying Durga's appearances and exploits is clear in the *Devi-mahatmya,* the most famous text extolling her deeds. Durga is said to underlie or pervade the cosmos; to create, maintain, and periodically destroy it according to the rhythmic sequences of Hindu cosmology; and to assume different forms from time to time when cosmic balance is threatened by enemies of the lesser gods. The *Devi-mahatmya* puts the matter succinctly: "Though she is eternal, the goddess becomes manifest over and over again to protect the world".

The *Devi-mahatmya* itself relates three of Durga's cosmic interventions on behalf of the gods : the battle with Madhu and Kaitabha; the battle with Mahisa and his army; and the battle with Sumbha and Nisumbha and their generals, Canda, Munda, and Raktabija. The text also refers specifically to five other appearances of the goddess and implies that she is incarnate in many more forms. The myths that are told in detail in the *Devi-mahatmya* conform to a structure that underlines Durga's role as the upholder and protector of the dharmic order. Because the myths are cast in traditional structure, they also make the point that Durga transcends the great male gods of the Hindu pantheon, who in other texts usually have the central role in these myths.

The structure to which the demon-slaying myths of Durga conform is found throughout Hindu mythological texts. In basic outline the structure is as follows : (1) a demon gains great power through doing austerities, is granted a boon as a reward, and becomes nearly invincible; (2) the demon defeats the gods and takes over their positions; (3) the gods prepare their revenge by creating a special being who can defeat the demon despite the boon, or else the lesser gods petition one of the great deities (Siva, Vishnu, or a great goddess) to intervene on their behalf; (4) the battle takes place and often includes the creation of helpers by the hero or heroine; (5) the demon is defeated, either slain or made subservient to the gods; (6) the gods praise the demon slayer. In the Madhu and Kaitabha myth and the myth of Sumbha and Nisumbha, Durga is petitioned to help the gods, whereas in the Mahisa myth she is specially created by the gods. In the Mahisa and Sumbha and Nisumbha myths the goddess takes a direct, active part in the battle itself, demonstrating her superior martial skills against her opponents. In the Sumbha and Nisumbha myth she also creates helpers in the form of ferocious goddesses. In all three episodes the gods collectively praise Durga during the battle or after she has defeated the demons.

The theology underlying Durga's cosmic interventions and the structure of the demon-slaying myths conforms to well-known Hindu ideas and forms. The idea of a deity's descending to the world from time to time in various forms to maintain the balance of cosmic order is a central Vaishnavite idea. Ever since the time of the *Bhagavad-gita* the idea of Vishnu's descending to the world in different forms in order to combat disorder has been well known in the Hindu tradition. Durga, in the *Devi-mahatmya,* is heir to this *avatara* theology. In fact, in many ways Durga is a female version of Vishnu. She, like him, creates, maintains, and destroys the world; intervenes on a cosmic scale whenever disorder threatens to disrupt the world in the form of certain demons; and is approached by the other gods as their savior in times of distress.

At the end of the *Devi-mahatmya,* after being petitioned by two of her devotees (part of whose petition has included offering their own blood to the goddess), she appears before them and grants their desires. To one she returns his wealth and kingdom and to the other she grants ultimate liberation. Durga, then, is not just a powerful, transcendent force whose sole concern is maintaining the cosmic rhythms, who is moved to action only when the world itself is threatened. She is attentive to the needs of her devotees and intervenes on their behalf if asked to do so. She is a personal savior as well as a great battle queen who fights to defeat the enemies of the gods.

Durga's distinctive nature also has to do with her identification with certain important Hindu philosophic ideas. The *Devi-mahatmya* and other texts extolling Durga state that she is identical with or associated with *sakti, maya,* and *prakrti.* This is to say that in some way Durga represents a dramatic illustration of these ideas or that these ideas can be discerned in her nature. *Sakti* is almost always understood to be the underlying power of the divine, the aspect of the divine that permits and provokes creative activity. *Sakti,* furthermore, is almost always understood to be a positive force. When viewed in concrete form, *sakti* is usually personified as a goddess. A common belief is that without his *sakti,* without his female counterpart, a male deity is ineffective, weak, and immobilized.

Durga as a personification of *maya* is most clearly seen in the Madhu and Kaitabha episode, in which she deludes the demons so that Vishnu can slay them and in which she is repeatedly referred to as Mahamaya and as Vishnu's *maya. Maya* has negative connotations in Hindu philosophy and mythology, as does Durga, particularly in this episode. *Maya* is that which deludes individuals into thinking themselves to be the center of the world, the power that prevents individuals from seeing things as they really are. *Maya* is that which impels individuals into self-centered, egotistical actions. *Maya* is the sense of ego, personal identity, and individuality which clouds the underlying unity of reality and masks one's essential identity with *brahman* or some exalted being such as Vishnu, Siva, or Durga. *Maya,* however, may also be understood as a positive, creative force not unlike *sakti. Maya* may be understood as the power that enables a deity to display or embody himself or herself and therefore as the power that enables a deity to act.

Durga's association or identification with *sakti, maya,* and *prakrti* lends to the great demon-slaying goddess an immediate, tangible dimension. As an expression of these ideas she is identified with the creation itself. Her presence is affirmed to pervade and underlie the actual world in which people live, and her power and strength are affirmed to imbue all creatures with the will to prosper and multiply.

Kali

The goddess Kali is almost always described as having a terrible, frightening appearance. She is always black or dark, is usually naked, and has long, disheveled hair. She is adorned with severed arms as a girdle, freshly cut heads as a necklace, children's corpses as earrings, and serpents as bracelets. She has long, sharp fangs, is often depicted as having clawlike hands with long nails, and is often said to have blood smeared on her lips. Her favorite haunts heighten her fearsome nature. She is usually shown on the battlefield, where she is a furious combatant who gets drunk on the hot blood of her victims, or in a cremation ground, where she sits on a corpse surrounded by jackals and goblins.

Many texts and contexts treat Kali as an independent deity, unassociated with any male deity. When she is associated with a god, however, it is almost always Siva. As his consort, wife, or associate, Kali's association with Siva, unlike Parvati's, seems aimed at exciting him to take part in dangerous, destructive behaviour that threatens the stability of the cosmos.

Kali's most famous appearances in battle contexts are found in the *Devi-mahatmya.* In the third episode, which features Durga's defeat of Sumbha and Nisumbha and their allies, Kali appears twice. Early in the battle the demons Canda and Munda approach Durga with readied weapons. Seeing them prepared to attack her, Durga becomes angry, her face becoming dark as ink. Suddenly the goddess Kali springs from her forehead. She is black, wears a garland of human heads and a tiger skin, and wields a skull-topped staff. She is gaunt, with sunken eyes, gaping mouth, and lolling tongue. She roars loudly and leaps into the battle, where she tears demons apart with her hands and crushes them in her jaws. She grasps the two demon generals and in one furious blow decapitates them both with her sword. Later in the battle Kali is summoned by Durga to help defeat the demon Raktabija, This demon has the ability to reproduce himself instantly whenever a drop of his blood falls to the ground. Having wounded Raktabija with a variety of weapons, Durga finds they have worsened their situation. As Raktabija bleeds more and more profusely from his wounds, the battlefield increasingly becomes filled with Raktabija duplicates. Kali defeats the demon by sucking the blood from his body and throwing the countless duplicate Raktabija into her gaping mouth.

In these two episodes Kali appears to represent Durga's personified wrath, her embodied fury. Kali plays a similar role in her association with Parvati. In general, Parvati is a benign goddess, but from time to time she exhibits fierce aspects. When this occurs, Kali is sometimes described as being brought into being. In the *Linga-purana* Siva asks Parvati to destroy the demon Daruka, who has been given the boon that he an only be killed by a female. Parvati then enters Siva's body and transforms herself from the poison that is stored in Siva's throat. She reappears as Kali, ferocious in appearance, and attacks and defeats Daruka and his hosts. Kali, however, becomes so intoxicated by the blood lust of battle that she threatens to destroy the entire world in her fury. The world is saved when Siva intervenes and calms her.

The *Vamana-purana* calls Parvati Kali (the black one) because of her dark complexion. Hearing Siva use this name, Parvati takes offense and undertakes austerities in order to rid herself of her dark complexion. After succeeding, she is renamed Gauri (the golden one). Her dark sheath, however, is transformed into the furious battle queen Kausiki, who subsequently creates Kali in her fury. So again, although there is an intermediary goddess (Kausiki), Kali plays the role of Parvati's dark, negative, violent nature in embodied form.

Iconographic representations of Kali and Siva nearly always show Kali as dominant. She is usually standing or dancing on Siva's prone body, and when the two are depicted in sexual intercourse, she is shown above him. It seems clear that she was never finally subdued by Siva and is most popularly represented as a being who is uncontrollable and more apt to provoke Siva to dangerous activity than to be controlled by him.

In general, then, we may say that Kali is a goddess who threatens stability and order. Although she may be said to serve order in her role as slayer of demons, more often than not she becomes so frenzied on the battlefield, usually becoming drunk on the blood of her victims, that she herself begins to destroy the world that she is supposed to protect. In relation to Siva, she appears to play the opposite role from that of Parvati. Parvati calms Siva, counterbalancing his antisocial or destructive tendencies. It is she who brings Siva within the sphere of domesticity and who, with her soft glances, urges him to moderate the destructive aspects of his *tandava* dance.

Kali attains a central position in late medieval Bengali devotional literature. In this devotion Kali's appearance and habits have not changed very much. She remains terrifying in appearance and fearsome in habit. She is eminently recognizable.

The approach of the devotee to Kali, however, is quite different in mood and temperament from the approach of the Tantric *sadhaka.* The Tantric adept, seeking to view Kali in her most terrible aspect, is heroic in approach, cultivating an almost aggressive, fearless stance before her. The Tantric adept challenges Kali to unveil her most forbidding secrets. The devotee, in contrast, adopts the position of the helpless child when approaching Kali. Even though the child's mother may be fearsome, at times even hostile, the child has little choice but to return to her for protection, security and warmth.

An analysis of the significance of Kali to the Hindu tradition reveals certain constants in her mythology and imagery. She is almost always associated with blood and death, and it is difficult to imagine two more polluting realities in the context of the purity-minded culture of Hinduism. As such, Kali is a very dangerous being. She vividly and dramatically thrusts upon the observer things that he or she would rather not think about. Within the civilized order of Hinduism, within the order of *dharma*, blood and death are acknowledged—it is impossible not to acknowledge their existence in human life—but they are acknowledged within the context of a highly ritualized, patterned, and complex social structure that takes great pains to handle them in "safe" ways, usually through rituals of purification. These rituals (called *sam-skaras,* "refinements") allow individuals to pass in an orderly way through times when contact with blood and death are unavoidable. The order of *dharma* is not entirely naive and has incorporated into its refined version of human existence the recognition of these human inevitabilities.

But the Hindu *samskaras* are patterned on wishful thinking. Blood and death have a way of cropping up unexpectedly, accidentally, tragically, and dangerously. The periodic flow of menstrual blood or the death of an aged and loved old woman (whose husband has cooperatively died before her) are manageable within the normal order of human events. But the death of an infant or a hemorrhage, for instance, are a threat to the neat vision of the order of *dharma*. They can never be avoided with certainty, no matter how well protected one thinks one is.

Kali may be one way in which the Hindu tradition has sought to come to terms, at least in part, with the built-in shortcomings of its own refined view of the world. It is perhaps best and even redemptive to recognize that the system does not work in every case.

Kali puts the order of *dharma* in perspective, perhaps puts it in its place, by reminding Hindus that certain aspects of reality are untamable, unpurifiable, unpredictable, and always a threat to society's feeble attempts to order what is essentially disorderly : life itself.

Kali's shocking appearance and unconventional behavior confront one with an alternative to normal society. To meditate on the dark goddess, or to devote oneself to her, is to step out of the everyday world of predictable dharmic order and enter a world of reversals, opposites, and contrasts and in doing so to wake up to new possibilities and new frames of reference. In her differentness, strangeness, indeed, in her perverseness, Kali is the kind of figure who is capable of shaking one's comforting and naive assumptions about the world. In doing this she allows a clearer perception of how things really are.

Kali allows (or perhaps forces) better perception by enabling one to see the complete picture. She allows one to see behind the bounteousness of the other goddesses who appear in benign forms. Kali reveals the insatiable hunger that logically must lie behind their amazing fecundity and liberality. Similarly, Kali permits individuals to see their overall roles in the cosmic drama. She invites a wider, more mature, more realistic reflection on where one has come from and where one is going. She allows the individual to see himself or herself as merely one being in an endless series of permutations arising from the ever-recurring cycles of life and death that constitute the inner rhythms of the divine mother.

The extent to which Kali invites or provokes one over the threshold from order to antistructure is seen in the roles she requires of those who would establish any intimacy with her. Iconographically, it is Siva who participates in the most intimate relations with Kali. In probably her most famous pose, as Daksinakali, she stands or dances upon Siva's prone body in the cremation ground. His eyes are closed in bliss, sleep, trance, or death—it is difficult to say which. His attitude is utterly passive and, whether he is dead or not, his appearance corpselike. The myth that explains the origin of this pose says that once upon a time Kali began to dance out of control on the battlefield after having become drunk on the blood of her victims. To stop her rampage, Siva lay down on the: battlefield like a corpse so that when she danced on his body she would stop, recognizing him as her husband. It is thus as a corpse, as one of her victims, that Siva calms Kali and elicits her grace.

In another myth it is the infant Siva who calms Kali and stops her rampage by eliciting motherly emotions from her. In this story Kali again has defeated her enemies on the battlefield and begun to dance out of control, drunk on the blood of those she has slain. To calm her and protect the stability of the world, Siva appears in the midst of the battlefield as an infant, crying out loudly. Seeing the child's distress, Kali stops her dancing, picks him up, and kisses him on the head. Then she suckles him at her breasts.

Both the dead and infants have a liminal nature. Neither has a complete social identity. Neither fits neatly or at all into the niches and structures of normal society. To approach Kali it is well to assume the identity of a corpse or an infant. Having no stake in the orderly structures of society, the devotee as corpse or infant is free to step out of society into the liminal environment of the goddess. The corpse is mere food for her insatiable fires, the infant mere energy, as yet raw and unrefined. Reduced to either extreme, one who approaches Kali in these roles is awakened to a perception of reality that is difficult to grasp within the confines of the order of *dharma* and a socialized ego.

Earth/India as a Goddess

An important aspect of the reverence for the divine feminine in the Hindu tradition is an awe for the sacrality of the land itself and for the Indian subcontinent as a whole. The most ancient expression of this in the Hindu tradition is found in the *Rig-veda* and its several hymns that praise the goddess Prithivi. It is clear that the hymns to Prithivi are grounded in reverence for the awesome stability of the earth itself and the apparently inexhaustible fecundity possessed by the earth. When Prithivi is described, characterized, or otherwise praised, the earth itself is usually the object of the hymn. Prithivi is the earth in a literal sense as much as she is a goddess with anthropomorphic characteristics.

An underlying implication of perceiving the earth as a great and powerful goddess is that the world as a whole, the cosmos itself, is to be understood as a great, living being, a cosmic organism. This idea is expressed in the central creation myth of the *Brahmanas,* which feature the deity Prajapati. The world was created, according to this scenario, when Prajapati undertook great austerities and subsequently released his immense stored-up energy. This great vigor became the underlying substance of the world, pervading it with life and energy. The aim of Vedic sacrificial ritual in the context of this myth is to reconstitute, replenish, rebuild, or reinvigorate Prajapati by gathering his dispersed energy. By gathering, nurturing, and feeding Agni (who is identified with Prajapati's released power), the participants in these rites understand that they are renewing Prajapati. Vedic rituals therefore become part of an ongoing cycle in which Prajapati creatively releases his ascetic power into the world and is then continually renourished in the sacrificial cult.

The idea of the earth as a personified goddess and the idea that the cosmos as a whole is a living being persist and are central in later Hindu mythology. Prithivi continues to be mentioned in medieval mythological texts, and reverence for Bhudevi (whose name literally means "the goddess who is the earth") becomes an important aspect of Vaisnavite mythology and iconography. When Bhudevi complains that she is being oppressed by a certain demon, Vishnu, attentive to the welfare of the earth, assumes the appropriate form and rescues the earth from her predicament.

Texts extolling the Mahadevi contain many examples of her identification with the world or the cosmos. The Mahadevi is often identified with *prakriti,* primordial matter or nature. The stuff of creation, the basic matter of the world, is affirmed to be a divine being. In the *Devi-mahatmya* the world is said to be filled by her; she is said to constitute every created thing. In the *Devi-bhagavata-purana* she is said to be present everywhere in the universe, from Brahma to each blade of grass.

The identification of the Devi with matter, the earth, or the cosmos is often expressed by identifying parts of the world with parts of her body. The *Devi-bhagavata-purana* calls the earth the Devi's loins. The same text speaks of the oceans as her bowels, the mountains as her bones, the rivers as her veins, and the trees as her body hair. The sun and moon are her eyes, and the nether worlds are said to be her hips, legs, and feet.

The fundamental conviction that the earth itself, or the Indian subcontinent itself, is a goddess, indeed, that she is one's mother, pervades the modern cult of Bharat Mata (Mother India), in which all Indians are called sons or children of India and are expected to protect their mother without regard for personal hardship and sacrifice.

Independent India still cultivates this theme of the motherland as a goddess. The Indian national anthem, composed by Rabindranath Tagore and first sung in 1911 at the Indian National Congress in Calcutta, is in the same vein as Chatterjee's "Bande Mataram."

Thou art the ruler of the minds of all people,
Dispenser of India's destiny.
Thy name rouses the hearts of Punjab, Sind, Gujarat and Maratha,
Of Dravida and Orissa and Bengal.
It echoes in the hills of Vindhyas and Himalayas,
mingles in the music of Jamuna and Ganges
and is chanted by the waves of the Indian Sea.
They pray for thy blessings and sing thy praise.
The saving of all people waits in thy hand,
Thou dispenser of India's destiny.
Victory, victory, victory to thee.

Concrete expressions of this reverence for India as a feminine deity are not difficult to find in modern India. In Banaras, the spiritual capital of Hinduism, there is a temple dedicated to Bharat Mata. Inside the temple, in the place where there would ordinarily be an anthropomorphic image of the goddess, there is a large, colored relief map of the Indian subcontinent. It is to this large map that pilgrims show reverence. Insofar as the nation-state represents, is identified with, or is associated with the land itself, it is due reverence. For the land itself is a sacred, nourishing, redemptive presence to those who are born from it and are nourished by it.

The Sakta Pithas

The myth and cult of the Sakta *pithas* is another vivid expression of the Hindu intuition that the Indian subcontinent itself is a goddess. India is covered with sacred places associated with prominent geographical features of the country. Mountains, hills, rivers, caves, and other sites having some geographical or natural peculiarity are often affirmed to possess sacred power or to be places where one may make contact with the divine. These sites are usually called *tirthas,* a term that means a place where one fords a river. The term is significant in regard to sacred places in two senses : (1) it indicates that rivers themselves are often the site of sacred power, and (2) such places are sites where one may cross over from the realm of the profane to the sacred, from the human to the divine, from this world to another world.

While it is difficult to establish historically how a given site has become popular as a sacred place, it seems clear that in many cases an awe or reverence for the geographical place itself was crucial in distinguishing it. Arduous pilgrimages to remote sites where the central religious rite is to bathe in the waters of a pool or river, enter a cave, or have a view of some geographical feature indicate that the great attraction of many sacred places is tied to the geography of the place. Although temples are often found in such places, the environment rather than the temple itself is usually the object of the pilgrim. The temple does not enhance the sacrality of the place so much as the place enhances the sacrality of the temple.

Looking at a map of the Indian subcontinent on which only the most famous sacred places are marked, we see that India bubbles with sacrality in every region. To a great extent these many *tirthas,* which are associated with Hindu mythology and epic history, have given India its sense of cultural and historical unity. India has rarely been under central rule. For the most part she has been ruled by several competing kingdoms. The sacrality of the land itself, rather than a unified political tradition, has cultivated among most Hindus the strong sense of Mother India.

Many sacred sites are specifically associated with, identified with, or presided over by a goddess. The pervasiveness of sites sacred to goddesses is suggested by the number of town, and villages that have names associated with different goddesses. Prof. Nihar Ranjan Ray observes.

"In this vast country, holy resorts of the goddess are innumerable and the popularity of her cult is proved even in the place-names of India. Referring to the Panjab region he says that few people pause to consider this social phenomenon, or to consider the significance of such toponyms in these regions as, for instance, Ambala which is derived from Amba, one of the many names of Durga, Chandigarh which is named after Candi, . . . Kalka which is a vulgarisation of Kalika, Simla which is Syamala Devi in its anglicised version. A careful and close look at the postal directories of the Punjab, Hariyana and Himachal would yield a long list of such toponyms from which one may draw one's own conclusion. Besides, throughout these regions one still finds a countless number of small, lowly shrines with all but shapeless or crude forms placed on their altars, which worshippers, lowly village folks, describe as Manasa, Chandi, Kali, Nayna, Durga, etc."

Many of these sites associated with goddesses are called *pithas,* "seats." Why the term *pitha* is used for those sites in preference to the more traditional and common term *tirtha* is not entirely clear. *Pitha* is preferred, perhaps because it tends to emphasize the rootedness of the goddesses associated with these places. Many of the goddesses are pre-eminently tied to the locales in which they are worshiped. They are perceived to be not so much transcendent, heavenly beings as beings whose power is firmly grounded in the earth itself.

Sometime in the medieval period an attempt was made to affirm the basic unity of all *pithas* sacred to goddesses. The assumption behind this attempt was that the Mahadevi underlies all the particular manifestations of goddesses residing at the many *pithas.* Mythologically this idea was expressed by adding an episode to the myth of Sati's self-destruction at Daksha sacrifice. In the expanded version of the myth Siva arrives at Daksha sacrifice having received the news that Sati has killed herself. He picks up her body and, racked with grief, begins to wander the cosmos. He is so distraught by Sati's death and so grieved by the presence of her corpse that he completely ignores his divine responsibilities. This threatens the stability of the world. Vishnu is called upon to remedy the situation. He slices pieces of her body off bit by bit, and so disposes of her body a bit at a time. When Siva discovers that Sati's body is gone, he recovers his divine composure and stops grieving. Where the parts of Sati's body fell, sacred places called *pithas* were then established. The number of *pithas* varies from 4 to 110 in the different accounts of the tale.

In most accounts of this myth and in most lists of the *pithas,* Sati's yoni is said to have fallen and been enshrined at Kamagiri in the region of Kamarupa in Assam, where the goddess is worshiped as Kamakhya. Although goddess worship is undoubtedly ancient in this part of India and although Kamarupa is mentioned in the Allahabad pillar inscription of Samudragupta (middle of the fourth century), the present temple of Kamakhya near Gauhati does not date beyond the sixteenth century. In the seventeenth century the Ahom kings of Assam encouraged the worship of Kamakhya on a grand scale, and her centrality in the *pitha* mythology probably originates around this time. In the Kamakhya temple at Kamagiri, the central image of the goddess is a yoni carved in stone.

Ganges

Geographical sacrality in the Hindu tradition is also dramatically expressed in the reverence shown to almost every river of the Indian subcontinent. This reverence extends all the way back to the *Rig-veda,* where the idea is expressed that earthly rivers have their origin in heaven. In the *Rig-veda* the Sarasvati River is praised as a mighty goddess who blesses her devotees with health, long life, and poetic inspiration. The earthly Sarasvati River is said to be only a partial manifestation of the goddess Sarasvati, for she is said to exist in heaven as well as on earth. The earthly river is an extension or continuation of divine waters that flow from heaven to earth.

Reverence for rivers in the Hindu tradition is nowhere more intense than in the case of the Ganges. Like the Sarasvati River in the Vedic tradition, the Ganges is said to have its origin in heaven. Many myths concerning the descent of the Ganges to earth emphasize this point. The oldest and probably best known concerns the restoration of the sixty thousand sons of King Sagara. According to this myth, Sagara's sons were dull-witted and impetuous, and while searching the world for their father's sacrificial horse they insulted and disturbed the tranquillity of the great sage Kapila. In anger, Kapila burned them all to ashes with the fire that he had generated as the result of his great austerities. Sagara's descendants, despite their piety and ascetic efforts, were unable to restore their incinerated forefathers until the saintly and mighty Bhagiratha, the great-great-great-grandson of Sagara, undertook the task. Giving his kingdom over to a trusted minister, Bhagiratha went to the Himalayas to do heroic austerities. After he had physically mortified himself for centuries, the Ganges appeared in bodily form and granted his wish: she would descend to the earth, provided that someone could be found to break her mighty fall, which otherwise would destroy the earth itself. Siva was persuaded to receive the Ganges on his head, and so the great heavenly river descended to earth, her mighty fall softened by Siva's massive tangle of hair. In his hair she became divided into many streams, each of which flowed to a different region of earth and sanctified that area. Her principal artery emerged from Siva's hair and came to India, and under Bhagiratha's guidance it cut a channel to where the ashes of Sagara's sons were piled. Moistened by her waters, the souls of the sixty thousand sons were purified and freed to undertake their journey to the land of their fathers, where they could be duly honored by their descendants.

The myths about the Ganges' coming to earth stress the river's heavenly origin, her essentially divine nature, and her association with the great male deities Brahma, Vishnu, and Siva. Spilling out of heaven from Vishnu's foot, containing Vishnu's liquified essence according to some myths, and falling onto Siva's head, where she meanders through his tangled locks, the mighty Ganges appears in this world after having been made more sacred by direct contact with Vishnu and Siva. The river then spreads the divine potency of these gods into the world when she flows onto the earthly plane. She gives their sacred presences to the earth in liquid form. The myths make clear that the earthly Ganges is only a limited part of the cosmic river that flows in heaven and descends to other regions and worlds as well as this one. As mighty as the Ganges appears here, the earthly river is only a limited aspect of a reality that transcends this world. The Ganges, these myths insists, points beyond itself to a transcendent, cosmic dimension that locates the source of the river in a divine sphere.

Although all rivers are revered as removers of pollution, the Ganges is preeminent among India's rivers as a purifying power. Hymns extolling the Ganges repeatedly emphasize the miraculously purifying powers of her waters. The *Agni-purana* says that the river makes those regions she flows through into sacred ground, that bathing in her waters is an experience similar to being in heaven, that those afflicted with blindness and other ailments become like gods after bathing in her waters, that the Ganges has made pure thousands of impure people who have seen, touched, or drunk her waters. To die while being immersed in the Ganges results in *moksa,* final spiritual liberation. Being brushed by a breeze containing even a drop of Ganges water erases all sins accumulated over lifetimes. In the *Brhaddharma-purana* a sinful king is said to have been spared an untimely death because he lived for a while with a merchant who used to bathe in the Ganges. The *Mahabhagavata-purana* tells the story of a robber who, though sent to hell after death, was subsequently sent to Siva's heaven because his flesh was eaten by a jackal who had drunk Ganges water.

Village Goddesses

India is primarily a village culture. The majority of Hindus live in villages of under a hundred thousand people, and there is little doubt that this has always been the case in the Indian subcontinent. In the context of village life one of the most (if not the most) significant and powerful divine presences is the *gramadevata,* a deity who is especially identified with the village and toward whom the villagers often have a special affection. It is not uncommon, in fact, for there to be several *gramadevatas* in a village, each of whom may have a specialized function. These village deities, more numerous than Indian villages themselves, are naturally diverse in character. Their names alone suggest diverse characteristics and functions. Some of these deities have a regional reputation, or at least the name of a certain *gramadevata* will be well known or popular throughout an entire region. The goddesses Mariyamman in South India and Manasa in North India are examples of this regional popularity. Other village deities may be known only to one small village.

Despite the number and variety of *gramadevatas,* several typical characteristics of these local deities have been noted. First, they usually are female.

Second, these deities are usually not represented by anthropomorphic images. They are usually represented by uncarved stones, trees, or small shrines that do not contain an anthropomorphic image. Sometimes no shrine is present at all except during special festivals, when temporary structures will be built to house or represent the deity.

Third, these deities, goddesses for the most part, capture the primary interest of the villagers and tend to be worshiped with more intensity than the great gods of the Hindu pantheon. Although the great gods are acknowledged to be in charge of distant, cosmic rhythms, they are only of limited interest to most villagers. The village goddess, in contrast, engages the villagers directly by being associated with their local, existential concerns. She is perceived to be *their* deity and to be concerned especially with *their* well-being and that of their village.

Finally, these village deities are often directly associated with disease, sudden death, and catastrophe. When the village is threatened by disaster, particularly epidemics, the local goddess is usually said to be manifesting herself. She erupts onto the village scene along with disasters that threaten the stability, and even the survival, of the village. Furthermore, her role vis-a-vis such epidemics or disasters is ambivalent. She is perceived both as inflicting these diseases and as protecting the village from them.

The close identity of the goddess with her village is also seen in her role as guardian of the village's boundaries. Her shrines or symbols are often erected at the boundaries of the village, where she acts to protect it from invasions of evil spirits and outsiders in general. Another expression of the intimate identity of the goddess with her village is her symbolic marriage to representatives of the village during her ceremonies.

Another indication of the identity of village and goddess is the participation of almost all members of a village in the goddess's festivals. In the case of the high or great gods, worship is often restricted to certain castes, usually the higher ones, or such deities may be particularly worshiped by *sampradayas* or movements that have restricted membership. The village goddess, however, is approached by the natural grouping of the local village itself and all those who constitute it. She is the goddess of the whole village, the physical place as well as the social and economic organism. Nearly all castes are represented at her festivals and to some extent mix freely. Her worship is a community effort, although particular castes may play more important ritual roles than others extent of the all-inclusive nature of local-goddess worship in villages is indicated by the participation of Brahmans and Muslims in these festivals. The point is that the local goddess is not so much a Hindu deity or a deity specially related to a caste or occupation, or even to a specific phenomenon such as disease, although all of these things might be the case to some extent. The point is that from the villagers' point of view the goddess is specifically their deity, their lady, as it were, who has their particular needs at heart.

The local rootedness of village goddesses, their special and narrow association with particular villages, is also suggested in the tendency during festivals in their honor to exclude outsiders. The exclusion of outsiders seems to be associated with the idea that they might benefit from the power of the goddess, which is intended for the local village. Her power is believed to be for her village, not for outsiders.

The basic relationship between the village goddess and her village seems quite straightforward. In return for the worship of the villagers the goddess ensures good crops, timely rain, fertility, and protection from demons, diseases, and untimely death. The arrangement is a local one with little or no room for outsiders. The power of the goddess does not extend beyond the village, so villagers leave her jurisdiction and protection when they venture beyond it. The relationship is localized and aims not so much at individual welfare as the welfare of the whole.

In fact, relations between village goddesses and their villages are more complicated. This is made clear by the association of these goddesses with disease and disruption, an identification that gives them an ambivalent character. For these goddesses are not usually peaceful, benign, and calm presences. Rather, they tend to be wild, rambunctious, independent, demanding, and destructive in their habits. This is evident in both their mythology and their ceremonies.

A mythical theme that emphasizes the village godesses' independence appears in the stories concerning Kanniyakumari. Kanniyakumari is prohibited from marrying Siva for various reasons. Although she is described as distressed at being prevented from enjoying Siva as her husband, the myths underline Kanniyakumari's perpetual virginity and her formidable power. Her great power seems to be directly related to her unmarried state and her celibacy. In the context of Tamil culture a woman's virginity, through which she withholds her sexual energy, is more or less equivalent to the building up of *tapas* in males when they retain their semen, which is magically transformed into powerful heat. Quite simply, Kanniyakumari is much more powerful as an unmarried maiden than she would be as a married woman. Although reluctantly unmarried, her independence from males gives her great power.

The great power possessed by goddesses and females who are independent of males is also a theme in many myths current in South India in which female deities are subjugated or tamed by gods. Probably the two best-known examples of this theme feature Minakshi, the goddess enshrined in Madurai and the fiercely wild goddess Kali. In the mythology concerning Minakshi the goddess is born with three breasts. Her disconcerted parents are instructed to raise the child like a male. She is brought up like a boy and ascends her father's throne when he dies. She then undertakes a campaign to subdue the entire world. She and her armies are invincible in battle until she comes to Mount Kailasa and challenges Siva himself. Seeing Siva, Minakshi's entire character is transformed. She becomes shy, and began to scrape the ground shyly with her toe. And so Siva reduces the powerful battle queen to a shy maiden.

Kali is subdued in a dance contest. In her independent form she is described as powerful, destructive, bloodthirsty, and fearsome. When she disrupts the meditation of one of Siva's devotees or otherwise attracts Siva's attention, he challenges her to a contest in which he tames her by defeating her in dance. Thereafter she is said to be his wife or to take on a benign form that becomes widely worshiped. In effect, she loses her power and becomes a weak, helpless female. "Kali acknowledged defeat; shyly . . . she worshiped the lord; she stood helplessly like a puppet, confused."

11

SONS OF SIVA AND PARVATI

Ganesha

Ganesha is usually regarded as the elder son of Siva and Parvati, but the Puranas differ very considerably in their accounts of his origin. All sacrifices and religious ceremonies, all serious compositions in writing, and all worldly affairs of importance are begun by pious Hindus with an invocation to Ganesha; a word composed of lsa, the governor or leader, and gana (instrument of Siva). Few books are begun without the words, 'Salutation to Ganesha;' and he is first invoked by Brahmans who perform the ceremony of the *homa* or sacrifice to fire. He is highly revered on the coast of Coromandel, not on any account would any one build a house without having placed on the ground an image of this deity. What is true of the Coromandel coast, is true of most parts of India so far as the worship of this deity is concerned.

Ganesha is the Hindu god of Prudence and Policy. He is the reputed eldest son of Siva and Parvati (the *Padma Purana* alone declares that he was the actual child of these deities), and is represented with an elephants head–an emblem of sagacity–and is frequently attended by, or is riding upon, a rat. He has generally four hands, but sometimes six, or eight, or only two. He is always described as being very corpulent; and pictures or images of him are seen over the doors of most shopkeepers.

The *Brahmavaivarta Purana* gives the following account of his birth: Parvati, after her marriage with Siva, being without a child, and very desirous to obtain one, was advised by her husband to perform the Panyakavrata. This is the worship of Vishnu, to be begun on the thirteenth day of the bright fortnight of Magha, and continued for a year, on everyday of which flowers, fruits, cakes, vessels, gems, gold, etc., are to be presented, and thousand Brahmans fed; and the performer of the rite is to observe most carefully a life of inward purity, and to fix the mind on Hari (Vishnu). Parvati having, with the aid of Sanat Kumara, as directing priest, accomplished the ceremony on the banks of the Ganges, returns after some interval, in which she sees Krishna, first as a body of light, and afterwards as an old Brahman, come to her dwelling. The reward of her religious zeal being delayed, she is plunged in grief, when a voice tells her to go to her apartment, where she will find a son who is the lord of Goloka, or Krishna, that deity having assumed the semblance of her son as a recompense for her devotions.

All the gods came to congratulate Siva and Parvati, and were allowed to see the infant. Amidst the splendid cohort was Sani, the planet Saturn, who, although anxious to pay his homage to the child, kept his eyes stedfastly fixed on the ground. Parvati asking him the reason of this, he told her that, being immersed in meditation upon Vishnu, he had disregarded his wife, and in resentment of his neglect, she had denounced upon him the curse that whomsoever he gazed upon he would destroy. To obviate the evil consequences of this imprecation, he avoided looking any one in the face. Parvati, having heard his story, paid no regard to it, but, considering that what must be, must be, gave him permission to look on her son. Sani, calling Dharma to witness, took a peep at Ganesha, on which the child's head was severed from his body, and flew away to the heaven of Krishna, where it re-united with the substance of him of whom it formed a part.

Durga, taking the headless trunk in her arms, cast herself weeping on the ground, and the gods followed her example, all except Vishnu, who mounted Garuda, and flew off to the river Pushpabhadra, where, finding an elephant asleep, he took off his head, and, flying back with it, clapped it on to the body of Ganesha. On the restoration of Ganesha to life, valuable gifts were made to the gods and Brahmans by the parents, and by Parvati's father, the personified Himalaya. The unfortunate Sani was again anathematized, and, in consequence of Parvati's curse, has limped ever since.

In another part of the same Purana, further particulars are given somewhat at variance with the above. Siva, offended with Aditya (the sun), slew him, and although he restored him to life incurred the wrath of the sage Kasyapa, who doomed his (Siva's) son to lose his head. The elephant whose head was placed upon Ganesha's body was Indra's elephant, which was decapitated because Indra threw over his neck the garland of flowers which the sage Durvasas gave him, and the disrespect of which, with the consequent degradation of Indra, is noticed in various Puranas, although with different results. Indra was no loser of an elephant by this transaction, as Vishnu, moved by the prayers of his wife, gave him another in place of that which he took away.

Ganesha has only one tusk, and hence is called Ekadanta. The reason of this is as follows: Parasurama, who was a favourite disciple of Siva, went to Kailasa to visit his master. On arriving at the inner apartment, his entrance was opposed by Ganesha, as his father was asleep. Parasurama nevertheless wanted his way, and, after a long dialogue, the two came to blows. Ganesha had at first the advantage, seizing Parasurama in his trunk, and giving him a twirl that left him sick and senseless. On recovering, Rama threw his axe at Ganesha, who, recognizing it as his father's weapon—Siva having given it to Parasurama—received it with all humility upon one of his tusks, which it immediately severed, and hence Ganesha has but one tusk. Parvati was highly incensed at this, and was about to curse Rama, when Krishna, of whom he was a worshipper, appeared as a boy and appeased her indignation. Brahma is said to have promised that her son should be worshipped before the other gods. This result of his contest with Rama was in consequence of a curse pronounced upon him by the sage Tulasi, with whom he had quarrelled.

We have quite a different account of the origin of Ganesha in the *Matsya Purana*. When Parvati was bathing, she took the oil and ointments used at the bath, together with the impurities that came from her body, and formed them into the figure of a man, to which she gave life by sprinkling it with the water of the Ganges. This figure had the head of the elephant. The *Siva Purana* relates that, after giving Ganesha life, Parvati placed him at her door to prevent intrusion whilst she was bathing. On his refusal to allow Siva to enter, a struggle ensued, in which that deity cut off Ganesha's head; but when Parvati showed her husband that it was by her orders that the door was closed, and wept because of the loss of her son, Siva ordered the first head that could be found to be brought to him; this happened to be an elephant's which he fitted to the headless trunk and resuscitated his son.

In the *Varaha Purana* Ganesha is said to have been produced by Siva alone. The immortals and holy sages observing that no difficulty occurred in accomplishing good or evil deeds which they and others commenced, consulted together respecting the means by which obstacles might be opposed to the commission of bad actions, and repaired to Siva for counsel, to whom they said: "O Mahadeva! God of gods, three eyed, bearer of the trident, it is thou alone who can create a being capable of opposing obstacles to the commission of improper acts.' Hearing these words, Siva looked at Parvati, and whilst thinking how he could effect the wishes of the gods, from the splendour of his countenance there sprang into existence a youth shedding radiance around, endowed with the qualities of Siva, and evidently another Rudra, and captivating by his beauty the female inhabitants of heaven.

Uma seeing his beauty was excited with jealousy, and in her anger pronounced this curse: 'Thou shalt not offend my sight with the form of a beautiful youth; therefore assume an elephant's head and a large belly, and thus shall all thy beauties vanish.' Siva then addressed his son, saying, 'Thy name shall be Ganesha, and the son of Siva; thou shalt be chief of the Vinayakas and Ganas; success and disappointment shall spring from thee; and great shall be thine influence amongst the gods, and in sacrifices and all affairs. Therefore shalt thou be worshipped and invoked the first on all occasions, otherwise the object and prayers of him who omits to do so shall fail.

The origin and purpose of Ganesha's existence are more fully taught in the *Skanda.* Siva addressing Parvati says, " During the twilight that intervened between the Dwapar and Kali Yugas, women, barbarians, Sudras, and other workers of sin obtained entrance to heaven by visiting the celebrated shrine of Someswara (Somnath). Sacrifices, ascetic practices, charitable gifts, all the other prescribed ordinances ceased, and men thronged only to the temple of Siva. Hence old and young, those skilled in the Vedas and those ignorant of them, and even women and Sudras, ascended to heaven, until at length it became crowded to excess. Then Indra and the gods, afflicted because thus overcome by men, sought the protection of Siva, and thus addressed him: 'O Sankara! by thy favour heaven is crowded with men, and we are nearly expelled from it. These mortals wander wherever they please, exclaiming, "I am the greatest, I am the greatest;" and Dharmaraja (Yama), beholding the register of their good and evil deeds, is lost in astonishment. The seven hells were intended for their reception; but, having visited thy shrine, their sins have been remitted, and they have attained to a most excellent future!' Siva replied, 'Such was my promise to Soma, nor can it be infringed; all men, therefore, who visit the temple of Someswara must ascend to heaven; but supplicate Parvati, and she will contrive some means for extricating you from this distress.'

"The gods then invoked Parvati in laudatory strains: 'Praise be to thee, O supreme of goddesses: Supporter of the universe, praise be to thee, who creates and destroys! Grant, us thy aid, and save us from this distress!' Having heard the prayer of Indra and the gods, thou O goddess! was moved with compassion; and gently rubbing thy body, there was produced a wondrous being with four arms and an elephant's head, and then thou didst thus address the gods: 'Desirous of your advantage, have I created this being, who will occasion obstacles to men, and, deluding them, will deprive them of the wish to visit Somnath, and thus shall they fall into hell.' Hearing this, the gods returned to their homes delighted.

"The Elephant-faced then, addressing Devi, said, 'Command, O lovely goddess! what shall I now do? Thou didst reply, 'Oppose obstacles to men's visiting Somnath, and entice them to give up such a purpose by the allurements of wives, children, possessions, and wealth. But from those who propitiate thee with the hymns do thou remove all obstacles, and enable them to obtain the favour of Siva, by worshipping his shrine at Somnath. And whoever invokes the god Vinayaka, no difficulties shall impede the attainment of his object, and a most beneficial result shall he derive from sacrifices, pilgrimages, and all other devotional acts."

Ganesha is said to have written the *Mahabharata* at Vyasa's dictation. In the Adiparva of that book it is declared that when the sage was about to compose it Brahma advised him to ask Ganesha to become his writer. Vyasa at first gave a few difficult sentences to puzzle him, which to this day the composer only and his disciple Suka have been able to understand. As Ganesha paused to think out the meaning of what he was writing, Vyasa composed other difficult passages.

Kartikeya

Kartikeya, the god of war, and general of the armies of the gods, though called the younger son of Siva and Parvati, according to most of the Purana legends, is their son only in the sense that they formed him. Brahma arranged for his birth in answer to the prayers of the gods for a competent leader of their forces. The *Ramayana* says: "While Siva, the lord of the gods, was performing austerities, the other deities went to Brahma and asked for a general like Mahadeva, who, it seems, had formerly acted in that capacity. 'He,' said they, 'whom thou didst formerly give as a leader of our armies (Mahadeva), is now performing great asuterities, along with Uma.' Brahma says that in consequence of the curse of Uma no son could be born of any wives of the gods, but that Agni should have a son by the river Ganga, who should be their general."

In the following extract from the *Mahabharata* is an explanation of the statement in the preceding paragraph that Agni was to be the father of this god. Kartikeya has just been installed as general, when, "the god whose banner is a bull (Siva), arriving with his goddess, paid him honour, well pleased. Brahmans called Agni Rudra, consequently he (Kartikeya) is the son of Rudra. Having seen him thus honoured by Rudra, all the deities consequently call him the son of Rudra. For this child was produced by Rudra when he entered into fire. Skanda (Kartikeya), that most eminent deity, being born of Agni, [who was] Rudra, and from Svaha (Uma) [and] the six wives [of the Rishis], was the son of Rudra."

The *Siva Purana* gives a different account of his origin, and teaches that he was produced to effect the destruction of Tarika. This demon, who was King of Tripura, was "exceedingly ambitious and oppressive. He forced Brahma, by his penance and austerities, to promise him any boon that he should demand. Among his austerities he went through the following series, each of the eleven specific mortification continuing 100 years:—1. He stood on one foot, holding the other and both hands up towards heaven, with his eyes fixed on the sun. 2. He stood on one great toe. 3. He took only water as sustenance. 4. He lived similarly on air. 5. He remained in water. 6. He was buried in the earth, but continued as under the last infliction, in incessant adoration. 7. The same in fire. 8. He stood on his head. 9. He hung on a tree by his hands. 10. He bore the weight of his body on one hand. 11. He hung on a tree with his head downwards.

Such merit was irresistible, and Indra and a host of demi-gods, alarmed lest their sovereignty should be usurped through the potency of this penance, resorted to Brahma for consolation. Brahma, however, said that, he would, after rewarding by granting the boon demanded, devise a method of rendering it ultimately ineffective.

The demand by Tarika was that he should be unrivalled in strength, and that no one should slay him but a son of Mahadeva. He now became so arrogant that Indra was forced to yield to him the white eight-headed horse Ukhisrava; Kubera gave up his thousand sea-horses; the Rishis were compelled to resign the cow Kamdhenu, that yielded everything that could be wished. The Sun in dread gave no heat, and the Moon in terror remained always at full. The Winds blew as he dictated, and, in short, he usurped the entire management of the universe.

Narada prophesied the marriage whence should arise the deliverer of the world; but at first Mahadeva could not be influenced with the passion of love. Indra persuaded Kama to lie in ambush, and contrived that Parvati should be seen by Siva while engaged in the amiable and graceful act of gathering flowers, wherewith to decorate his image. Kama, accompanied by his wife Rati (Desire), and his bosom friend Vasant (the Spring), took his aim, and launched an arrow at Mahadeva, who, enraged at the attempt (to interrupt his devotion), reduced Kama to ashes by a beam of fire that issued from his third eye. At length, however, by ardent devotion and austerities, Parvati propitiated Siva, and the deity consented to espouse his persevering devotee.

For some time after their marriage, as there was no child born to them, the distressed and disappointed deities who had been anxiously expecting a deliverer, renewed their lamentations and complaints.

Agni arrived in the presence of Mahadeva, having been deputed to express the desires of the other gods, that he would provide them with a son, who should destroy Tarika. Siva had just left his wife, and Agni, assuming the form of a dove, received from Mahadeva the germ from which Kartikeya arose. Unable to carry it further, he let it fall into the Ganges, on the banks of which river arose a boy, beautiful as the moon, and bright as the sun, who was called Agnibhuva (produced from Agni), Skanda, Kartikeya, etc.

It happened that six daughters (the Pleiades) of as many Rajas coming to bathe, saw the boy, and each called him her son; and, offering the breast, the child assumed to himself six mouths, and received nurture from each; whence he is called Sasthimatriya (having six mothers). But in fact the child had no mother, for he came from his father alone. In course of time a conflict ensued between Kartikeya and Tarika, in which the demon was slain.

A story is told showing how Kartikeya was outwitted by his brother Ganesha. As the two brothers fell in love with two ladies named Siddhi and Buddhi, it was agreed that whoever first travelled round the world should have them. Ganesha proved by his logical talents and aptness at quotation that he had done this, and obtained the prize long before his brother returned from his weary pilgrimage, to the disquiet of both families when Ganesha's sophistry was discovered.

There is another account of the origin of Kartikeya: "Siva emitted sparks of fire from his eyes, which, being thrown into the lake Saravana, became six infants, who were nursed by the wives of the Rishis, who are seen in the sky as the Pleiades. When Parvati saw these children, she was transported with their beauty, and embraced all of them together so forcibly that their six bodies became one; while their six heads and twelve arms remained."

Kartikeya is better known in South India under the name of Subramanya. The *Skanda Purana* gives a full account of his war with Sura, and relates how he was sent by his father to interrupt Daksha's sacrifice; and how at the instigation of the latter, he was delayed on his journey by beautiful damsels, who entertained him with dance and song. Hence it is the practice for dancing girls to be betrothed and married to him; and, though allowed to prostitute themselves, cannot marry any one.

12

CREATION AND THE DIVINE SAGES

Before passing on to the divine sages, an account of the creation will be given. As in the case of the deities, the germs are found in the older books of what is told at considerable length in the more recent ones. The following from the *Rig-Veda* describes the primal condition of things before the creative power was exercised :

"There was neither aught nor naught, nor air, nor sky beyond.
What covered all? Where rested all? In watery gulf profound?
Nor death was then, nor deathlessness, nor change of night and day,
The One breathed calmly, self-sustained; nought else beyond it lay.

"Gloom, hid in gloom, existed first—one sea, eluding view.
That One, a void in chaos wrapt, by inward fervour grew.
Within it first arose desire, the primal germ of mind,
Which nothing with existence links, as sages searching find.

"The kindling ray that shot across the dark and drear abyss—
Was it beneath? or high aloft? What poet can answer this?
There fecundating powers were found, and mighty forces strove—
A self-supporting mass beneath, and energy above.

"Who knows, who ever told, from whence this vast creation rose?
No gods had then been born—who then can the truth disclose?
Whence sprang this world, and whether framed by hand divine or no—
Its lord in heaven alone can tell, if even he may not know."

This hymn contains perhaps the earliest speculations of the Hindus respecting the creation that have come down to us; and the wise conclusion was arrived at that God alone knew how the world came into being. But as time went on this confession of ignorance did not satisfy the cravings of the human mind : hence succeeding ages sought by its conjectures to throw light upon the unknowable.

The next quotation is from the *Purusha Sakta* of the *Rig-Veda,* which from its thought and language is generally believed to be of much later origin than the preceding hymn.

"Purusha has a thousand heads, a thousand eyes, a thousand feet. On every side enveloping the earth, he overpassed (it) by a space of ten fingers. Purusha himself is this whole (universe), whatever has been and whatever shall be. He is also lord of immortality, since by food he expands. All existences are a quarter of him, and three-fourths of him are that which is immortal in the sky. With three-quarters Purusha mounted upward. A quarter of him was again produced here. From him was born Viraj; and from Viraj, Purusha. When the gods performed a sacrifice, with Purusha as the oblation, the spring was its butter, the summer its fuel, and the autumn its (accompanying) offering. From that universal sacrifice were provided curds and butter. From that universal sacrifice sprang the Rik and Saman verses, the metres and the Yajus; from it sprang horses and all animals with two rows of teeth, kine, goats and sheep. When (the gods) divided Purusha into how many parts did they cut him up ? The Brahman was his mouth, the Rajanya was made his arms, the Vaisya was his thighs, and the Sudra sprang from his feet. The morn sprang from his mind, the sun from his eye, Indra and Agni from his mouth, and Vayu from his breath. From his navel arose the air, from his head the sky, from his feet the earth, from his ear the (four) quarters; in this manner (the gods) formed the worlds."

Now follows an extract from the *Satapatha Brahmana*, which gives the words used at the creation. "(Uttering) 'bhuh,' Prajapati generated this earth. (Uttering) 'bhuvah,' he generated the air; and (Uttering) 'svah,' he generated the sky. This universe is coextensive with these worlds. Saying 'bhuh,' Prajapati generated the Brahman; (saying) 'bhuvah,' he generated the Kshattra; (and saying) 'svah,' he generated the Vis. All this world is as much as the Brahman, Kshattra and Vis. (Saying) 'bhuh,' Prajapati generated himself; (saying) 'bhuvah,' he generated offspring; (saying) 'svah,' he generated animals. This world is so much as self, offspring, and animals."

The *"Taittiriya Brahmana"* says, "This entire (universe) has been created by Brahman and gives an account of the creation of the *asuras, pitris* (or fathers) and gods. "Prajapati desired, 'May I propagate.' He practised austerity. His breath became alive. With that breath (*asu*) he created *asuras*. Having created the *asuras,* he regarded himself as a father.

After that he created the fathers (*pitris*). That constitutes the fatherhood of the fathers. Having created the fathers, he reflected. After that he created men. That constitutes the manhood of men. He who knows the manhood of men becomes intelligent. To him, when he was creating men, day appeared in the heavens. After that he created the gods."

The *Satapatha Brahmana* relates the creation of men and animals. "Prajapati was formerly this (universe) only. He desired, 'Let me create food, and be propagated.' He formed animals from his breaths, a man from his soul, a horse from his eye, a bull from his breath, a sheep from his ear, a goat from his voice. Since he formed animals from his breaths, therefore men say, 'The breaths are animals.' The mind is the first of breaths. Since he formed a man from his mind, therefore they say, 'Man is the first of the animals and the strongest.' The mind is all the breaths; for all the breaths depend upon the mind. Since he formed man from his mind, therefore they say, 'Man is all the animals;' for all these are man's."

In another passage this *Brahmana* gives quite a different account. Purusha, as the soul of the universe, was alone. Hence "he did not enjoy happiness. He desired a second. He caused this same self to fall asunder into two parts. Thence arose a husband and wife. From them men were born. She reflected, 'How does he, after having produced me from himself, cohabit with me. Ah! let me disappear. She became a cow, and the other a bull; from them kine were produced. The one became a mare, the other a stallion; the one a she-ass, the other a male-ass. From them the class of animals with undivided hoofs were produced. The one became a she-goat, the other a he-goat; the one an ewe, the other a ram. From them goats and sheep were produced. In this manner pairs of all creatures whatsoever, down to ants, were created."

Manu's account of the creation most probably follows the preceding one in order of time; and it will be noticed that he has developed some germs of thought expressed there. "He (the self-existent) having felt desire, and willing to create various living beings from his own body, first created the waters, and threw into them a seed. That seed became a golden egg, of lustre equal to the Sun; in it he himself was born as Brahma, the parent of all the world. The waters are called narah, for they are sprung from Nara; and as they were his first sphere of motion (*avana*) he is therefore called Narayana. Produced from the imperceptible, eternal, existent and non-existent cause, that male (*purusha*) is celebrated in the world as Brahma. After dwelling for a year in the egg, the glorious being, by his own contemplation, split in twain. . . . Having divided his own body into two parts, the lord (Brahma) became, with the half a male, and with the half a female; and in her he created Viraj. Know, O most excellent twice-born men, that I, whom that male Viraj himself created, am the creator of all this world."

The Puranas enter very minutely into the details of the creation. It is one of the specified topics of which a Parana ought to treat. The first book of the *Vishnu Purana* is largely filled with this.

The account in the *Vishnu Purana* was originally imparted by the great father of all (Brahma) in answer to the questions of Daksha and other venerable sages, and repeated by them to Purukutsa, a king who reigned on the banks of the Narmada. "Who can describe him who is not to be apprehended by the senses? He is Brahma, supreme, lord, eternal, unborn, imperishable. He then existed in the form of *Purusha* and of *Kala*. *Purusha* (Spirit) is the first form of the supreme; next proceeded two other forms, the discreet and indiscreet; and *Kala* (time) was the last. These four—*Pradhana* (primary or crude matter), *Purusha* (Spirit), *Vyakta* (visible substance), and *Kala* (time)—in their due proportions, are the causes of the production of the phenomena of creation, preservation, and destruction. The supreme Brahma, the supreme soul, the substance of the world, the lord of all creatures, the universal soul, the supreme ruler Hari (Vishnu), of his own will having entered into matter and spirit, agitated the mutable and immutable principles, the season of creation having arrived, in the same manner as fragrance affects the mind from its proximity merely, and not from any immediate operation upon mind itself; so the supreme influenced the elements of creation."

After giving an account of the creation, or rather the evolution of the elements, the *Vishnu Purana* goes on to say : "Then (the elements) ether, air, light, water and earth, severally united with the properties of sound, and the rest existed as distinguishable according to their qualities as soothing, terrific, or stupefying; but possessing various energies, and being unconnected, they could not without combination create living beings, not having blended with each other. Having combined, therefore, with one another, they assumed, through their mutual association, the character of one mass of entire unity; and from the intellect, and the rest, to the gross elements inclusive, formed an egg, which gradually expanded like a bubble of water. This vast egg, compounded of the elements, and resting on the waters, was the excellent natural abode of Vishnu in the form of Brahma; and there Vishnu, the lord of the universe, whose essence is inscrutable, assumed a perceptible form, and even he himself abided in it in the character of Brahma. Its womb, vast as the mountain Meru, was composed of the mountains; and the mighty oceans were the waters that filled its cavity. In that egg were the continents and seas and mountains, the planets and divisions of the universe, the gods, demons, and mankind.

"Affecting then the quality of activity, Hari the lord of all, himself becoming Brahma, engaged in the creation of the universe. Vishnu, with the quality of goodness and of immeasurable power, preserves created things through successive ages, until the close of the period termed a Kalpa; when the same mighty deity, invested with the quality of darkness, assumes the awful form of Rudra, and swallows up the universe. Having thus devoured all things, and converted the world into one vast ocean, the supreme reposes upon his mighty serpent couch amidst the deep : he awakes after a season, and again, as Brahma, becomes the author of creation."

The Purana next gives an account of the creation in the present Kalpa or age. This is a secondary creation, for water and the earth also are already in existence; it is not creation properly speaking, but the change of pre-existing matter into their present forms. Vishnu knew that the earth lay hidden in the waters; he, therefore, assuming the form of a boar, raised it upon his tusks.

In answer to a request for a full account of the creation of gods and other beings, the following occurs :—"Created beings, although they are destoryed (in their original forms) at the periods of dissolution, yet, being affected by the good or evil acts of former existence, are never exempted from their consequences; and when Brahma creates the world anew, they are the progeny of his will, in the fourfold condition of gods, men, animals, and inanimate things. Brahma then, being desirous of creating the four orders of beings—termed gods, demons, progenitors, and men—collected his mind into itself.

"Whilst thus concentrated, the quality of darkness pervaded his body, and thence the demons (the *asuras*) were first born, issuing from his thigh. Brahma then abandoned that form which was composed of the rudiment of darkness, and which, being deserted by him, became night. Continuing to create, but assuming a different shape, he experienced pleasure, and thence from his mouth proceeded the gods.

The form abandoned by him became day, in which the good quality predominates; and hence by day the gods are most powerful, and by night the demons. He next adopted another form in which the rudiment of good men also prevailed; and thinking of himself as the father of the world, the progenitors (or *Pitris*) were born from his side. The body, when he abandoned it, became the Sandhya, or evening twilight. Brahma then assumed another person, pervaded by the quality of foulness; and from this, men in whom foulness (or passion) predominates, were produced. Quickly abandoning that body, it became the dawn. At the appearance of this light of day men feel most vigour; whilst the progenitors are most powerful in the evening.

"Next from Brahma, in a form composed of the quality of foulness, was produced hunger, of whom anger was born; and the god put forth in darkness beings emaciated with hunger, of hideous aspect and with long beards. These beings hastened to the deity. Such of them as exclaimed, 'Oh, preserve us,' were thence called *Rakshasas* (from *Raksha*, to preserve); others who cried out, 'Let us eat,' were denominated from that expression *Yakshas* (from *Yaksha*, to eat). Beholding them so disgusting, the hairs of Brahma were shrivelled up, and first falling from his head were again renewed upon it; from their falling they became serpents, called *Sarpa* from their creeping, and *Ahi* (from Ha, to abandon), because they had deserted the head. The creator of the world, being incensed, then created fierce beings, who were denominated goblins, *bhutas,* malignant fiends, and eaters of flesh. The Gandharvas (choristers) were next born : imbibing melody, drinking of the goddess of speech, they were born, and hence their appellation.

"The divine Brahma, influenced by their material energies, having created these beings, made others of his own will. Birds he formed from his vital vigour ; sheep from his heart; goats from his mouth; kine from his belly and sides; and horses, elephants, sarabhas, gayals, deer, camels, mules, antelopes, and other animals from his feet: whilst from the hairs of his body sprang herbs, roots, and fruits." In this manner all things are said to have sprung from Brahma; they were with him in the egg. The creation of man, as divided into four castes, is described in this Purana, in similar terms to those in Manu.

Following this is the account of the mind-born sons of Brahma—Bhrigu, Daksha, and others—nine in number, who became the progenitors of men. Next "Brahma created himself as Manu Swayambhu, born of, and identical with, his original self for the protection of created beings:

and the female portion of himself constituted Satarupa, and whom the divine Manu Swayambhu took to wife." After this follows a long-account of the descendants of these mind-born sons ; and it is then shown how by the production of the *amrita* at the churning of the ocean the gods obtained immortality, and the work of creation for this age was complete.

With some variations this is the story of the creatior as told in the Puranas. In some, greater prominence is given to parts that are only lightly touched upon in this account; whilst other incidents are more fully described here than in the other Puranas.

Puranic Divisions of Time

The three main divisions of time employed in the Hindu Scriptures are Yugas, Manvantaras, and Kalpas.

There are four Yugas, which together extend to 12,000 *divine* years. Their respective duration is as follows :

The Krita Yuga = 4,800 divine years.
The Treta Yuga = 3,600 divine years.
The Dvapara Yuga = 2,400 divine years.
The Kali Yuga = 1,200 divine years.

"One year of mortals is equal to one day of the gods." As 360 is taken as the number of days in the year—

The Krita Yuga = 4,800 × 360 = 1,728,000 years of mortals.
The Treta Yuga = 3,600 × 360 = 1,296,000 years of mortals.
The Dvapara Yuga = 2,400 × 360 = 864,000 years of mortals.
The Kali Yuga = 1,200 × 360 = 432,000 years of mortals.

One Mahayuga, or Great Age, including the four lesser Yugas, therefore, being 12,000 divine years = 4,320,000 years of mortals. "A thousand such Mahayugas are a day of Brahma," and his nights are of equal duration; a *Kalpa,* therefore, or Day of Brahma extends over 4,320,000,000 ordinary years. "Within each Kalpa 14 Manus reign; a Manvantara, or period of a Manu, therefore, is consequently one-fourteenth part of a Kalpa, or day of Brahma.

"In the present Kalpa, six Manus, of whom Swyambhuva was the first, have already passed away; the present being Vaivasata. In each Manvantara (period of a Manu), seven Rishis, certain deities, an Indra and a Manu, and the kings, his sons, are created and perish. A thousand systems of the four Yugas occur coincidentally with these fourteen

Manvantaras, and consequently about 71 systems of four Yugas elapse during each Manvantara, and measure the lives of the Manus and the deities of the period. At the close of this day of Brahma, a collapse of the universe takes place, which lasts through a night of Brahma, equal in duration to his day, during which period the worlds are converted into one great ocean, when the lotus-born god (Brahma), contemplated by the Yogis and gods in Janaloka, sleeps on the serpent Sesha. At the end of that night he awakes and creates anew.

The dissolution of existing beings is of three kinds : "incidental, elemental, and absolute." The first is *naimittika,* occasional, incidental, or brahmya as occasioned by the intervals of Brahma's days; the destruction of creatures, though not of the substance of the world, occurring during the night. The second is the general resolution of the elements into their primitive source, or *prakriti,* the Prakritika destruction, and occurs at the end of Brahma's life. The third, the absolute, or final, Alyantika, is individual annihilation, *Moksha,* exemption for ever from future existence.

The process of destruction is as follows :—

"At the end of a thousand periods of four ages the earth is for the most part exhausted. A total death then ensues, which lasts a hundred years, and in consequence of the failure of food all beings become languid and inanimate, and at last entirely perish. The eternal Vishnu then assumes the character of Rudra, the destroyer, and descends to reunite all his creatures with himself. He enters into the seven rays of the sun, drinks up all the waters of the globe, and causes all moisture whatever, in living bodies or in the soil, to evaporate, thus drying up the whole earth. The seas, the rivers, the mountain-torrents, and springs are all exhaled, and so are all the waters of Patala, the regions below the earth.

"Thus fed, through his intervention, with abundant moisture, the seven solar rays dilate to seven suns, whose radiance glows above, below, and on every side, and sets the three worlds and Patala on fire. The three worlds, consumed by these suns, become rugged and deformed throughout the whole extent of their mountains, rivers, and seas; and the earth, bare of verdure and destitute of moisture, alone remains, resembling in appearance the back of a tortoise. The destroyer of all things, Hari, in the form of Rudra, who is the flame of time, becomes the scorching breath of the serpent Sesha, and thereby reduces Patala to ashes. The great fire, when it has burnt all the divisions of Patala, proceeds to the earth and consumes it also."

The *Vayu Purana* is more explicit. "Those sainted mortals who have diligently worshipped Vishnu and are distinguished for piety, abide at the time of dissolution in Maharloka, with the *Pitris,* the Manus, the seven Rishis, the various orders of celestial spirits and the gods. These, when the heat of the flames that destroy the world reaches to Maharloka, repair to Janaloka in their subtle forms, destined to become re-embodied in similar capacities, when the world is renewed, at the beginning of the succeeding Kalpa. This continues throughout the life of Brahma; at the expiration of his life all are destroyed; but those who have then attained a residence in the Brahmaloka, by having identified themselves in spirit with the Supreme, are finally resolved into the sole existing Brahma."

The *Vishnu Purana* continues as follows : "Janarddana, in the person of Rudra, having consumed the whole world, breathes forth heavy clouds. Mighty in size, and loud in thunder, they fill all space. Showering down torrents of water, these clouds quench the dreadful fires which involve the three worlds, and then they rain uninterruptedly for a hundred years and deluge the whole world. The world is now enveloped in darkness, and all things, animate and inanimate, having perished, the clouds continue to pour down their waters for more than a hundred years."

The four Yugas mentioned above—viz. the Krita, Treta, Dvapara, and Kali—have characteristic qualities. The Krita is the golden, and Kali the iron age. The *Mahabharata* gives these characteristics very distinctly. Hanuman, is the speaker, describing the four ages to Bhimasena, one of the Pandus.

"The Krita is that age in which righteousness is eternal. In the time of that most excellent of Yugas (everything) had been done *(Krita),* and nothing (remained) to be done. Duties did not then languish, nor did the people decline. Afterwards through (the influence of) time, this Yuga fell into a state of inferiority. In that age there were neither gods, Danavas, Gandharvas, Yakshasas, Rakshasas, nor Pannagas; no buying and selling went on, no efforts were made by men; the fruit (of the earth was obtained) by their mere wish; righteousness and abandonment of the world (prevailed). No disease or decline of the organs of sense arose through the influence of age ; there was no malice, weeping, pride, or deceit; no contention, no hatred, cruelty, fear, affliction, jealousy, or envy. Hence the Supreme Brahma was the transcendent resort of these Yogins. Then Narayana, the soul of all beings, was white. In that age were born creatures devoted to their duties. They were alike in the object of their trust, in observance, and in their knowledge. At that period the castes, alike in their functions, fulfilled their duties, were unceasingly devoted to one deity, and used one formula (*mantra*), one rule, and one rite. They had but one Veda.

"Understand now the Treta, in which sacrifice commenced, righteousness decreased by a fourth, Vishnu became red ; and men adhered to truth, and were devoted to a righteousness dependent on ceremonies. Then sacrifices prevailed, with holy arts and a variety of rites. In the Treta men acted with an object in view, seeking after reward for their rites and their gifts, and no longer disposed to austerities, and to liberality from (a simple feeling of) duty. In this age, however, they were devoted to their own duties and to religious ceremonies.

"In the Dvapara age righteousness was diminished by two quarters, Vishnu became yellow, and the Veda fourfold. Some studied four Vedas, some three, others two, and some none at all. The scriptures being thus divided, ceremonies were celebrated in a great variety of ways; and the people, being occupied with austerity and the bestowal of gifts, became full of passion *(rajasi)*. Owing to ignorance of the one Veda, Vedas were multiplied. And now from the decline of goodness *(sattva)*, few only adhered to truth. When men had fallen away from goodness, many diseases, desires, and calamities, caused by destiny, assailed them, by which they were severely afflicted, and driven to practise austerities. Others, desiring enjoyments and heavenly bliss, offered sacrifices. Thus, when they had reached the Dvapara, men declined through unrighteousness.

"In the Kali, righteousness remained to the extent of one-fourth only. Arrived in that age of darkness, Vishnu became black; practices enjoined by the Vedas, works of righteousness, and rites of sacrifices ceased. Calamities, diseases, fatigue, faults, such as anger, etc., distresses, anxiety, hunger, fear, prevailed. As the ages revolve, righteousness again declines; when this takes place, the people also decline. When they decay, the impulses which actuate them also decay. The practices generated by this declension of the Yugas frustrate men's aims. Such is the Kali Yuga, which has existed for a short time. Those who are long-lived act in conformity with the character of the age."

It is interesting to notice that in the account of the Krita Yuga, or Age of Righteousness, it is said that the castes were alike in their functions. This must evidently mean that the modern caste distinctions did not then exist, and that all were devoted to the worship of one deity with one rule and one rite, evidently pointing to the time when their forefathers were monotheists.

THE DIVINE RISHIS

Bhrigu

Vishnu Purana says : "When Brahma wished to populate the world, he created mind-born sons, like himself; viz. Bhrigu, Pulastya, Pulaha, Kratu, Angiras, Marichi, Daksha, Atri, and Vasishtha: these are the nine Brahmas or Brahmarishis celebrated in the Puranas." Originally seven only were mentioned in the Mahabharata; but the lists found in different parts of that Epic do not agree with each other. These seven are supposed to be visible in the Great Bear, as their wives shine in the Pleiades. These Brahmarishis are also called Prajapatis (lords of offspring), Brahmaputras (sons of Brahma), and Brahmanas. The *Vishnu Purana* teaches that Bhrigu married his niece Khyati, a daughter of Daksha, who bore to him Sri or Lakshmi; but as it was the common belief that she was one of the products of the churning of the ocean, the reciter of the Purana is asked to explain this discrepancy. The substance of his answer was, that "of gods, animals, and man, Hari is all that is called male, Lakshmi is all that is termed female."

In his account of the creation, Manu mentions ten Maharishis as having been created by himself, one of whom is Bhrigu, who in his turn created seven other Manus, from whom all that is has sprung. The *Mahabharata* says : "Six great Rishis are known as the mind-born sons of Brahma;" but Bhrigu is not named amongst them. In another passage it describes him as a son of Varuna, but Brahma is there identified with Varuna. At a sacrifice at which Brahma officiated, a portion of Varuna was thrown into the sacrificial fire, whence there arose three men endowed with bodies. Bhrigu sprang first from *bhrik* (the blazing of the fire), Angiras from the cinders, and Kavi from a heap of ashes. The god called Mahadeva, Varuna, and Pavana, claimed these three as his own. Agni and Brahma also claimed them. It was agreed that Bhrigu was Varuna's son. Agni received Angiras, and Brahma took Kavi. In another part of that poem it is said, "We have heard that the great and venerable Rishi Bhrigu was produced by Brahma from fire at the sacrifice of Varuna." The *Bhagavata Purana* says that "he sprang from the skin of the Creator;" and the *Mahabharata,* in another verse, declares that "the venerable Bhrigu, having split Brahma's heart, issued forth."

At the great sacrifice of Daksha, to which Siva was not invited, Bhrigu officiated as priest; and because he reviled that god and his followers, and justified Daksha in slighting him, he suffered the loss of his beard.

The *Mahabharata* gives a legend of Bhrigu cursing Indra. The Indra of that age, named Nahusha, being filled with pride, lost the benefit of his previous good works, and in his presumption caused the Rishis to carry him about. When it came to Agastya's turn to carry him, Bhrigu said to him, "Why do we submit to the insults of this wicked king of the gods ?" Agastya replied that none of the Rishis had cursed Nahusha, because he had received as a boon the power to subject to his service any on whom he fixed his eye; but that at the same time he was quite ready to act upon any suggestion Bhrigu might make. Bhrigu then told him that he had been sent by Brahma to take vengeance on Nahusha, who would that very day attach Agastya to his car and kick him; but incensed at this insult, he (Bhrigu) would by a curse condemn the oppressor to become a serpent.

The mighty Nahusha summoned Agastya from the banks of the Sarasvati to carry him. The glorious Bhrigu then said to Maitravarum (Agastya), "Close thy eyes, whilst I enter into the knot of thy hair!" With the view of overthrowing the king, Bhrigu hid himself in the hair of Agastya, who then stood motionless as a stock. Nahusha came to Agastya, when the sage desired to be attached to the vehicle, and agreed to carry the king of the gods wherever he pleased. Nahusha attached him, but Bhrigu did not venture to look at him, knowing his power of subduing by a glance. Agastya kept his temper; even when urged by a goad, he remained unmoved. The king at last kicked him; then Bhrigu, invisible in the hair of Agastya, became enraged, and violently cursed him : "Since, fool, thou hast in thine anger smitten the great Muni on the head with thy foot, therefore become a serpent, and fall swiftly to the earth." Thus cursed, Nahusha fell to the earth; had the sage been seen by Indra, he would have been unable to punish the oppressor.

Bhrigu on another occasion cursed Agni. The *Mahabharata* says:—A woman named Puloma was betrothed to a demon; Bhrigu, seeing her beauty, married her according to Vedic rites, and carried her off. The demon, by the aid of Agni, discovered the bride's hiding-place, and took her away to his home. For rendering the demon this assistance, Bhrigu, cursing Agni, said, "From this day, you shall eat everything." Agni asked Bhrigu why he had cursed him, seeing that by speaking the truth he had simply done his duty; and reminded him that "when a person is asked a question, and intentionally speaks what is false, he, with seven preceding and seven succeeding generations, is cast into hell; and that he who withholds information is equally guilty." He goes on to say, "I, too, can curse, but respecting Brahmans restrain my anger. I am really the mouth of the gods and ancestors. When *ghi* is offered to them, they partake of it through me as their mouth; how then can I be said to eat everything ?" Bhrigu hearing this consented to modify his curse, by saying that, "as the Sun by his light and heat purifies all nature, so Agni should purify all that passed through him."

Bhrigu is said to have performed a most wonderful deed; the transforming of a Kshattriya king into a Brahman. The *Mahabharata* gives the following account of this unique work:— "Divodasa, King of Kasi (Benares), was attacked by the sons of Vitahavya, and all his family slain in battle. The afflicted monarch therefore resorted to the sage Bharadvaja, who performed for him a sacrifice, in consequence of which a son named Pratardana was born to him. Pratardana, becoming an accomplished warrior, was sent by his father to take vengeance on the Vitahavyas. Vitahavya had now to fly to another sage, Bhrigu, who promised his protection. The avenger Pratardana, however, followed, and demanded that the refugee should be given up. Bhrigu, the most eminent of religious men, filled with compassion, said, 'There is no Kshattriya here; all these are Brahmans.' Hearing this true assertion of Bhrigu, Pratardana was glad, and, gently touching the sage's feet, rejoined, 'Even thus, O glorious saint, I have gained my object, for I have compelled this king to relinquish his caste.' This Vitahavya, by the mere word of Bhrigu, became a Brahman Rishi, and an utterer of the Vedas."

In the *Ramayana* there are not many references to Bhrigu; he is there called a Maharishi; and, Rama is induced to slay a female demon by the remembrance that Vishnu slew Bhrigu's wife when she aspired to Indra's throne. He is the saint whom the childless wives of Sagar worshipped in order to obtain a son; and he gave to one lady one, to the other sixty thousand. Parasurama was one of his most illustrious descendants.

Pulastya

Pulastya, another of Brahma's mind-born sons, is reverenced because it was through him that the Puranas were made known to men. The reason of his being regarded as the Revealer of Scripture is taught in the *Vishnu Purana*, where the narrator Parasara, in answer to a question of his disciple Maitreya, says: "You recall to my mind what was of old narrated by my father's father, Vasishtha. I had heard that my father had been devoured by a Rakshas, employed by Visvamitra : violent anger seized me, and I commenced a sacrifice for the destruction of the Rakshasas; hundreds of them were reduced to ashes by the rite, when, as they were about to be entirely extirpated, my grandfather Vasishtha thus spake to me: 'Enough, my child; let thy wrath be appeased; the Rakshasas are not culpable : thy father's death was the work of destiny.' "

Parasara ceased from his sacrifice, and his grandfather was pleased; then Pulastya coming said to him : "Since, in the violence of animosity, you have listened to the words of your progenitor, and exercised clemency, you shall become learned in every science. Since you have forborne, even though incensed, to destroy my posterity, I will bestow on you another boon; you shall become the author of a summary of the Puranas, shall know the true nature of the deities, and your understanding through my favour shall be perfect and free from doubts." Parasara relates the Purana as told him formerly "by Vasishtha and the wise Pulastya."

Pulastya married Prithi, a daughter of Daksha, by whom he had a son, the sage Agastya; the *Bhagavata* calls his wife Havisbhu, whose sons were Agastya and Visravas, the father of Kubera, Ravana, and other Rakshasas.

The reason of Parasara's attack upon the Rakshasas is given in a legend in the *Mahabharata.* King Kalmashapada, meeting with Sakti (Parasara's father) in a narrow path in a forest, wished him to get out of his way. This the sage refused to do; whereupon the king-thrashed him with his whip; in return Sakti cursed him, and he became a Rakshas. When in this form, the king killed and ate Sakti and all the other sons of Vasishtha. Sakti's wife being pregnant at the time of his death, Parasara was born soon after and brought up with his grandfather. When he grew up, he commenced the slaughter of the Rakshasas, but was restrained by Vasishtha, Pulastya, and others.

Pulaha

This Rishi does not figure largely in Hindu mythology. He married a daughter of Daksha named Kshama (Patience), by whom he had three sons.

Kratu

Kratu is no more widely known than Pulaha. He married Ṣannati (Humility), another daughter of Daksha, by whom he had "sixty thousand

Balakhilyas, pigmy sages no bigger than the joint of the thumb; chaste, pious, and resplendent as the rays of the sun."

Angiras

Angiras is famed as the author of several hymns of *Rig-Veda*. He first married Smriti (Memory), by whom he had four daughters, and afterwards he married Swaddha (Oblation) and Sati, also Daksha's daughters. His so-called daughters, the Pratyangirasa Richas, are thirty-five verses addressed to presiding divinities. There is some ambiguity in the use of his name; it comes from the same root as Agni of which deity it is used as an epithet; it is also used of Agni's father, and is the name of a son of Agneya, Agni's daughter. Angiras is supposed to have been associated with Bhrigu in introducing fire-worship into India.

Marichi

Marichi is better known through his descendants than from any work of his own, his most illustrious child being Kasyapa, whose son was Vishnu, in his incarnation as a dwarf. Amongst Kasyapa's thirteen wives were Diti and Aditi, who became the mothers of gods. The *Vishnu Purana* states:— "there were twelve celebrated deities in a former age called Tushitas, who, on the approach of the present period, or during the reign of the last Manu Chakshusa, said amongst themselves, 'Come, let us quickly enter into the womb of Aditi, that we may be born in the next Manvantara, for thereby we shall again enjoy the rank of gods. Accordingly they were born the sons of Kasyapa, the son of Marichi by Aditi; thence named the twelve Adityas, whose names were Vishnu, Sakra, Aryaman, Dhuti, Tvastri, Pushan, Vivasvat, Savitri, Mitra, Varuna, Ansa, and Bhaga."

An explanation of the fact that gods undergo successive births is found in the *Vayu Parana*. In the beginning of the Kalpa, twelve gods, named Jayas, were created by Brahma as his deputies and assistants in creation. They, lost in meditation, neglected his commands, on which he declared that they should be reborn in each Manvantara until the seventh. The *Vishnu Purana* tries to explain this fact : "These classes of divinities are born again at the end of a thousand ages according to their own pleasure, and their appearance and disappearance are spoken of as a birth and death; but they exist age after age in the same manner as the sun sets and rises again."

By his wife Diti, Kasyapa had two sons, Hiranyakasipu and Hiranyaksha, whom Vishnu, incarnated to destroy; these mortal enemies were therefore cousins.

Atri

Atri was the author of many Vedic hymns, especially those "praising Ạgni, Indra, the Asvins, and the Viswadevas." He married Anasuya, who bore him Durvasas, the sage who was slighted by Indra. Soma, the moon, is said to proceed from the eyes of his father Atri.

When this sage and his wife were old, they received a visit at their hermitage from Rama, Sita, and Lakshman, who were then wandering from place to place—

"He came to Atri's pure retreat,
Paid reverence to his holy feet,
And from the saint such, welcome won
As a fond father gives his son."

Atri, in introducing his wife to his illustrious guests, thus describes her—

"Ten thousand years this votaress, bent
On sternest rites of penance, spent;
She, when the clouds withheld their rain,
And drought ten years consumed the plain,
Caused grateful roots and fruits to grow
And ordered Ganga here to flow;
So from their cares the saints she freed,
Nor let these checks their rites impede.
She wrought in heaven's behalf, and made
Ten nights of one, the gods to aid."

Anasuya then joins with her husband in welcoming the exiles to their hermitage, and, delighted with the princess, tells her to ask a boon. As, however, Sita appeared to want nothing particular, the aged saint said—

"My gift to-day
Thy sweet contentment shall repay :
Accept this precious robe to wear,
Of heavenly fabric, rich and rare;
These gems thy limbs to ornament,
This precious balsam sweet of scent.
O Maithil dame ! this gift of mine

Shall make thy limbs with beauty shine,
And, breathing o'er thy frame, dispense
Its pure and lasting influence.
This balsam, on thy fair limbs spread,
New radiance on thy lord shall shed,
As Lakshmi's beauty lends a grace
To Vishnu's own celestial face."

Daksha

Daksha, the father of Uma, the consort of Siva, has attained pre-eminence amongst his brethren largely through the greatness of his son-in-law. He, too, is a mind-born son of Brahma; or, according to other accounts, sprang from the thumb of his father. He is one of the chief Prajapatis. Before speaking of Daksha, as the term Prajapati is of frequent occurrence, it will not be out of place here to describe the position of these beings.

The term Prajapati means a lord of creatures; the Prajapatis, therefore, are regarded as the progenitors of mankind. Sometimes Brahma alone is intended by the term Prajapati; he is the "lord of creatures;" sometimes it is employed for the first-formed men from whom the human race sprang. The word was originally employed as an epithet of Savitri and Soma, as well as of Hiranyagarbha, or Brahma. It afterwards, however, came to denote a separate deity, who appears in three places in the *Rig-Veda* Prajapati is sometimes identified with the universe, and described (in the same way as Brahma) as having alone existed in the beginning, as the source out of which creation was evolved : "*e.g.* Prajapati was this universe; Vak was a second to him. She became pregnant, she departed from him, she produced these creatures. She again entered into Prajapati." At the same time he is sometimes described as a secondary or subordinate deity, and treated as one of thirty-three deities.

By the time Manu wrote, creation had come to be regarded as the special work of Brahma, hence the term Prajapati is applied to him in the *Dharmasastra,* and in the later writings it is given to those who sprang from him, and carried on his work of populating the world.

The *Mahabharata* gives two distinct accounts of the origin of Daksha:—"Daksha, the glorious Rishi, tranquil in spirit, and great in austere fervour, sprang from the right thumb of Brahma. From the left thumb sprang the great Muni's wife, by whom he begot fifty daughters."

"Born with all splendour, like that of the great Rishis, the ten sons of Prachetas (another Prajapati) are reputed to have been virtuous and holy, and by them the glorious beings (trees, plants, etc.), were formerly burnt up by fire springing from their mouth. From them was born Daksha Prachetasa; and from Daksha, the parent of the world, (were produced) these creatures. Cohabiting with Virini, the Muni Daksha begat a thousand sons like himself, famous for their religious observances."

Fuller particulars of Daksha's origin are in the *Vishnu Parana*. From Brahma, were born mind-engendered progeny, with forms and faculties derived from his nature. But as they did not multiply themselves, Brahma, created other mind-born sons like himself, viz. Bhrigu, etc. Considerable variety prevails in this list of Prajapatis, but the variations are of the nature of additions made to an apparently original enumeration of but seven, whose names generally occur. The names mentioned in all the Puranas make up altogether seventeen.

The *Vishnu Parana* also speaks of Daksha as a son of the Prachetasas, and gets over the difficulty by the statement that he was born first as a son of Brahma, and afterwards as the son of the Prachetasas. These progenitors of Daksha were the sons of a mighty patriarch named Prachinaverhis, so called "from his placing upon the earth the sacred grass pointing to the East." At the termination of a season of rigid penance, he married Savarna, the daughter of the ocean, who had by him ten sons, styled Prachetasas, who were skilled in military science; "they all observed the same duties, practised religious austerities, and remained immersed in the bed of the sea for ten thousand years." The reason for this prolonged penance was the fact that their father had been enjoined by Brahma to increase the human family. In harmony with his promise of obedience, he told his sons that the performance of severe penance was the best way of fulfilling Brahma's order; "for whoever worships Vishnu, the bestower of good, attains undoubtedly the object of his desires : there is no other mode."

As the sons were immersed in the ocean, intent on the worship of Vishnu, that deity appeared to them, and, hearing their request, said, "Receive the boon you have desired; for I am content with you." Whilst the Prachetasas were absorbed in their devotions, "the trees grew and overshadowed the unprotected earth, the people perished, the winds could not blow, the sky was shut out from view by the boughs, and mankind unable to labour for ten thousand years. When the sages saw this, wind (which tore up the trees) and flames (which then consumed them) issued from their mouths, and the forests were soon cleared away.

Soma, the sovereign of the vegetable world, seeing nearly all the trees destroyed, went to the patriarchs and said, 'Restrain your indignation, and listen to me. I will make an alliance between you and the trees. Prescient of futurity, I have nourished this maiden, the daughter of the woods. She is called Marisha, and, as your bride, she shall be the multiplier of the race of Druva. From a portion of your and my lustre the patriarch Daksha shall be born, who, endowed with a part of me and composed of your vigour, shall be resplendent as fire, and shall multiply the human race.' "

Soma then informs the brothers respecting Marisha's origin. "There was formerly a sage named Kandu, eminent in wisdom and austerity, on the banks of the Gomati. Indra sent, the nymph Pramlocha to divert the sage from his devotions : they lived together for 150 years, during which time the Muni was given up to pleasure. The nymph at the close of this period asked leave to depart, but the Muni entreated her to continue with him. And though at the end of several centuries she preferred the same request, again and again she was asked to remain.

"On one occasion, as the sage was going forth from their cottage in a great hurry, the nymph asked where he was going. 'The day,' he replied,' is drawing fast to a close. I must perform the Sandhya worship, or a duty will be neglected.' The nymph smiled mirthfully as she rejoined, 'Why do you talk, grave sir, of this day drawing to a close; your day is a day of many years, a day that must be a marvel to all: explain what this means.' The Muni said, 'Fair maiden, you came to the river-side at dawn. I beheld you then, and you entered the hermitage. It is now the revolution of evening, and the day is gone. What is the meaning of this laughter ? Tell me the truth.' Pramlocha answered, 'You say rightly, venerable Brahman, that I came hither at morning dawn, but several hundred years have passed since the time of my arrival. This is the truth.' " She informed him that they had lived together nine hundred and seven years, six months, and three days. The Muni sees now that the nymph must have been sent by Indra purposely to interrupt his devotions, and deprive him of the divine knowledge he had desired. And though very angry with her at first, he bids her depart in peace, as he says, "The sin is wholly mine."

"Thus addressed by the Muni, Pramlocha stood trembling, whilst big drops of perspiration started from every pore, till he angrily cried to her, 'Begone, begone !' She then, reproached by him, went forth from his dwelling, and, passing through the air, wiped the perspiration from her person with the leaves of the trees. The nymph went from tree to tree, and as with dusky shoots that crowned their summits she dried her limbs, which were covered with moisture, the child she had conceived by the Rishi came forth from the pores of her skin in drops of perspiration. The trees received the living dews, and the winds collected them into one mass. 'This,' said Soma, 'I matured by my rays, and gradually it increased in size, till the exhalation that had rested on the tree-tops became the lovely girl named Marisha. The trees will give her to you, Prachetasas; let your indignation be appeased. She is the progeny of Kandu, the child of Pramlocha, the nursling of the trees, the daughter of the wind and moon.' "

Soma then informs the Prachetasas that Marisha, in her previous birth, was the widow of a prince, but left childless. She therefore earnestly worshipped Vishnu, who told her to desire some boon. She replied, "I pray thee that in succeeding births I may have honourable husbands, and a son equal to a patriarch among men, ... and may I be born out of the ordinary course." Vishnu promised her : "In another life you shall have ten husbands of mighty prowess, and renowned for glorious acts; and you shall have a son magnanimous and valiant, distinguished by the rank of a patriarch, from whom the various races of men shall multiply, and by whose posterity the universe shall be filled. You, virtuous lady, shall be of marvellous birth, and delighting the hearts of men." Thus having spoken, the deity disappeared, and Soma informs his hearers that it was this princess who was born as Marisha.

"Soma having concluded, the Prachetasas took Marisha, righteously to wife, relinguishing their indignation against the trees, and upon her they begot the eminent patriarch Daksha, who had (in a former life) been born as the son of Brahma. This great sage, for the furtherance of creation and the increase of mankind, created progeny. Obeying the command of Brahma, he made movable and immovable things, the bipeds and quadrupeds, and subsequently by his will gave birth to females, ten of whom he bestowed on Dharma, thirteen on Kasyapa, and twenty-seven, who regulate the course of time, on Soma (the moon). From that period forward living creatures were engendered in an ordinary manner; before the time of Daksha, they were variously propagated by the will, by sight, by touch, and by the influence of religious austerities by devout sages and holy saints."

Daksha's first attempts at populating the world were unsuccessful. A thousand sons were born to him by Asikni, but these were induced by Narada not to propagate offspring. A thousand other sons by the same wife were born, who also were advised by Narada not to be troubled with children. The Prajapati, incensed, cursed Narada, and proceeded to create sixty daughters by Asikni, whom he gave to various husbands, by whom they had children. At length, when a time of peace and prosperity prevailed on the earth, and the gods had their proper places assigned to them, to Daksha was given the position as chief of the Prajapatis —progenitors of mankind.

Vasishtha

Vasishtha, together with Pulastya, is said to have narrated the *Vishnu Purana*, and he, too, is believed to have been the writer of many of the Vedic hymns. It was he who allayed the anger of Parasara when that sage was about to extirpate the Rakshas race, because one of their kings had slain his father. He is said to have been the Vyasa, or arranger of the Vedas, in the Dvapara Age; this work of arranging having a different agent in each age.

Vasishtha served as the family priest of several kings. One of these, named Saudasa, when out hunting, seeing a couple of tigers, shot one of them with an arrow. It happened that these tigers were really Rakshasas, for, as the one shot by Saudasa was dying, it assumed a fiendish shape; the other, threatening vengeance, disappeared. Not long after this, as the king was engaged in a sacrifice, Vasishtha being out of the room, the Rakshas who escaped, assuming the form of Vasishtha, came to the king and said, "Now that the sacrifice is ended, give me something to eat; let it be cooked, and I will presently return." The Rakshas next transformed himself into the cook, and, having prepared a dish of human flesh, brought it to the king. When the real Muni entered, the king offered him the dish; but he discovered by the force of meditation, that it was human flesh that was presented to him. Indignant at the insult, cursing the king, he said, "Your appetite shall be excited by similar food to that now offered me." The king was astonished at this outburst of anger, and Vasishtha, seeing this, by further meditation, discovered the whole trick; but as he could not entirely recall the effects of his curse, he modified it so that it was to work for twelve years only. It was this same king who was cursed by Vasishtha's son Sakti to become a Rakshas, and who, in that state, devoured the sage that cursed him.

Vasishtha also cursed a king named Nimi. As the king was about to commence a sacrifice that was to continue for a thousand years, he asked Vasishtha to officiate as priest; but the Muni being engaged in a similar work for Indra, he could not do so for the next five hundred years. The king proceeded with his sacrifice; engaging Gautama as priest. As soon as his engagement was over with Indra, the sage, coming to conduct Nimi's sacrifice, found another priest had been appointed. He was so angry that, cursing the king, he declared that he should cease to exist in a bodily form. On learning what was done, the king in return pronounced a similar curse upon the sage. Both took effect; but as Vasishtha's spirit became united to the spirits of Mitra and Varuna, when these deities were smitten with the beauty of the nymph Urvasi, the spirit of the sage fell from them, and he became again incorporated through her. A verse in'the *Rig-Veda* ascribes Vasishtha's birth to Mitra and Varuna, in harmony with the legend just quoted: "Thou, O Vasishtha, art a son of Mitra and Varuna, born a Brahman from the soul of Urvasi. All the gods placed in the vessel thee—the drop which had fallen through divine contemplation."

There are several stories of quarrels between this sage and Visvamitra, who was anxious to obtain the position of priest to Saudasa, which was held by Vasishtha. At another time, when he was priest to Harischandra, he was so greatly incensed at the treatment the king had received at Visvamitra's hands that he cursed him, and he became a crane. His rival returned the compliment, and he too became a bird. In this form the sages fought so violently that it was necessary for Brahma to pacify them. The real cause of all this unpleasantness was the fact that Visvamitra was a Kshattriya by birth, who, by penance and various rites, had obtained admission into the Brahmanical caste. Previous to his exaltation he was a king. Being desirous of obtaining a wonderful cow that belonged to Vasishtha, which had the power to grant whatever her owner desired, as he could not overcome the Brahmans, owing to their superhuman power, he first sought to raise himself to equality with them, and at length his efforts were crowned with success.

Narada

Narada's name is not found in the list of Brahma's sons in the *Vishnu Purana*, yet he is generally regarded as one, though, according to some authorities, he had a different origin. He is the messenger of the gods, and is often described as imparting information that was only known to them.

It was he who persuaded the sons of Daksha not to beget offspring, and who was cursed for his interference; it was he who informed Kansa of the approaching birth of Krishna, which led that king to slay the children of Vasudeva: hence his common name is Kalikaraka, the strife-maker, and in modern plays he is introduced as such. The name Narada is frequently used to describe a quarrelsome, meddling person.

The accounts of Narada's origin vary considerably. According to the *Bhagavata,* he was the third incarnation of Vishnu. Manu declares that he was one of the Maharishis whom he created at the beginning of the age. The *Siva Purana* teaches that Narada sprang from the thigh of his father: "Brahma, in view of peopling the world, produced four beings, who, being refractory, caused their parent to weep. To comfort him, Siva, in the character of Rudra, issued from a fold in his forehead, with five heads and ten arms, and, endowing Brahma with additional might, he (Brahma) produced Bhrigu and the seven Rishis and after that Narada from his thigh."

In another birth Narada was the son of Kasyapa and a daughter of Daksha. Daksha was greatly incensed when he dissuaded the Prajapati's sons from peopling the world, and declared that he should not have a resting-place; hence his wandering nature.

On one occasion Narada was cursed by his own father, and he in return cursed Brahma. "Brahma exhorted his son Narada to take a wife, and assist in peopling the world. Narada, who was a votary of Krishna, becomes angry, affirms that devotion to that god is the sole way to attain felicity, and denounces his father as an erring instructor. Brahma, in reply, curses Narada, and dooms him to a life of sensuality, and subjection to women. Narada pays back the imprecation as follows : 'Wretch ! become no object of adoration : how shall any one be devoted to the forms of thy worship ? Thou shalt without, doubt lust after her who is no fit object of thy desires!' Through this curse of Narada, the creator of the world ceased to be an object of worship. Beholding the beauty of his daughter, he ran after her.

In the *Mahabharata,* Narada figures as a religious teacher; and in the *Uttara Kanda* of the *Ramayana* is a specimen of his teaching. A Brahman, carrying the dead body of his son, came to the door of Rama's palace at Ayodha; and bewailing his loss, as he himself was unconscious of any fault, he believed it to be owing to some misconduct on the part of the king. Rama summoned his councillors, when the divine sage Narada spoke as follows : "Hear, O king, how the boy's untimely death occurred;

and, having heard the truth regarding what ought to be done, do it." The story, briefly told, is as follows: "A presumptuous Sudra, paying no regard to the fact that during the age in which he lived the prerogative of practising self-mortification had not descended to the humble class to which he belonged, had been guilty of seeking to secure a store of religious merit by its exercise. Rama; after considerable search, comes upon a person who was engaged in the manner described by Narada. The Sudra avows his caste, and his desire to conquer for himself the rank of a god, by the self-mortification he was undergoing. Rama instantly cuts off the offender's head; the gods applaud the deed, and, having been encouraged by them to ask a boon, Rama requests that the Brahman's boy may be resuscitated. He is informed that he was restored to life the very moment that the Sudra was slain."

Narada was the friend and companion of Krishna, and was famed for his musical talents, but, becoming presumptuous on account of them, he emulated the divine strains of Krishna, who severely punished him for his presumption by placing his *vina* in the paws of a bear, when it emitted sounds far sweeter than those of the mortified musician. Krishna played many practical jokes on his friend; on one occasion he went so far as to metamorphose him into a woman.

Great honour is given to Narada because he is said to have revealed to Valmiki the *Ramayana,* which opens as follows :—

"To sainted Narad, prince of those
Whose lore in words of wisdom flows,
Whose constant care and chief delights
Were scripture and ascetic rites,
The good Valmiki, first and best
Of hermit saints, these words addressed
In all the world, I pray thee, who
Is virtuous, heroic, true ?
Firm in his vows, of grateful mind,
To every creature good and kind?
Bounteous and holy, just and wise,
Alone most fair to all men's eyes?
* * * *
Grant, saint divine, the boon I ask,
For thee, I ween, an easy task,

To whom the power is given to know
If such a man breathe here below.'
Then Narad, clear before whose eye
The present, past, and future lie,
Made ready answer!"

Narada proceeds to narrate the life of Rama to Valmiki, who feels that the task of writing down what was told him is too great a work for his powers, until Brahma himself appears, and encourages him to proceed—

"Then come, O best of seers, relate
The life of Rama, good and great;
The tale that saintly Narad told
In all its glorious length unfold."

13

SYMBOLISM OF GODS AND GODDESSE

Art of God Symbolism

Conceptual thinking is hard for many. To contemplete upon the formless and therefore the Transcendental Essence is given to a few. The majority needs some grosser expression of the Pure and the Infinite, for their mind to conceive It and their intellect to contemplate upon It. These "symbols" of the Eternal Ground, the Supreme Truth, are called idols.

Thus, an idol represents an ideal. When we do not know the ideal which a given idol represents, it is something like seeing a portrait in a studio. If it were my beloved's portrait I would have seen in it more than what the picture represents.

In the same way the religious symbols and idols have a deeper depth for us to discover, over and above their mere external shape, the general forms of the symbol and, in each, even the exact arrangements of its various aspects.

To bring out eloquently the voiceless beauty and joy of the Infinite, through unsaid significances of Its finite expressions and symbols, is called Mysticism. All religious idols are mystic–symbols. To learn the art of interpreting them is to experience a harmony in our devoted contemplations heard without ears, seen without eyes.

Melody carved in stone is scupture. Sculpture in melody is music. In colours it becomes painting. And this medium of word painting has been chosen by the poet–seer, Vyasa, to describe the Indescribable, in the Puranas.

The theme of the *Upanishads* is too subtle for the average intellect to comprehend and when one is not able to appreciate an ideal one would necessarily fail to apply one's mind to it. Unless the student is capable of clearly visualising a concept and continuously meditating upon it, he will not be able to experience the highest beatitude that has been promised as the achievable final goal in all the scriptures of the world.

In order to help children to understand their country we use maps The map is a physical guide for the students intellectual growth. In the same way, in order to help the seeker comprehend the Infinite Reality and the philosophical concepts of Vedanta, Vyasa, the teacher, felt the need for supplying some conceivable representations and these are provided in the word-pictures and the stories in the *Puranas.*

These representations, we find very often, have normal forms, but it is not unusual for Vyasa to take even impossible anatomical features and structures to describe the All-Pervading Essence of the Self; for, the One Infinite Reality Itself has become the world of endless forms and, naturally, therefore, every form in the universe is, in a sense, but a representation of the Primeval Truth.

Thus, these Puranic stories were written for the benefit of the early students of Spiritual Truth, and, in his pages, the irresistible philosopher and Man of Realization in Vyasa could not remain permanently hidden. Now and then the mask of the teacher falls off and the theme of the *Upanishads* unconsciously flows out of his pen. As we read the Purana we find that the drab description,of the man-like deities are enhanced by Vyasa adding effulgent strokes of the Upanishadic concepts to make the gods directly reveal their real essence as the Eternal Soul of the Universe.

In the *Upanishads* we find very many methods of meditation *(Upasanas)* which are all techniques to develop the seeker's powers of concentration, which each student has to practise by bringing his entire thoughts channelized into the given line of contemplation. As time passed, the population increased and, consequently, the competition for existence became more and more severe. In a competitive society, the individual mind gets more and more shattered and, under such continuous tensions, it is difficult for the mind to discover the necessary poise for pursuing the methods of concentration prescribed in the *Upanishads.* By the time of Vyasa, a psychological situation had arisen wherein it was found necessary that the teacher must provide the students with a fresh technique. In the *Puranas* Vyasa had so successfully concieved these new deities and the easier methods of meditating upon them that the Vedic methods fell almost completely into disuse, and in their place the Pauranic gods and goddesses got accepted as the most popular. Herein I proposed to point out the symbolism of a few of the deities most popularly worshipped.

Nothing has so directly helped the Hindus to feel their common religious bond as the worship of these deities, the most important and popular of them being Rama, Krishna, Siva, Vishnu, Narayana and Devi. In the temples of these gods, Hindus of all classes and persuasions together worship and feel the exhilaration of the Spirit. For centuries these temples and the common worship of these deities held the Hindu society together, providing a common bond of love and devotion, creating among them a great sense of pride and brotherhood.

Symbolism in Hindu Mythology

The term "Symbol" signifies a *mudra,* a seal or a mark, imparting certain implications and ideas. In the term mudra lies concealed, an expression of Truth through a suggestive pose or posture of the body or a limb, capable of depicting a vast source of wisdom underlying the same. For example, Shri Sankaracharya the great saint, is said to have held the *bhadra mudra,* a combination of the tip of the forefinger and the thumb. He was silent in the midst of his disciples seated under the shade of a Banyan tree giving them a very eloquent speech in absolute silence while holding up the *bhadra mudra* before them to clear their doubts, reveal the ultimate Truth, and lead them to the aim and destiny of the human soul. He was more eloquent in silence than in speech in deference to the general principle "the more we talk, the more the confusion, the lesser we talk, the lesser the confusion, and if we do not talk, there is no possibility of any confusion at all," because everyone is left to himself to have his doubts cleared according to his own light and intellectual development at the given time.

Symbolism is employed to simplify human effort to expose the ultimate Truth and the underlying principles, giving adequate opportunities to the aspirants to interpret it in a way in which they will get their answers from and in themselves. Such and other devices are nothing new to other religions either because the ultimate aim and end of man is expressed only through symbolism. The Cross of Christianity is symbolic enough to impart the idea that Jesus Christ sacrificed his life at the instance of heretics and truth should always be prepared to face and endure martyrdom at the hands of heretics and non-believers. Symbolism is the most effective way of propagating the Truth because it can be appreciated and enjoyed by the truly deserving devotees, each according to his or her light and vision.

A mass of ideas are indicated in a symbol. A man makes himself better understood by signs and symbols and, if language fails to prove his case or cause, he establishes the same through the movements of his limbs or to supplement or emphasise his arguments. In Kerala there is a highly developed folk-dance called *Kathakali,* wherein the different characters effectively play their parts and communicate with each other, only through *mudras* or symbols and not through words. The ideas contained in the background songs are expressed through the movements of the body and the limbs, and they are all well understood, highly appreciated, and thoroughly enjoyed by all those in the audience who know the techniques of the art. All sentiments of the human mind are thus expressed effectively.

In this connection, let us consider the Hindu trinity and their spouses. Siva, is represented with matted hair, tiger-skin apparel, triple-eyed, adorned with snakes, besmeared with ashes all over, residing at the top-most point on the earth on the Himalayan peak called Kailas, perhaps also the coldest part of the earth in proximity to human habitation. The place is covered with snow and everything is snow-white. He has a trident in His hand, and the other hand is held in *chinmudra*. The matted hair proclaims the length and intensity of his *tapas*, and the cobra around his matted hair signifies that even the most poisonous become harmless because the one that has identified himself with the Supreme has gone beyond all the effects of matter on his senses or organs and has become immune even to the deadliest of poisons. The third eye in the midst of the forehead represents the concentration of *jnana* (knowledge) and therefore the absolute power to destroy *tamas* (laziness) and all its manifestations. The blue colour of the neck symbolises the pervasiveness of *maya* or *avidya* (ignorance) upto the neck. Blue colour represents distance. This can as well warn us about the vast distance that we'll have to traverse from the realms of the body and the heart to the realms of the intellect and beyond. The ashes that besmear the body recalls to us that this body of which we are proud and obsessed is ultimately bound to end up merely as ashes. This realisation is really the starting point in the march towards the final emancipation. It can also mean the complete dehydration of all the *vasanas* (perterbrations) at the mental level. The Trident stands for *sama* (equality), *dama* (self-control) and *vairagya* (dispassion) which dispel and destroy the six qualities which pull us down, namely *kama, krodha, lobha, moha, mada* and *matsarya* (lust, anger, greed, delusion, intoxication, envy). By directing the trident mercilessly against these weaknesses, one becomes conscious of the worthlessness of this wordly existence and this awakening helps one to forge ahead to the summum bonum of human birth and existence – Liberation. He revels in the cremation ground, the place of death and the haunting grounds of ghosts and evil spirits. Siva, by his *tapas,* austerities, and consequent wisdom, has conquered the concept of death and all its hideous retinue, and they are all under his overlordship and command. The tiger-skin apparel stands for *vairagya* and absolute unconcern for the body and its supposed needs. The *chinmudra* in which he holds his hand teaches us that our ego – which is concentrated on the index finger – must bend and that our individuality must end as represented by the symbol 'zero' which the index finger produces when it bends and touches the middle of the thumb in the thumb in the *mudra.* So, the form of Siva is depicted in such a way that each and every aspect of his personality has a much deeper significance to convey. The eternal truth is expressed more in dignified silence than in vociferous eloquence.

Siva's spouse is represented as Parvati (Durga) who is said to be invincible. She is the manifesting power of Siva, both potential and dynamic, functioning through the means and medium of Siva. Siva left to himself is impotent and inactive, and it is only through association with her *sakti* that He becomes efficient of manifestation. The Devi cult of worship is anterior to the Deva cult because the saints and the sages worshipped Power more than Form. As the electric energy is creative, sustaining and destructive at the same time, so also the primordial power functions through different forms and names in different aspects. Her name differs according to the functional names of Siva, as when he is Rudra she is Rudrani, and she is Bhavani when he is Bhava, etc. She is pure white, when she is *santi durga*, and blesses her *upasakas* with *bhakti* (devotion) and *mukti* (liberation). She becomes multi-headed and multi-armed when she is engaged in fighting with Mahishasura, Chanda, Munda, etc., which only represent the multitude of undivine qualities to conquer which a multi-faced and multi-pronged attack is necessary. She can change her form at will, as conditions and circumstances demand and she is named after her success in the warfare. So she is called 'Mahishasura Mardini', 'Chandika', 'Chamundi', etc.

Vishnu is represented as the lord of protection, with four hands, with four symbols, with a crown, and a spouse who is called Lakshmi,the goddess of prosperity. Her feet are on a .fully-blossomed lotus - which stands for the *sahasrara kamala*, the fully-blossomed seat of divine prosperity. She is with four hands representing the four *purusharthas* – *dharma, artha, kama* and *moksha* – the four spiritual virtues and values of life which every spiritual aspirant is enjoined to adopt and practise as laid down in the scriptures. Her personal charm is par excellence, and around her is the aura of divine happiness and prosperity. Her smiling face with a look of compassion is the prize which the devotees seek for mental consolation, mundane contentent, and spiritual satifaction. Her one palm which is spread downwards represents her character of *daana* (giving, offering) and the other palm held up stands for encouragement and spiritual blessings. Born of the ocean of milk, she is the essence and personification of purity, chastity and generosity, and represents magnanimity and depth of love and compassion. She is integrated with Vishnu who has become Narayana only due to her association - known as Lakshmi-Narayana, the resort and refuge of all for material prosperity and spiritual redemption.

The conch - the *samkha* – in the hand of Vishnu represents the source of the primal sound the *pranava* – the *nada brahman* – the source of all knowledge, the Vedas, and stands for the call to the devotees to listen to the voice of the divine in them. The *chakra* – the discus – is the wheel of time, which turns at His will and decision, under the revolution of which everything is changed and transformed according to the requirement of time. The fully-blossomed lotus in one hand stands for the *sahasrara*, – the thousand petalled lotus-which, according to the yoga system, is the point where the divine wisdom dawns in man. The *mace* in the fourth hand symbolises the authoritative and punishing capacity and aspect to those who stand in need of the same to turn them godward and on to the spiritual path and the higher values of life. The palm turned upwards assures protection to the distressed and the dissipated and the *bhadra mudra* signifies that spiritual'prosperity and divine bliss await the devoted and the virtuous. The devotee feefs his oneness with God, in respect of time, place and proximity. All His incarnations assure us that He is present everywhere,in all forms and names to protect the virtuous and uphold *dharma* according to the requirement of time, conditions and emergency.

Brahma, the creator (as distinct from Brahman the Supreme),is the seat of knowledge and hence creation. He is situated on a fully-blossomed lotus which represents spiritual wisdom, with the power of projection and procreation. He is the physical form of the invisible principle. His two eyes represent the sun and the moon, and his nose the cosmic wind. His four hands stand for the four *purusharthas,* and the four faces are the four Vedas or the sources of knowledge. The garland of beads in one hand points to his incantation of the holy mantra "OM" from which the whole universe has evolved. His spouse is the goddess Saraswati, the mother of learning and wisdom. She is the seat of all the sixty-four *kalas* or accomplishments in the various branches of arts and sciences, and holds a book in her hand to show that the study of the sacred scriptures is indispensable to know her depth and extent, as also to show that knowledge is endless, as even the mother of wisdom still needs to hold a book. She is depicted as playing on a lute to mean that she sings, the melody of life, and invites the devotees to merge into *nada brahman.* All students and seekers after material knowledge and spiritual wisdom, invoke and worship the goddess Saraswati. Even today, great scholars- and orators are invoking the power of Saraswati through *japa, dhyana* and *upasana,* for their effectiveness, superiority, and invincibility.

SYMBOLISM OF IMAGES

Brahma

Brahma is the first member of the orthodox Hindu triad; Vishnu being the second and Siva, the third. Brahma is the God of creation.

In Vedanta, the cosmic-subtle-body called *Hiranya-garbha* is considered to be the creator, Brahma. An individual's subtle body is constituted of his mind and intellect, *i.e.* his entire thoughts. The subtle body of an individual is responsible for the creation of his gross physical body and the world of objects that he experiences. In other words, it is the mind-intellect equipment that projects the physical body and the world. When this equipmeat is absent, there can neither be a physical body nor the world. Hence, the sum of all the subtle bodies of all the living beings, the *Hiranyagarbha,* is said to be the creator of the entire universe.

The manifested world of plurality has emerged from the unmanifest Reality. To indicate this, Brahma, the creator, is described as being born from the navel (*nabhi*) of Vishnu (who represents the eternal reality) , when He is shown underlying on the great serpent *ananta* in the milky ocean.

One of the earliest iconographic descriptions of Brahma is that of a four-faced God seated on a lotus. The Lord has in his four hands a water-pot (*kamandalu*), a manuscript (*Vedas*) , a sacrifical implement (*sruva*) and a rosary (*mala*). He wears the hide of a black antelope and his vehicle is a swan (*hamsa*) .

This description of Brahma, like those of the other deities in Hinduism, bears a mystic symbolism. The Lord sitting on a lotus indicates that He is ever rooted to the infinite reality. Lotus represents the reality, which is the foundation upon which his personality exists.

The four faces of Brahma represent the four Vedas. His four hands, like those of other Gods, stand for the four aspects of man's inner personality (*antahkarana*) *viz.* the mind (*manas*), intellect (*buddhi*), ego (*ahamkar*) and conditioned consciousness (*chitta*). These four are the manifestations of the pure consciousness.

The deer skin worn by him indicates that a seeker, who desires to reach the supreme state of Brahma, must first observe austerities like a *brahmachari.* Observing such austerities, the seeker must carefully study and reflect upon the scriptural truths which are suggested by holding the manuscript (*Vedas*) in one hand representing the *buddhi* (intellect). With such self-control and discipline and having the knowledge of the *sastras* (scriptures), he must use his physical body in selfless and dedicated service (*karma-yoga*) for the general prosperity of all. This is indicate the sacrificial implement held in the second hand (*ahamkar*/ego). When these three spiritual practices are adopted, the mind of the seeker is withdrawn from its preoccupation with the sense pursuits in the external world. Such a mind, which has become introvert and relatively tranquil, alone is suitable for concentration (*dharana*) and *japa* (chanting with the *rosary – mala*) provided in the third-hand (*manas*/mind) . Meditation is the last process by which the seeker is transported from his finite limited individuality into the infinite transcendental state of god-realisation. This is indicated by the holding of the water-pot (*kamandalu*) - a symbol of *sanyas* - in the fourth hand (*chitta*/conditioned consciousness).

Brahma uses the swan (*hamsa*) as his vehicle. Its significance is that a man-of-realization moves about in the world with the unique faculty that a swan possesses. A *hamsa* (swan), as described in the Hindu mythology, has the faculty to separate pure milk from a sample of milk mixed with water. Similarly, a man-of-perfection recognises the one supreme truth inherent in the entire pluralistic phenomena.

The Lord of creation must necessarily possess the knowledge to create. Creation presupposes the possession of a know-how of the process of creation. Hence it is that Brahma is said to be wedded to the Goddess of Knowledge, Saraswati.

Life in this world is a manifestation of the three principles of construction, destruction and sustenance. In fact, these three are inter-connected. The apparent destruction is only an essential forerunner to all construction. Destruction and creation go hand in hand and they are like the two sides of a coin. For example, destruction of the morning is the creation of the evening and the destruction of the evening is the creation of the night. This chain of continuous destruction and construction maintains the day. Hence, the three Gods of the Trinity, *viz.* Brahma, Vishnu and Maheshwara, representing creation, maintenance and destruction, are essentially one and the same principle of existence.

The above idea is well portrayed in Dattatreya, in whose form the three Gods are combined. Dattatreya, has three faces of Brahma, Vishnu and Maheswara (Siva) to indicate that the three principles for which they stand are inseparable. Dattatreya is always shown with four dogs following Him. The four dogs represent the four *Vedas*. A dog is one of the most faithful animals in the world and it follows its master in all environments and circumstances. So too, the *Vedas* said to follow all the actions, thoughts and desires of a man-of-redisation is in perfect accord with the principles enunciated in the *Vedas*.

Brahma is not popularly worshipped in India. This is so, because the idea of creation is repugnant to a seeker of truth. It is the creation of thoughts that has veiled the infinite reality. The attempt of all spiritual seekers is to destroy the existing thoughts and maintain this state until the Truth reveals Itself. Hence, Siva (God of destruction) and Vishnu (God of maintenance) are worshipped more than Brahma. In fact, there are very few temples of Brahma - one in Rajasthan and another in Orissa - compared to numerous shrines of Siva and Vishnu existing all over India.

Vishnu

Vedanta analyses the human being and declares the pure consciousness to be the core of his personality, which manifests through his body, mind and intellect and experiences the world of objects, emotions and thoughts. The consciousness, functioning as the spark of existence in living beings, is the one eternal reality which is the substratum of the entire cosmos as well. This Supreme Reality, which pervades the microcosm and the macrocosm, is described by the sage,Vyasa in the *Vishnu Purana* as Vishnu.

Vishnu is shown as in yogic-sleep (*yoga-nidra*) , in an ocean of milk (*ksheerabdhi*) , on a great serpent (*Ananta*), which has its body coiled up to form His bed. The serpent has a thousand heads and its hood is turned inward looking at its own coiled body. Lakshmi, the consort of the Lord, sits at His feet, serving Him.

Vishnu (Narayana) represents the pure consciousness deep within one's personality beyond-the five layers of matter *viz.* the food, vital, mental, intellectual and blis sheaths. This picture of Narayana lying on the serpent bed in the milky ocean suggests ways and means of recognizing Him as the consciousness in the innermost recesses of one's own heart.

The ocean of milk, in which Narayana rests, represents the purity of one's bosom. White colour represents nobility and purity. The whiteness of the milk indicates one's *sattwic* (noble and pure) tendencies or qualities. The serpent of the mind and its thousand heads represent the infinite variety of thoughts that the mind entertains. When a serpent comes into contact with its victim, it injects poison from its fangs into the body of its victim. If, however, the serpent remains coiled up around itself, there is no letting out of the poison. So too, when man's mind is extrovert, i.e. seeking the world of objects, it develops ego and egocentric desires, which veil the divine self in him. On the other hand, when a *sattwic* (pure) mind turns its attention inward, *i.e.* towards his Self, it develops a tranquility whereby there are no longer any desires or passions arising within him.

The thousand heads of the coiled up serpent are all turned inwards to indicate that the thoughts in a tranquil mind are directed to single pointed meditation upon the Self, the Reality. If such meditation is prolonged in a pure, *sattwic* attitude (ocean of milk), the meditator locates therein the infinite reality, Vishnu.

The Lord is shown to be in yogic-sleep. It means that the realized One, who has reached the state of pure consciousness, is no longer aware of the pluralistic phenomena of perceptions, emotions and thoughts. He has awakened to the infinite, all-pervading reality and He seems to be asleep so far as the terrestrial world is concerned. Hence, it is called *yoga-nidra* (yogic-sleep). Yoga, derived from the root yuj (to join), indicates that He is attuned to the infinite reality; *'nidra'* sleep and it indicates his transcendence to the infinite from the finite realm of experiences of the limited man.

As Narayana is thus lying down on the body of the serpent, Ananta, His consort Lakshmi, sits at His feet and serves Him. Lakshmi symbolises wealth, power and glory. A man-of-realization, who through meditation has thus experienced the highest, is disinterested in the world of objects and achievements. Nevertheless, wealth, power and glory follow him and remain always at his feet. He may use them or reject them without the least thought, because he is ever rooted and revelling in the supreme truth.

Vishnu is the eternal infinite reality. The manifested world of plurality, which man experiences, has emerged from this unmanifest reality. To indicate this, Brahma, the creator, is described as being born from the navel (*nabhi*) of Vishnu. The navel portion represents the psychological centre (*chakra*) from where sound originates in the form of *para vak* (transcendent speech). The inaudible sound passes through two more stages of development, *viz. pashyanti* and *madhyama* before it becomes audible gross speech called *vaikhari*. This audible sound is the quality of space (*akash*), which is the first of the five elements that constitute the entire universe. The production of sound, therefore, symbolises creation. This idea is illustrated by Brahma emerging from the navel of Vishnu.

Vishnu is one of the Gods of the Trinity. He represents the power of sustenance. In order to maintain anything in life, one must have the means to do so. This is indicated by the marriage of Vishnu with Lakshmi, the Goddess of wealth. Unless Vishnu is associated with wealth, how can there be proper maintenance of the created world? In terms of esoteric philosophy, Lakshmi stands for spiritual wealth and auspiciousness.

Vishnu is shown blue in colour and clothed in yellow. He wears a crown and stands upon a lotus. He has four hands and He holds in them a conch (*sankha*), a discus (*chakra*), a mace (*gada*) and a lotus (*padma*). All these are significant symbollisms employed to indicate that Vishnu is none other than the supreme self – the changeless reality around which all the terrestrial changes take place – the imperishable Essence in the perishable world.

The blue colour of Vishnu indicates His infinite stature. Blue colour is associated with the infinite since immeasurable entities like the cloudless sky or the deep ocean appear blue in colour. Yellow represents the earth for two reasons *viz.* (*i*) earth (silica) glows with a yellow colour when introduced in a colourless flame and (*ii*) anything that is buried in the earth for a long period of time gathers a yellowish colour. Vishnu, who is blue in colour and clothed in yellow, therefore represents the descent of the infinite, immeasurable, transcendental truth to the terrestrial realm,i.e. the earth. In other words, Vishnu is the infinite manifesting Himself in a finite form.

When the infinite expresses through a finite form, there is a manifestation of an individual (*jeeva*). The individual comes in contact with and reacts to the world with the help of four subtle equipments in him. They are the four constituents of his subtle body, *viz.* the mind (*manas*), the intellect (*buddhi*) the ego (*ahankar*) and the conditioned-consciousness (*chitta*). The four hands of Vishnu represent these four.

The crown on Vishnu's head signifies His supreme sovereignty and lordship over the entire world of plurality. He is the One who maintains and protects all things and beings in the entire universe.

The deity stands upon a lotus. Lotus represents the Truth. 'Standing upon the lotus', therefore means that the ground or substratum which supports a man-of-perfection is the Brahman, *i.e.* a man-of-perfection is ever rooted in the supreme truth.

In one of His four hands, Vishnu carries a lotus. The lotus indicates the final goal of human evolution. Vishnu invites mankind to reach this goal of perfection,which is the pure self within. The Lord blows His conch (*sankha*) calling mankind to live the higher and nobler values of life so that they may turn their attention away from their preoccupations with the material world and realise the Self within. This call is the whisperings of the inner conscience, which advises man to give up his sensuous appetites and extrovert living and seek the eternal reality. But man does not heed this sacred voice within. He continues with his passionate living until at last he gets knocked down by disappointment and dissatisfaction with life as such. This 'knocking down' is also done by the kindly hand of the Lord using His mace (*gada*). If man, despite the growing sense of restlessness and agitations in his bosom, still persists in his sensual indulgence and does not turn towards the spiritual path, the Lord uses the annihilating power of His discuss (*chakra*). The discus is meant to destroy man's presennt equpment so that he may start afresh, with better equipment and in a more appropriate and conducive environment, for seeking the truth.

Narayana

Analysing the human personality, the Vedanta takes the student to discover the state of pure consciousness in the innermost depth of his being, which is the one source at once for all his perceptions, feelings and thoughts.

Vyasa describes this great reality in his the *Vishnu Purana* as Narayana. Narayana has been shown as resting in yogic-sleep in an ocean of milk (*ksheerabdhi*) Narayana lies in *yoga-nidra* on a great serpent-bed (Ananta), protected by the hood of the serpent. He is served by Lakshmi, His consort, who is ever at His feet.

Deep in the recesses of our personality (*vaikuntha*) lies the infinite truth (Vishnu) upon the serpent-Ananta (the mind) who is depicted as thousand-headed. The serpent represents the vicious mind which, at one and the same time, can think a thousand thoughts. In life it is found that the hooded cobra, to strike its victim, turns its hood away from his body. When the mind is turned towards the world of objects outside, it is capable of spilling its poison on to the world outside.

Here in the description, the hoods are turned upon the body of the serpent and it is lying coiled upon itself, forming a soft bed upon which reclines Vishnu. When the multi-headed human mind turns its attention inward upon itself, and the mind lies coiled upon itself, there is the state of a meditator. The Lord is in "yogic-sleep". It means that, looking from the pure consciousness, the world known to us, constituted of the perceptions, emotions and thoughts, is not there at all; just as in our sleep we do not recognize the world-of-plurality. But this is not the ordinary sleep, (*nidra*); it is a moment of positive experience of the all-pervading reality, and hence it is called the *yoga-nidra*.

Such a vision of the Lord can be experienced by the mind when it turns upon itself; and the mind can gain this steady introvertedness only in an atmosphere of supreme purity. Hence it is described that He is resting in the "milky-ocean".

Lakshmi (wealth, power and glory) rests at His feet, serving Him. A man of realization, who through meditation has thus experienced the soul of the universe in himself, does not thereafter run after the wealth of the world of objects; all glory follows him at his heels, wanting to serve him as his dutiful mistress.

Narayana is the one among the Trinity, representing the power-of-sustenance. He is the one who manifests Himself in the world among mankind at appropriate eras in His various incarnations to rid life of its evil propensities and to make the world ready for greater evolution. When this benign Lord wakes up from His yogic-sleep and comes down to bless those who are His devotees, He assumes the form of Narayana, and the description.of Him is given in a dozen places in the *Vishnua Purana.*

His hands are never empty - each is holding a symbol, together indicating how He carries out his divine duties as the preserver of the universe. He blows the conch, calling man to live the nobler values of life so that he may preoccupations and ultimately reach Him and receive from Him the infinite bliss of unbroken peace and perfection. This "final goal" is represented in Hindu tradition as the lotus.

We many even consider the 'hand that holds the conch' as the intellect (*buddhi*), the 'hand that holds the discus' as the ego, 'that which holds the mace' as the mind (*manas*), and 'that which holds the lotus' as the consciousness (*chitta*). The discriminating intellect gives us the call and points out a more rewarding way of life, and in case we ignore this silent whisper of the heart the mind gives endless knocks to that personality. If even then, we are not able to realize our folly the arrogant ego fattened by these stupidities of the mind in revolt against the intellect, ultimately drives the individual to his total doom.

Siva

For ages past, the Indian people have been celebrating Sivaratri (the sacred night of Siva). The Hindus associate with it several religious and mythological anecdotes, which give it an aura of pious ceremony. On this occasion, the observance of a fast followed by the worship of Siva during the four quarters of the night, is enjoined.

The conception is that, on Sivaratri Siva manifests Himself in the form of a vast linga (*Jyotirlingam*). Another conception of Siva is that of Ardhanareeswara – half male and half female. In fact there is a biological enunciation according to which both male and female hormones are inherent in each individual organism. The latest researches in psychology reveal that every man has a woman in his mind and each woman has a man inherent in her consitution. This is known as the principle of animus and anima. Nature has made every individual as an Ardhanareeswara. To speak in the language of the ancient symbolism each individual is Brahma *i.e.* Prajapati or the creator unto himself and creates for himself a mind-born daughter who functions as his energy for all creativity. She typifies the principles of intelligence (*buddhi*) by which the individual obtains his extension that may be termed as the *mandala* of his life. This female energy or the principle of intelligence and intellection is the element that makes up the Ardhanareeswara form of each individual.

In the ancient scriptures, we see an increasing importance attached to Siva. He is invoked as the Master of Life and Death and we find that those aspects of his character which inspire terror and strike dread are exalted in preference to that beneficence of nature which distinguishes Him most in the hymns of the Vedas. He is more frequently identified with Agni, Fire, conceived as an element of destruction. By his side appear *Bhava* - the Prosperous; and *Sarva* - the Archer, both of whom are destined to merge in the person of the God; and *Kaala* or Time which produces and devours all things and which shall also became one of the elements or 'forms' of Siva is invoked as the first principle of all that exists. In the Puranas, Siva is called 'Isaana', 'Iswara', the Lord, and 'Mahadeva' or the 'Great God'. We also meet with the legends that relate to His birth, His triumphs over the *Asuras,* whose Tripura He destroys, 'The Triple City', namely Earth, Air and Heaven, as well as others which exhibit Him as breaking into the midst of the gods and taking violent possession of the offerings made in sacrifice to them.

Siva is the God with three eyes: *Triambaka Deva* – the Sun, the Moon and Fire are said to be the three eyes of the Deity, typifying the triple constitution of the life principle or consciousness, and corresponding to the three-fold fires of the sacrifice. The principles of matter, vital powers (*prana*) and consciousness (*chitta*) are combined in the conception of Siva. The perfect integration of the physical man, the vitalman and the mental man, constitute the ideal of a perfect yogi; and Siva is the embodiment of that ideal.

Siva appears with all the criteria of a Deity of purely popular origin, in vital relationship with all the aspects of the rough and tumble of life, which has from time immemorial distinguished India. He and His *ganas,* the troops under His command, are invoked as protectors of the house, the fields, the herds, and the roads. He is the patron of craftsmen, cartwrights, carpenters, smiths, potters, hunters, and is himself a crafty merchant; but he is also the head of the army, the God of the brave, of foot soldiers, and of those who fight in chariots, of all those who live by the bow, the sword and the spear. It is his cry that echoes in the thick of the battle, and his voice which resounds in the war-drum. He is the patron of thieves and of all those who go by night in troops and live on plunder. He is also the God of the beggars and the *faquirs,* of those who wear long and matted hair, as well as those who shave the head. By himself or by the numberless spirits at his back, he is omnipresent, in the houses and the fields, in the rivers and the fountains, in the wind and the passing clouds, in the grass as it springs up, in the tree as it grows green, and in the leaf as it falls. But his dwelling is especially in forests and solitary places, and he reigns over the mountains. He sits enthroned on Kailas,the fabulous mountain of the North, beyond Himavat, surrounded and waited on by the *yakshas* and a large number of spirits of different forms. By His side sits enthroned Uma, His spouse, the daughter of Himavat. Like Her husband of whom She is the exact counterpart, She has many names and assumes many forms. She is worshipped as Devi, Goddess Parvati, the daughter of the Mountain, Durga the bright one, Sati the devoted wife, Bhairavi the terror-inspiring, Kali the black one, Karala the horrible one, and countless other designations, which express Her two-fold nature as Goddess of Life and Goddess of Death.

Lord Siva is said to have the bull for his vehicle. What is the meaning of this and what is the symbolism contained in it? Every individual is an expression of the principle of *ananda*. As the holy books reveal, all creatures are processed to the mysterious chemistry of *ananda*. The most subtle and refined form of *ananda* is *kama*. Siva typifies the divine principle of *kama,* not as its slave but as its master; and the bull, as its name Nandi implies, represents the same principle of *ananda* incarnating in matter and this is the vehicle of Siva. It is said that the bull, the life principle, inheres in Mahadeva, the Great God, the immortal divine amongst all mortal beings. Each individual is the Nandi bull, the vehicle and agent of Lord Siva, the instrument of His creative powers.

Siva is a development of the Vedic wind or the storm-god, Rudra. He inspires love and reverential fear and wins the affections of human hearts and is worshipped emotionally. He is not only dreaded but also revered, as the destroyer of evil and evil-doers, hatred, diseases, and is a nourisher who bestows long life. Says the *Rig-Veda.*

Rudra! thou smiter of workers of evil,

The doers of good, all love and adore thee!

Preserve me from injury and every affliction,

Rudra! the Nourisher!!

Siva-Nataraja

Symbols in Indian civilisation have always been powerful representations of the higher reality. The principle has been understood by the support of its symbolic counterpart on our plane of existence. The link between the worlds, the outer and inner, the higher and the lower, is through the language of symbols. How else can a reality where 'sight cannot go, nor the mind, where we cannot know, we cannot understand' be comprehended?

The dance has been one of the most powerful vehicles for this representation and the dancer is fortunate that, through her entire being, she is an expression of infinity. The images of our deities each manifest, in their visible structures, one particular aspect of the world. But the genius of Indian thought found a marvellous unity of science, art and religious fervour in the sculpture of the dancing Siva, Nataraja.

The deep significance underlying this image needs to be clearly understood – not only because this symbol has been alive for six thousand years, but because the message is still significant today.

The upper right hand holds aloft the *damaru*, representing *nada*, the sound, the evolution of the universe. From sound came all language, all music, all knowledge. The shape of the' drum, with its two triangles, tells us of nature and energy which combine together for all creation. The upper left hand in the half moon gesture holds a tongue of flame.

Why does Siva hold the hope of creation in one hand, and the flame, the fire that destroys, in the other? For, creation and destruction are the counterparts of His own Being. They are the two aspects of our life, for as we are surely born, so do we surely die. What then is the answer? The right hand, held in front, in the wondorous gesture of protection and peace, tells us, 'Look, God's grace is ever with you.'

Whether it be Siva or Krishna, Buddha or Christ, every manifestation of the Supreme, uses this *hasta* called *abhaya hasta* in the language of the dance. But let us go on questioning. 'How can we attain that grace, how may we be for ever in Thy care'? The left hand points the way. It lies across the body, directing the gaze to the foot. The hand is in the *gaja hasta,* the sign of the elephant hand. This is the hand movement depicting the trunk of the elephant and herein is a still deeper meaning. The trunk is discriminating. It can pick up and break the heaviest of objects, as well as handle the most delicate. It can choose between the two. So too, should we choose between the higher and the lower, and be discriminating. And to help us, He who owns the trunk, Ganesh,remover of all obstacles, is ever present.

The left foot is raised, telling man that as the Dancer raises His foot, so can man raise himself and attain salvation. While one foot is raised, the right foot upon which balances the whole body of the universe, that which,at this eternal moment of dance, precariously balances the fate of the world, that foot is not on the firm ground, but upon the body of a struggling dwarf, a man who is the embodiment of all that veils truth from falsehood, the *apasmara purusha,* made up of ignorance and forgetfulness. This is the *purusha* within us, which prevents us from realizing our own essential divinity. It is for us to firmly crush out the ignorance, if we are to attain the supreme joy which is our true nature, the eternal bliss that man calls God. Around Natraja, is a ring of flames, the *prabha mandala,* the dance of nature, all initiated by the Self in the centre, all emanating from Him, and all dissolving within Him.

While Shiva dances, His matted locks hold the sacred river Ganga, the power and the source of all movement in life, with its waters that purify mankind.and the crescent moon delicate as a new-born babe with its promise of life in all its radiance and glory.

What is perhaps most significant of all in the image is the combination of this God Ascetic, the Solitary One, Master of Meditation, with the frenzied dancer- the Yogi and the Artist. A dancer becomes the being that he impersonates on the stage. In the dance are aroused the entire energy of body, mind, intellect and soul. It is a complete surrender to God. Thus, a dancer is similar to the Yogi, who gives his all to the Lord.

This is a dramatic and vivid comparison. But look at the face of Natraja in the sculpture. It is serene, the epitome of inward absorption. While the body moves in a frenzy like the world with its tumult, Siva Himself is undisturbed by the activity, depicting most wonderfully the mortal life and the divine self. His face, calm and immobile, is a spectator in the external play of His own creative impulse, while He teaches, His eternal self remains apart, watchful and tender. It is the secret of life open to us all to read, so magnificently portrayed in this masterpiece of sculpture. A seeker of the truth, need search no further for a symbol of the highest reality. He only needs to look with eyes that see.

Nataraja the Guru

Every name and form in which the lord is worshipped has a special symbolic significance of its own. The inner meaning of these symbols is often very grand and poetic, and to enter into and understand it, will certainly be a privilege to those who are striving to realise for themselves the truths of philosophy; for these symbols were devised simply as aids to imagination and many men have employed them with advantage. The meanings of these symbols differ of course according to the standpoint adopted, and the highest, *viz.,* the Vedantic will be the one from which we shall study them.

Nataraja means the lord of the stage. The idea is that the world is a stage, a puppet-show which presents the vision of life and activity through the power of the all-pervading Atman or God, the unseen Lord of the stage.

The Atman or Self being the real teacher of the human mind, Nataraja is meant to represent the teacher or guru. There are two kinds of gurus – the apparent and the real, the seen and the unseen. The former is the teacher who instructs the disciple and takes him along the path - this is what we usually mean by the word guru; but all teaching really comes from inside, not merely in the sense that the outward apparent teacher is but the instrument employed by Atman or God, but also in the sense that all growth is from within. The plant, for example, grows from within; the manure, water, etc., are simply aids to its growth. In the same way, the mind has to grow only from within, Assimilating of course the teachings from outside. Nataraja, then, is the real guru concretely represented. One of the functions of the guru, perhaps the most important, is to be what he teaches-to enforce his teachings by example. It is this idea that is the key-note to the Nataraja symbol.

The little drum in one of the right hands is meant to express the idea that God or guru holds the cause of all the world, i.e., sound, in His hand. In other words, all the world is in His hand, to be folded or unfolded at

His own will. To the *gnani* or wise man the world exists only if he chooses and not otherwise. The deer on one side is the mind, because the latter leaps and jumps from one thing to another as wildly as that animal. The Atman is far beyond the reach of the deer-like mind; and so the deer in the picture is placed near the legs. Nataraja wears the skin of a tiger which He Himself slew. *Ahankara* or the skin of egoism is that tiger; it is beastly and ferocious and fiercely fights when attacked, but it has to be killed and Nataraja or guru alone can kill it. On His head He wears the Ganges, i.e., chit sakti or wisdom,which is most cool and refreshing, and the moon which represents the ethereal light and blissfulness of the Atman. One foot is planted over and crushes the giant Mayalaka, i.e., *Maha Maya*, the endless illusion which is the cause of birth"and death, while the other foot is raised upward and represents the *turiya* state, which is beyond and above the three states of waklng, dream and dreamless sleep, and leaves behind, the mind, *Maya* and the world. The second right hand,representing the idea of peace,indicates the blessed calmness,which is the glorious privilege of wisdom. In one of the left hands, is held Agni (fire), i.e., the guru brings in the light of the Atman itself to attest the truth of His teaching. The idea is that the truth of the guru's teaching can only be fully understood on practical realisation in experience (*anubhava*). The place of the dance, the theatre is *thillaivanam,* i.e., the body (of the individual as well as of the Cosmos) spoken of as *vanam* or forest on account of the multitude of its components. The platform in that theatre is the cremation ground, i.e., the place where all passions and the names and forms that constitute the vision of the world have been burnt away; pure consciousness devoid of attachment to anything outside and devoid of illusion.

The above are some of the leading features of the Nataraja symbol. The guru teaches that *maya* – illusion – should be crushed down, that the world should become subject to us and not we to the world, that the deer-like mind should be left behind, and *ahankar* (egoism) be destroyed, and that man should ascend to the region of pure, unconditioned consciousness free from passion and free from deception, and enjoy the calmness which is his birthright, and bliss, the light and the truth that form the Self. Viewed in the light of this inner meaning,the image of Nataraja is no more a meaningless idol, a piece of stone or copper but a symbol of the highest teaching, an object that can inspire and elevate.

Ganapati-Vinayak

Shiva's first son is described as the supreme leader (*Vinayaka*) or as the leader of the *ganas* (*Ganapati*), who attends upon and follows at all times Lord Shiva, or as the Lord of all Obstacles (*Vighneswara)*. These names clearly show that He is a master of all circumstances and not even the divine forces can ever obstruct His path. Since He is thus the lord of all obstacles, no Hindu ritual or auspicious act is ever undertaken without invoking Him. With His grace, it is believed that no undertaking can fail due to subjective or objective obstacles.

Ganapati is said to have two spouses, *Buddhi* (intellect) and *Siddhi* (achievement). Thus He is the master of knowledge and achievement.

In this characterisation Shri Ganapati represents a possessor of perfect wisdom. Some are shocked to see people revere a form which is so ridiculous and absurd. But the elephant-headed Lord indeed represents the highest and the best. To a Vedantic student, since his "path of knowledge" is essentially intellectual, he mjust have a great head to conceive and understand the logic of Vedantic thought and, in fact, the truth of Vedanta can be comprehended only through listening to a teacher and, therefore, *sravana* (listening) is the initial stage to be mastered by the new initiate. Therefore, Ganapati has large ears representing continuous and intelligent listening to the teacher.

After "listening" (*sravana*) to the truths of the Upanishads, the Vedantic student must independently "reflect" (*manana*) upon what he has heard, for which he needs a sensitive intelligence with ample sympathy to dicover in himself sufficient accomodation for all living creatures in the universe.

His intellect must have such depth and width in order to embrace in his vision the entire world-of-plurality. Not only must he, in his visualisation, embrace the whole cosmos, but he must have the subtle discriminative power (*viveka*) in him to distinguish the changing, perishable, matter-vestures from the Eternal, Immutable, all-Pervading Consciounsness, the Spirit. This discrimination is possible only when the intellect of the student has consciously cultivated this power to a large degree of perfection.

The trunk, coming down the forehead of the elephant-face, has got a peculair efficiency and is a "tool" which can at once uproot a tree or pick up a pin from the ground. The elephant can lift and pull heavy weights with his trunk and, at the same time, it is so sensitive at its tip that the same instrument can be employed by the elephant to pluck a blade of grass. The mechanical instruments cannot have this adaptability. The spanner that is used for tightening the bolts of a wheel cannot be used to repair a lady's watch. Like the elephant's trunk, the discriminative faculty of an evolved intellect should be perfect so that it can use its discrimination in the outer world for resolving gross problems, and at the same time, efficiently discriminate the subtle realms of the inner personality.

The discriminative power can function only where there are two factors to discriminate between; these two factors are represented by the tusks of the elephant as the trunk is between them. Between god and evil, right and wrong, and all other dualities must be discriminated. Shri Vinayaka is represented as having lost one of His tusks in a quarrel with Parasurama, a great disciple of Siva. This broken tusk indicates that a real Vedantic student of subjective experience is one who has gone beyond the pairs-of-opposites (*dwandwaatita*).

He has the widest mouth and the largest appetite. In Kubera's palace, He cured Kubera's vanity that in his riches he had become the "Treasurer of the Heavens'. When Kubera offered Him a dinner He ate up all the food prepared for the dinner. Thereafter, He started eating the utensils and then the decorative pandal, and still He was not satisfied. Then His Father, Lord Siva, approached Him and gave Him a handful of "puffed rice". Eating this he became satisfied.

The above story narrated in the *Puranas,* is very significant that a man of perfection has an endless appetitie for life – he lives in the consciousness and to him every experience, good or bad, is only a play of the infinite, alone can satisfy the hungers of such sincere students by giving them a handful of "roasted rice", representing the "baked *vasanas*", burnt in the fire of knowledge.

A man of perfection must have a big belly to stomach peacefully, as it were, all the experiences of life, auspiciousand and inaspicious.

When such a mastermind sits dangling his foot down, it is again significant, in the symbolism of the *Puranas*. Generally we move about in the world through the corridors of our experiences on our two feet, or the inner subtle body, the mind and the intellect. A perfect man of wisdom has integrated them both to such an extent that they have become One in him – an intellect into which the mind has folded and has become completely subservient.

At such a great Yogi's feet are the endless eatables of life-meaning, the enjoyable glories of physical existence. All powers come to serve him, the entire world of cosmic forces are, thereafter, his obedient servants, seeking their shelter at his feet; the whole world and its environment is waiting at His feet for his pleasure and command.

In the representation of Sri Vinayaka we always find a mouse sitting in the midst of the beautiful, fragrant ready-made food, but if you observe closely, you will find that the poor mouse is sitting looking up at the Lord, shivering with anticipation, but not daring to touch anything without His command; and now and then He allows the mouse to eat.

A mouse is a small little animal with tiny teeth, and yet, in a barn a solitary mouse can bring disastrous losses by continuously gnawing and nibbling at the grain. Similarly, there is a "mouse" within each personality, and this mouse is the power of desire. The man of perfection is one who has so perfectly mastered this urge to acquire, possess and enjoy this self-annihilating power of desire, that it is completely held in obedience to the will of the Master.

The lord of obstacles, Sri Vighneswara, has four arms representing the four-inner-equipments (*antahkarana*). In one hand He has a rope, in another an axe. With the axe, he cuts off the attachments of His devotees to the world-of-plurality and thus ends all the consequent sorrows, and with the rope, pulls them nearer and nearer to the truth, and ultimately ties them down to the highest goal. In his third hand he holds a rice ball (*modaka*) representing the reward of the joys of *sadhana* which He gives His devotees. With the other hand he blessess all His devotees and protects them from all obstacles in their spiritual path of seeking the Supreme.

The above three or four examples clearly brings to mind the art employed by Vyaya in his mystical word paintings. It is evidently clear that the representations given in the various symbolisms are not as many different deities, but they are vivid pen-portraits of the subjective Truth described in the Upanishadic lore.

Subramanya – Karthikeya

The second son of Siva and Uma is known as Subramaniam or Kartikeya or Shanmukha. The picture of Subramaniam, like other Deities in the Hindu mythological literature, has a deep mystic significance, which not only indicates the ultimate Reality but also prescribes the path to be taken by a seeker to reach that Reality.

Shanmukha is represented in the human form with six faces ('*shat*' means 'six' and *mukham* means 'face'). He is blue in colour. He holds a trident, a sort of spear or javelin (*sakti*) in his hand. His vehicle is the peacock. The peacock grips a snake with its claws.

Blue colour is generally attributed to infinity. All infinite expanses in nature appear blue in colour to the human perception; for example, the sky and the ocean. The blue colour of Subramaniam, therefore, indicates the infinite reality which exists as the spiritual essence in all human beings. In a human being, this supreme reality expresses itselt through the media of the five sense organs and the mind-intellect. This idea is represented by the Lord having six faces. The infinite reality by itself has no expression; however, when it functions through the six equipments there is a manifestation of life, such manifestation being like a multi-faceted jewel reflecting light from its different facets.

Again, the peacock-vehicle of Shanmukha is also blue in colour. Another characteristic of a peacock, which is significant here, is its vanity. The peacock is acclaimed to be the vainest living creature. How evident this is during the peacock's lengthy dancing with its colourful feathers propped up in a delightful form!

The suggestion here is that the seeker of Truth must also develop extreme vanity in his supreme self. This idea is figuratively represented by Kartikeya using the peacock as His vehicle. The vehicle on which man moves about at present is his egocentric mind which conceives only the limited individual. Man's attention is constantly focussed upon his body, mind and intellect. Identifying with them, he believes himself to be a 'perceiver' at the physical level, a 'feeler' at the mental level and a 'thinker' at the intellectual level. Thus, limiting his personality, he develops the vanity of the 'perceiver-feeler-thinker' and becomes unaware of his infinite potentiality. The deity of Kartikeya is meant to invoke in man the vanity of his supreme self and thereby he will conceive his infinite stature. The one who practises this art of withdrawing his mind from its pre-occupations with the material equipments of the body, mind and intellect and succeeds in maintaining the concept of the Infinite Self, that one becomes the blue-coloured Kartikeya – a God-man on earth.

The deity also gives the seeker a practical suggestion on how to reach the abode of the supreme reality. This suggestion lies in the peaock clutching the serpent with its claws. The peacock is the greatest enemy of the serpent. It can destroy the serpent if it wishes to, but the serpent is held here in captivity without being destroyed. The serpent represents the ego, which tempts him to use his material equipments for seeking the fleeting pleasures of the pluralistic world. Like the serpent, the ego crawls in darkness created by man's ignorance of the Supreme Light. The serpent carries poison in its fangs but it is interesting to observe that the poison is for its own protection. Similarly, the ego carries with it the poisonous mind, which, when focussed on one's material vestures, assumes the vanity of 'I-ness' and 'mine-ness'. The same mind can be intelligently used for evolving oneself by changing its focus from body, mind and intellect to the supreme self. By this process one unfolds and recognises one's own real nature. It is important, therefore to note that the ego is not destroyed. The same ego which lures man to the pluralistic world can be channnelised to discover the supreme self. This idea is symbolised in the serpent being held firmly by the peacock.

Lord Subramania represents such a man-of-perfection who has discovered the supreme self. To proclaim his infinite status he carries in his hand the *sakti*. The weilding of this instrument of annihilation symbolises the destruction of all negative tendencies (*vasanas*) which veil the divine self.

Devi as Consort and Shakti

Saraswati

The Vedic tradition in India from time immemorial has given women the highest respect and recognition. Thus, we find our scriptures referred to as 'Mother Sruti'. the Bhagavad Geeta as 'Mother Geeta' and knowledge itself personified as a feminine deity, goddess Saraswati.

Saraswati literally means 'the one who gives the essence (*sara*) of our own Self (*swa*),' Goddess Saraswati is represented as sitting on a lotus, holding the sacred scriptures in one hand and a lotus in her second hand. With the other two hands she plays the Indian lute (*veena*).

The goddess of knowledge and learning is depicted here as one who has not only the experience of the supreme reality but is also the embodiment of the philosophy of the Upanishads. These two are the essential qualities of a guru, a spititual teacher. The goddess, therefore, represents the ideal guru who possesses both these qualities. 'Sitting on the lotus' symbolises that the teacher is well established in the subjective experience of the truth. 'Holding the scriptures in her hand' indicates that she holds that the knowledge of the scriptures alone can take us to the truth.

The four hands of the Goddess, represent the four aspects of the inner personality of man, *viz.*, *manas* (mind), buddhi (intellect), *chitta* (conditioned consciousness) and *ahamkar* (ego).

The goddess's *chitta-hand* holds the scriptures. With the other two hands, representing the mind and the intellect, she plays the lute (*veena*). The suggestion is that a truly qualified teacher tunes up the mind and intellect of the seeker and draws out of him the music and melody of life. *i.e.*, the seeker learns to be in perfect harmony with the world. If such tuning is not done, man suffers mental agitations in life and remains ever in disharmony with the world.

Thus, when a seeker lives a life of intelligent self-control (*tapas*), deep study (*swadhyaya*), continuous reflection (*manana*) and steady meditation (*nidhi-dhyasana*), his erstwhile limited ego attains liberation (*moksha*). This state of absolute liberation experienced by the individual ego when it rediscovers the supreme self within is symbolised by the lotus held by the goddess in her '*ahamkar*' hand.

Saraswati is wedded to the creator. Brahma. The creator needs to be associated with the goddess of knowledge, since creation has to be supported by the 'knowledge to create'. All creative endeavours can spring forth from and sustain themselves only by the knowledge of what and who to create.

Lakshmi

Lakshmi is the consort of Lord Vishnu. Vishnu represents the power of maintenance. In order to maintain anything in life, one must possess the wealth to do so. An earning member alone can maintain his family. The god of maintenance has therefore, necessarily to be associated with the goddess of wealth.

Wealth in this context does not mean only money. It also includes the nobler values of life, the power of the mind and the intellect, moral and ethical qualities, etc., which constitute the spiritual wealth. These are the types of wealth to be acquired before one's initiation into actual spiritual learning and knowledge.

Lakshmi is expressed as *swarnahasta* by virtue of the fact that she pours out wealth to the community. This wealth is gained by invoking the goddess. Wealth, however, does not come to anyone of its own accord. The capacity to earn wealth remains as an inherent power in man and it has to be drawn out through self-effort (*purushartha*). This idea is well brought out in the allegory of 'the churning of the ocean of the milk'.

The story given in the *Bhagavata Purana* is that of the churning of the ocean of milk by the gods (*devas*) and the demons (*asuras*) for obtaining the nectar (*amruth*). One of the many precious things that came out of the ocean, while it was being churned, was Lakshmi. The emergence of Lakshmi from the ocean symbolises the creation and development of ethical and cultural values of life in one's bosom when one's pure, sattwic mind is churned by the process of reflection and contemplation upon the higher self.

Lakshmi is sometimes represented with four arms, but more often with two. She is described as seated on a lotus. She also holds a lotus in Her hand. The realisation of the self is the supreme goal to be gained by man. This is symbolised by the lotus in the hand of the goddess.

Uma

Uma is the consort of Siva, the lord of constructive destruction. Uma represents *prakriti* (matter). The power of destruction has always to be associated with destructible matter in order that this power could manifest. In other words, destruction ceases to have any meaning without destructible objects. The god of destruction has, therefore, chosen Uma to be His partner.

The God and the Goddess are the first self-revelation of the absolute, the male being the personification of the passive aspect and the female, the activating energy (*sakti*) goddess Parvati (Uma) represents this universal Power. Uma and Parvati are Her maiden names; and Mrudani and Ambika are Her post-marriage names.

The Goddess is also referred to as Annapurana meaning 'bestower of food'. 'Anna', though translated as 'food', has a wider connotation and includes all material objects/wealth, which are food for the five sense organs. The Goddess is possessed of all types of 'food' to offer Her devotees.

All the three Goddesses together are represented by the fierce-looking goddess Durga or Kali. She is shown in a fearful form. Kali is worshipped by a seeker to invoke her latent power of destruction and thereby annihilate all his negative tendencies and qualities which veil his higher self.

Durga

Durga is the power which manifested out of the eternal truth, which is complete and so has in itself all powers.

Man, the imperfect, the bound, the sorrowful, has a thousand enemies within. He is riddled with negative thoughts, fears, yearnings. These are selfishness, jealousy, meanness, prejudice and hatred – just to mention a few. The *sadhak* must get rid of these lawless villains within. With Kali's blessings these destructive masters are to be annihilated. No amount of soft persuasions can avail. The forces of Rudra must be applied. There must be a deep, determined resolve, and a fight-royal within, as sanguine as Kali's ferocious sword dripping with blood; and unless the *sadhak* is ready to wear about his neck the skull-*mala* of these murdered false values there can be no peace or order within.

Invoke the Mother to help us annihilate within ourselves all negative forces; all weaknesses, – all little-ness. It is these that have removed us from our own selves.

Now a mere elimination of our weakness in itself is no permanent achievement, for, if the bosom is empty, again they will enter by the 'back-doors'. In short, a mere negative *sadhana* alone is impotent. We must equally emphasise the positive side in our right effort – then only does the *purushartha* become complete and whole.

Dasavatara Symbollism

Puranic literature in Hinduism is well-known to be only an exposition of the highest Advaitic principles in the form of stories which can be understood and appreciated even by the common mass of people in the light of their own life's experiences.

The Dasavataras of Vishnu have been a source of inspiration and solace to millions of Hindus through the centuries, and the ideals embodied therein have kept them in the straight and narrow path of *dharma,* even when sorely tempted to stray by alluring forms of *adharma.* To the spiritual *sadhak* however, they convey quite another secret import. To that soul who is all set to climb the mighty peak of self-realisation, the serious student and practitioner of Vedanta, these symbolic stories show the stages in the spiritual journey to perfection. This path, one has to traverse all alone to the Alone.

The ten Avataras of Vishnu are :

1. Matsya or the Fish
2. Kurma or the Tortoise
3. Varasha or the Boar
4. Nrusimha or the Man-Lion
5. Vamana or the Dwarf
6. Parasurama – Rama with the axe
7. Sree Rama – The Ideal
8. Sree Krishna – The Perfect Joy
9. The Buddha – The Enlightened
10. Kalki – The ruthless striker of the evil

Moksya

The ego of the *sadhak,* before he becomes one, is wallowing in the mire of sensuality and gross ignorance. It is encompassed by the dark night of *tamas,* and almost drowned in the ocean of *samsara* with its various trials and tribulations. At this moment comes a very faint light and the Lord in his own bosom manifests, as a desire to do *sadhana* in some form. He seeks a guru, and does spiritual practice, taking the first tottering steps on the path to God. A faint ray of divine light leads him ever onward to save him from the slime and dirt all around.

Kurma

Having started on the path. the *sadhak* is told to do daily introspection and self-analysis to discover his weaknesses. A multititude of evil tendencies are discovered, some even masquerading as divine traits. The good is found to be minimal, almost negligible. A divine desperation urges him not to yield but fight out the battle with all his might. Resolving to do intense *tapas*, he fixes the rope of his mind to the churning rod of his own discriminative intellect and begins to churn out the ocean of *vasanas* in himself, to draw out the nectar of Immortal Bliss. And in this *purashartha* or self-effort, it is the Lord in him that serves as the solid rock of support to the intellect, to guide and help, even as the Kurma *avatara* supported the churning rod of the mountain Mandhara during the churning of the ocean by the gods and the demons.

Varaha

Thereafter, the *satwic* tendencies, become predominent in the seeker, for by constant *abhyas* or practice, he has by now learnt to stand apart from his own ego. But even now there are lurking desires, deeply hidden evil traits which have to be literally dug out of the subconscious before they can be eliminated. This calls for intense self-analysis, rigorous inner probing, unpleasant though the process may prove.

This is the symbolism of the Varaha or the boar diving down into the very bowels of the earth to discover the demon Hiranyaksha and destroy him. So deeply entrenched are some *vasanas* that they have to be dug out painfully from deep within and eliminated. Else, further progress is impossible.

Nrusimha

The seeker now stands well-up on the stage of evolutionary growth, half-god half-man, as shown in the Nrusimha avatara. Many god-like qualities, love, compassion, kindness, have developed in the head and heart, he is towering above the common level of mankind. A few *rajasic* qualities, however, still continue to plague him – spiritual arrogance, pride of learning, etc., – which have to go before he can forge ahead, so comes the next stage.

Vamana

The dwarf boy-saint comes to the great king Bali to beg for three feet of land. The Vamana avatar emphasises the important role of humility in the *sadhak.* Until and unless he has overcome pride in his own progress and sublimated the spiritual arrogance, he is bound to be humbled by a great fall, when he least expects it. The seeker must always be humble enough to recognise his weakness and obey the words of wisdom of elders and teachers in the spiritual field. Had Bali obeyed his guru Shri Sukracharya, who warned him against granting the boon to the dwarf-child *vamana*, he could not have been crushed as he was.

Parasurama

Truly humble and sincere through he be, in the last phase of his spiritual Odyssey, the seeker has to give battle to a horder of *rajasic* traits symbolised by the *kashtriya* kings annihilated by Parasurama in a blood-bath. This *avatara* also highlights the intense detachment which must be available in the inner personality at this stage, for did not Parasurama kill his own mother on the command of his father and guru? The strongest bond of affection has to be thus overcome, before perfection is attained.

The *rajasic* elements to be conquered are no longer the gross one like lust and anger that were prominent earlier. These are subtler enemies, truly kingly in stature. Pride of mastery of the Vedas, complacency in being able to hold large audiences spell-bound by the power of oratory, occult powers, etc., come to tempt the *sadhak*, and he must resolutely say a no to them and kill them ruthlessly. Only then can man become the super-man or the next avatar.

Rama

Grown perfect now, the god-man emerges as the culminating ideal Rama, the perfect ideal man, born only to show suffering humanity, how man may truly live as a god on earth. An ideal son, husband, brother, king, the acme of perfection is thus the Rama *avatara*.

And when the sadhak has passed through all the previous stages of *sadhana*, he emerges as the prince among seekers, a completely enlightened soul.

Krishna

And after perfection is achieved, it is all joy, for ever after. Supreme, scintillating, permanent ecstasy all around and within himself, for he has beome the eternal Self in all selves of the Universe. Who or what can contain Him? This abounding joy is symbolised by the *leelas* of Krishna, His enchanting divine pranks, which held the Gopi maidens in thrall. The Krishna *avatara* is one where not a tear was shed ever. The smilling Lord laughed his way through all His splendid colourful life of intense activity.

Buddha

And after this deep unchanging ecstasy has been lived and experienced as a permanent reality, the now Self-realised saint is transformed into the deeply compasionate Buddha. He yearns to help others, actually his own reflections, to become or rather *be* what he is. The teacher of the world, the *sadguru* emerges, even as the Buddha did, his only reason for his existence being to teach and show others the path leading to unending joy. He may choose to be silent like Ramana or walk the path of lecture tours like Vivekananda, and yet both are there only to teach those who are seeking the path and the goal.

Kalki

Last, and yet to come, is the stage where riding the horse of his own dynamic personality, the saint becomes a force to be reckoned with battling for the cause of the right and striking down all evil anywhere and everywhere; the world looks on in wonder and amazement at the saint-man, who is God in his own right; strong and perfect as *Sat-Chit-Ananda* (Existence-Consciousness-Bliss).

May the eternal principle within all of us grow and manifest through all these stages of *Sadhana* to produce at length the God-man which is only His Self made manifest. As the *Upanishad* says.

"From the unreal leads us to the Real

From darkness lead us to Light

From death lead us to Immortality".

INDEX